D0296345

LIVING TWICE

By the same Author:

CRIME AND PUNISHMENT (1950)
TOWARDS MY NEIGHBOUR (1950)
PERSONAL IDENTITY (1956)
THE HUMAN SUM (1957)
COMMONSENSE ABOUT CRIME AND PUNISHMENT (1961)
THE TRIAL OF LADY CHATTERLEY (1961)
(*With Arthur Koestler*) HANGED BY THE NECK (1961)
ALL THOSE IN FAVOUR? (*The ETU Trial*) (1962)
THE POLICE AND THE PUBLIC (1962)
LAW AND THE COMMON MAN (1967)
BOOKS IN THE DOCK (1969)
KINGSLEY: THE LIFE, LETTERS AND DIARIES OF
    KINGSLEY MARTIN (1973)
BELIEVE WHAT YOU LIKE (1973)

The author today

LIVING TWICE

An autobiography

by

C. H. ROLPH

LONDON
VICTOR GOLLANCZ LTD
1974

Printed in Great Britain by
The Camelot Press Ltd, Southampton

CONTENTS

Part I

BREAD AND BUTTER

Part II

THE BETTER LIFE

LIST OF ILLUSTRATIONS

PART I

BREAD AND BUTTER

Chapter 1

"A CHILD IS HUNGRY ALL OVER"

QUEEN VICTORIA AND I just missed each other. Between 22 January 1901 when she died at Osborne House, and 23 August in the same year when I was born in what was then called a "dwelling" on the site of the old Marshalsea Prison, English history presents a disfiguring gap of seven months. What was going on? It turns out that the British Army under Lord Kitchener was still systematically destroying Boer farms by way of giving guerillas nowhere to hide; that the House of Lords was hatching its famous judgment (in the Taff Vale Railway Case) that a trade union should be made to pay for losses resulting from a strike; and that Edward VII had added to his title, in a phrase destined to live little longer than the Taff Vale decision, the words "and of the British Dominions Beyond the Seas". Freud published his *Psychopathology of Everyday Life*, Rachmaninov his second piano concerto, Maeterlinck his *Life of the Bee*. And my mother nearly died because I weighed twelve and a half pounds and struggled.

We moved to Finsbury Park (I am told) just before my first birthday anniversary. I can't remember that; but since it is commonly held that the conscious human memory retains nothing that happens before the age of two years, I take some pleasure in offering this evidence to the contrary. At Marshalsea Road, Southwark, the flat underneath ours was occupied by an uncle, my mother's brother, who was a Post Office sorter and whose name was Herbert Speed. (He was also one of the sweetest characters I have ever known.) One day I was allowed to go down there for tea, and was placed in one of those high chairs fitted with a semi-circular tray which ingeniously serves two purposes: it locks you into your elevated seat and it gives you something to bang with your fists when the service is inferior. I do not know how old I was, only that it must have been less than twelve months; but I do remember that I had not yet decided that walking was preferable to crawling. Hence I was not invited to join a procession (elder brother, cousin, and two girls from across the landing) which after tea marched round the kitchen table with empty tins revolving on the ends of brandished sticks. One of the tins flew off, knocked over the oil lamp on the dresser, and started a fire. I watched with stolid but uncomprehending interest as the china cups on the dresser hooks turned black instead of catching fire. I was told long afterwards that it took fifteen frantic minutes to put out the flames, and I doubt that I should have remembered the episode at all but for the panic and excitement of a number of grown-ups who had suddenly appeared from nowhere.

That is one of two early and utterly genuine recollections. The other, a slightly later one, is the word freenigin. It must have been in constant use by my family at the time. It meant nothing to me, it was one of the noises with which grown-ups amused each other. (I understood biscuit, milk, water, dirty, nice, sleep, and pram, and this seemed an adequate vocabulary for the time being.) It was years before I discovered that freenigin must have been Vereeniging, the Transvaal town where the Boers signed a Peace Treaty with Britain on 12 May 1902, and thus became British subjects. On that date I was nine months old. No doubt people went on saying freenigin for some time after that; but the odd thing is that after those very early days I never heard Vereeniging mentioned again. Have *you* ever heard of it?

My father, who at this time was a sergeant of police, had spent some of his boyhood in South Africa and would, I imagine, have talked about the Boer War incessantly. He also had an intense admiration for Cecil Rhodes, which in due course I found myself unable to share; and I was christened Cecil Rolph Hewitt, partly to the glory of Rhodes and partly as a tribute of some kind to a Rolph in the family whom everyone has now forgotten. (Years later Kingsley Martin found himself unable to put up with the "Cecil" and re-christened me Bill because, he said ambiguously, I looked like one.) My father greatly influenced me on the subject of colonial peoples, and had a romantic admiration for the Zulus, even though they had killed his father (a private in the South Wales Borderers) at the Battle of Isandhlwana, near Rorke's Drift, on 22 January 1879. I grew up to regard that date as even more important than 1066. And although I have read numberless accounts of the battle, or rather the massacre, in which the second battalion of the South Wales Borderers were ambushed and wiped out by a vast army of Zulus, I have not seen an account so vivid or so appalling as that given by the late R. F. Delderfield in his *Theirs Was the Kingdom*.[1]

My father used to say that although it was Rorke's Drift that all the history books talked about (because there the British won), it was strategically unimportant. Isandhlwana and its 900 British dead showed "the blacks" that spears and courage could win against rifles, and that well-trained *impis* could outwit upper-class English duffers like Lord Chelmsford. I came to think that he was a bit hard on Lord Chelmsford, who recovered with astonishing speed from the Isandhlwana disaster to defeat a Zulu army 20,000 strong at Ulundi, the place of residence of the Zulu kings. But we never heard much about Ulundi, though it marked the end of the Zulu War. My Grandma Hewitt, back in England, thought it was an outrage that in 1883 the British reinstated Cetywayo as Chief over most of his old dominions. She had a way of saying "Cetywayo" as if she were spitting.

My family had a military history. Accordingly, man of peace as I've always been, I have since early childhood winced to see marching bodies of men, with drums or bands (or both) to help them along, coming down on the wrong foot. Stage armies always do this—I wonder why? The procession in *Aida*, even with that tremendous composition to march to, unfailingly brings down its right foot on the main beat of each bar and I have to close my eyes, missing all the pageantry. Foreign armies do it, of course, but they are, after all, foreign and actually drive their vehicles on the wrong side of the road. I don't know whether a military ancestry is enough by itself, without army training, to make a man square his

[1] Hodder and Stoughton, 1971.

shoulders when he walks, half-close his fists when swinging his arms (instead of letting the fingers hang like beef sausages), and always walk in step with a companion, however shambling the companion may be. But men who fail thus to comport themselves have always provoked in me a disapproval bordering on contempt; an irrational feeling, with consequences throughout my life to which I will return. I mention it now because it seems to be something I was born with.

The Finsbury Park house was at 101 Woodstock Road, and at one period it must have been distinguished from all the other houses (with which it was otherwise drably identical) by the presence of a ladder placed, it seemed to me permanently, against a first-floor window-sill. This was the means by which my uncle got into his bedroom in the small hours of the morning when his postal duties had kept him on "late shift". I never regarded this as in any way out of the ordinary. Painters went up ladders, and window cleaners and firemen. You never saw them walking through doorways. I had then no idea what my uncle did for a living, why he was so often home very late, or why he went up a ladder when he did get home. I probably supposed that people who didn't stay at home in the day-time went to school, like my elder brother and my cousin Herbert Speed (junior). I may have thought my uncle went to night school. I learned later that my security-minded father was unwilling to leave the front door unbolted at night, and that the ladder was agreed upon as a compromise solution. Then my father began to worry about the ladder's being in position all through the dark evenings, as a sort of qualified invitation to everyone. So another compromise was agreed upon: a six-foot plank was padlocked to the lower rungs, so that climbing might be as awkward as possible for an intruder. I don't know how long this went on, but I believe that when my father came home from *his* duties (as he sometimes did) in the small hours, he used no ladder. He came in by the front door. From what I remember of his lifelong single-mindedness, I would bet my last coin that my poor mother got up and unbolted for him.

Frederick Thompson Hewitt (if he had to write his full name he would often give the "Thompson" an enormous

"P", probably because someone had once left it out) was as good a father as any man ever had. He was born in Sheffield in 1869, his father then being a private in the 24th Regiment of Foot, the South Wales Borderers.

My father was always an alert-looking, distinguished man with a brown bony face and a deep scar under his chin, the acquisition of which involved a story that my two brothers and I never tired of hearing. (Anyway we were not supposed to tire of it.) His father's regiment was stationed at Gibraltar in 1874 on its way to India, and his daily walk to school was round the base of the Rock. One day he decided to do some climbing on the way home, and was suddenly seen by a sentry from 200 feet below. The sentry's loud challenge and the fear of being shot so frightened him that he lost his foothold, fell 80 feet and was knocked out. A stretcher party took him home to a mother whose frantic concern lasted until he had recovered consciousness and had his chin stitched up, and then turned to the righteous anger that I came to know so well myself— and to provoke so often. My Grandma Hewitt was a tartar.

My father had a widely dispersed succession of fairly primitive schools, as the South Wales Borderers moved from Gibraltar to Secunderabad in India, from India to Natal, Natal to Cape Colony, and so on, taking some of its women and children everywhere. After the Zulu War the widowed mother brought my father and his four sisters home to England, and took a job as resident housekeeper to one of the officials in the Tower of London. She also worked as a "monthly midwife", a job for which, so far as I know, she possessed no qualification other than having mothered five children herself. Soon afterwards, as a soldier's orphan, my father was admitted to the Duke of York's School in King's Road, Chelsea (it is now at Dover), and his sisters were dispersed among various schools in the Home Counties. When, on holiday from school, he slept in the servants' quarters at the Tower of London, he was frequently terrified at night by the heavy approaching footsteps of sentries patrolling the iron landings, which he took to be the steps of executed traitors carrying their heads underneath their arms.

From what my brothers and I were told about his schooldays

at the Duke of York's, one thing is uppermost in my memory: the ceremonial floggings of recalcitrant boys before the whole of the school at morning assembly, which seem to have been about as regular as morning prayers, the two sacraments being designed to inculcate the same moral principles through opposite ends of the body. The boys' own code of practice bound them not to oblige the authorities by looking on, so they all sat with their eyes defiantly closed during a flogging, except for one deputed boy at the end of each line, who watched his row of faces to see whether anyone raised a head and tried to snatch a glimpse of what was going on. If anyone did, he was afterwards knocked about by a kind of strong-arm gang. . . . I don't know whether it is fanciful, but I have sometimes liked to attribute to this odd example of gang discipline a noticeable disposition on my father's part, and even more on mine, to avert the eyes from acts of cruelty or obscenity.

His sisters were a handsome lot, and all grew up to be attractive, self-reliant, and rather wilful young women, each with a constantly changing retinue of expendable young men. Sophie was my favourite because I knew her the best and also (I think) because to me she looked like Queen Alexandra. She had a daughter of my own age, who was also called Sophie and was one of the prettiest girls I have ever known. When we were both about sixteen we spent some time going around hand-in-hand. I remember that I spent rather more time trying to find out the genetic reasons against marrying a cousin, and then, having found them, sweeping them angrily aside. There will be more about Sophie later on.

Isabel and May were twins, born in Cape Colony in an Army bullock-waggon on the march during the Zulu War; a glimpse of motherhood on active service which must have been rare even in the heyday of imperialism. May was a tomboy, whose rare visits to our household (before she married and went to America) were vastly enjoyed. Once my brothers and I (all then under twelve) linked arms at the foot of the stairs and told her she would not be allowed to go up to her room unless she uttered some truly shocking swear-word. We generously left the choice to her (we wanted to find out what kind of words she would know). I don't know what we expected to hear though our playground vocabulary was by that time extensive enough to sustain an informed criticism. But our adored Aunt May, having for some time smilingly refused, suddenly gave voice to a string of expletives that might even commend themselves to a modern playwright; and we all collapsed on the stairs in astonishment and admiration. . . . Isabel, whom everyone called Bella, was the frailest and lived the longest: as I write this she has just died at the age of ninety-five. She had spent her childhood and early adolescence with her twin sister May at a "School for the Daughters of Non-Commissioned Officers" near Wandsworth Common. (My grandfather wasn't an N.C.O. when he was killed, but he had been Regimental Sergeant Major, and resumed service as a private in recognition of his devoted drunkenness. The school authorities must have stretched a point here.) And in view of the harrowing pictures of Victorian orphanages bequeathed to us by Frances Hodgson Burnett and other writers it is pleasant to record that my Aunt Bella assured me, shortly before she died, that she remembered being "utterly happy" there. She was also happy when she "went into service", on leaving school, with a wealthy family named McCorquodale, then recently home from India and living in Wimbledon.

Elizabeth, who (rather surprisingly) liked to be called Lizzie, seemed to me a gentle and delicate creature with an extraordinarily generous nature and an unexpectedly fiery temper. Never once did she omit, on her visits to our house, to bring us each a sixpenny bundle of little chocolate bars wrapped in silver paper and parcelled up with a narrow coloured ribbon. There was more sadness in her shortish life than anyone deserves, and it was an odd consequence of my affection for her that I always associated grief and weeping with little bundles of silver-papered chocolate. I still do.

My mother, Edith Mary Speed, was one of a family of eight children, whose father died when the oldest was thirteen; which has often made me wonder how many children there would have been if he had lived. They rented a small house in Oakley Street, Chelsea, and another later in Flood Street. The oldest girl was Caroline, who from thirteen onwards helped to mother the family and sewed on buttons for a local shirt-maker. Caroline and Edith made my father's acquaintance (in the King's Road, Chelsea) through the railings of the Duke of York's School playground, when he was fourteen, Caroline a year older and Edith two years younger. They were among the girls who were occasionally "chatted up" by the Duke of York's scholars. But it would surely have surprised all of them to know then that he was to marry Edith in 1897 and then, when she died in 1910, to marry Caroline—among the first marriages made legally possible by the Deceased Wife's Sister Marriage Act of 1909. Among the brothers and sisters of Edith and Caroline was Herbert, who in due course figured in my life as "Uncle Bert" the postman, and shared houses with us at Southwark and Finsbury Park.

My father had been in the Duke of York's School drum-and-fife band and was showing promise as a flautist. At fourteen he was given a place at the Royal Military School of Music (Kneller Hall) at Twickenham, and was trained there to a high standard of proficiency in "flute and piccolo". It was, as it turned out, a development of great importance to me. The whole of my childhood had a background of flute and piccolo practice. There are people who hate the sound of an unaccompanied flute—and my father at practice was always unaccompanied, for there was no piano in the house for many years to come. I loved it always, whether it was the "soft complaining flute" of Dryden, the rushing gymnastics of *Leonora No. 3* or the obbligato in Bishop's "Lo, Here the Gentle Lark". He became a very good flautist, and for some years after I was old enough to take any interest he was much in demand by amateur orchestras. His love of music was infectious and it gave my life an important dimension.

He left Kneller Hall after three years and went to do his soldiering in Ireland—at Buttevant in County Cork and later in Dublin (Curragh Camp) and Londonderry. Already imbued with a Regular Army, imperialist attitude to the "natives" in Dominion territories, he saw the Irish as feckless, likeable, comic, slightly mad and potentially homicidal. The "Irish Problem" called neither for a solution nor for any special enquiry as to how it began. It was a natural phenomenon.

Its two main sides, the recognisable sides, were represented in Dublin by Mountjoy Prison and what was still called the Viceregal Lodge, at both of which he frequently found himself on guard duty. After eight years, totally fed up, he bought himself out of the Army, borrowing most of the money from the Colour Sergeant; I think it was only about £40 but it took him seven years to pay it back. In England he got a job as a uniformed attendant at the Natural History Museum in South Kensington, where he beguiled the hours with such obsessive calculations as the number of footsteps it took to walk right round the gigantic skeleton of the *ceteosaurus*, while he silently and assiduously practised the "triple tonguing" essential to good flute playing. Then he saw in an advertisement that the City of London Police Band wanted a flute and piccolo player, who, alas, must be six feet tall because he would also have to be a policeman and six feet was then the minimum height. His height was 5' 8⅜". He went along to try. "Have you got your piccolo?" they asked him. He had. "Can you play *The Wren*?" He could, and there and then he did, unaccompanied but with consummate ease. He was in. And because he was so small, and had high cheekbones and a stiff bearing, he was christened Togo Hewitt, a name which clung to him for the next twenty-eight years. (Togo was a Japanese Admiral then much in popular use as a convenient personification of the Yellow Peril.)

But someone at the Duke of York's School had given him a grounding in the grammar of the English language so fundamental—and, I should suppose, so unimaginative—that throughout his long life the bricks-and-mortar of the language (as distinct from the architecture, which was something to be added, optionally, afterwards) remained an obsession with him. He seldom missed an opportunity at home to lay down the law about grammar, spelling and punctuation; and my two brothers and I in conversation with him, or with each other (if he was close enough to overhear), were made, kindly but firmly, to conform to all the rules. If you began an excited sentence with "He was bigger than me . . ." you would have to start again, and keep on starting again until you got it right—and until all the excitement had gone and you wanted to drop the subject. Accordingly unless you were bursting with the information you wanted to impart, you didn't start at all. When, near bedtime, you said "Can I stay up and just finish this chapter?" he would reply, "You can, but you *may* not." So you went to bed (always in the dark) and finished it with the aid of an electric torch.

In their travels with the regiment his family had grown accustomed to the help of "native" servants—in India and South Africa particularly. (I have often wondered how my Grandma Hewitt must therefore have felt when, in her widowhood, she had to go back into domestic service.) When I was two years old we acquired a "servant" in a rather different way. One very wet and cold night at Woodstock Road a woman of about twenty-seven knocked at our front door and told my father in a very high-pitched voice that she was homeless and needed somewhere to rest for an hour. He soon discovered that she was also stone deaf. He took her into the kitchen, and while he got her some food my mother found some dry clothes—she was wet to the skin. Having seen to it that she was fed and clothed, he went to the front door to see if the weather was fit for her to move on. Then it was found that she had nowhere to go anyway. In answer to written questions from my father, she told him in the shrill and rather muddled voice of the totally deaf that she had been in domestic service, and had lost the job when she finally lost her hearing. She had known that deafness was coming on and that when she could no longer conceal it her only prospect would be the workhouse. My elder brother Harold, who remembered all this better than I, used to recall that she broke down completely under the impact of what seems to have been the first kindness she had known, and begged to be allowed to stay. She would do all the housework, she sobbed, all the cooking, all the shopping, look after the children, anything, everything; and she would want no money—only her bed and some food. My parents decided that she must at any rate stay for the night. She stayed for twenty years.

Her name was Annie Palmer. I never knew where she came from. It has always been on my conscience that, many years later (my parents now too old to look after her and she too unreliable to look after anyone), she did go into a London County Council workhouse called Luxborough Lodge in Marylebone Road (though by that time it didn't call itself a workhouse); and died there in 1930, two days before I belatedly traced her. I shall never forget the powerful smell of carbolic in that huge, echoing place, and how it seemed to blight the flowers I had taken with me as a propitiatory offering. There's no doubt that she had utterly devoted herself to the care of my brothers and me as children, and little doubt that Harold and I, at all events, behaved like little boors towards her, taking advantage of her deafness in all sorts of inexcusable ways—and for our own heartless amusement. I believe she was pretty useless in the house: one of those "home helps" who need helping even more than the home does, who in fact need someone to go round after them undoing most of the things that they have just done. My father made no secret of this in the exasperated things he said about her in our presence, and I don't doubt that we thought we were taking our cue from him. Roland, my younger brother, was her special favourite; no doubt because, apart from being the youngest, he was by nature a gentler person and incapable of unkindness.

In the days before the First World War there were many people in the sad plight of Annie Palmer (deafness apart) when she first came knocking on our door. In my early childhood I watched many a pair of ragged parents shuffling along the middle of our road—there never seemed to be any traffic to incommode them—holding the hands of three or four barefoot children as they sang or croaked their lugubrious hymn-tunes. Always, literally always, hymn tunes, and nearly always the ones in a minor key like "Jesu, Lover of My Soul" (sung to *Aberystwyth*). As I watched from our front room window I was always more interested in the children than in the parents. Why were they not at school like my brother? Did they ever play games? (They were often crying, no doubt from boredom; and usually their noses were running.) If my father was at home he would sometimes go to the door and beckon to them. Then he would bring the whole family into the kitchen and give them hunks of bread and jam—

it seemed always to be bread and jam: we had no butter. Many years later I came to know that you could hire these children from their real parents, sometimes indeed from an orphanage, the fee being a percentage of whatever charitable proceeds their paraded misery had coaxed from the pockets of the public into your own.

But raggedness, visible poverty, and especially deformity were far commoner then; and seemed to excite less sympathy. Even my mother used to quote the words of Jesus as a kind of comfort:[1] "You have the poor among you always, so that you can do good to them when you will: I am not always among you." And I remember an incident involving poor deaf Annie that left me puzzled then, and puzzles me now. I was with her in a horse-tram at Seven Sisters Road, waiting excitedly for it to begin. I was four; and I believe it was the only time I ever in my life went in one of those entrancing vehicles. As I knelt on the seat looking out of the window a man walked by, a horribly crippled man, dragging and wriggling his feet and hands in the slow contortions which I later came to recognise as those of *locomotor ataxia*. I watched him with dreadful absorption and pity. Then I saw that four children, not much older than I, were following him, in single file and flopping their feet and hands in the same way, giggling with shared delight. I was incredulous at first, and then incoherent with rage. I scrambled down from the seat and struggled with Annie to get out of the tram—to do I know not what, but I felt literally murderous. I screamed and cried with rage, and pummelled away at poor Annie until the tram started. When we got home she described the episode to my parents, in her shrill deaf voice, and was laughing so much that the tears ran down her cheeks. Oh, it was funny, that line of cruelly mocking children. Funny to poor deaf Annie, to the children, and I suppose to more people then than would be amused by it now. But at least those children were free, not hired and exploited for their poverty or brutishness.

By 1908 the law had caught up with this. A Children Act made it an offence to "cause a child to be in the street for the

_____
[1] Mark 14: 7.

purpose of begging—whether or not there is any pretence of singing, playing, performing, or offering anything for sale". And it was laid down then, and re-enacted in 1933,[1] that this applied to a child who had been "lent or hired out" for such a purpose. But by 1908 the school attendance officers had caught up with it too, and child-decoys of this kind must have been hard to come by. I'm glad I didn't at the time apprehend the disgust that these little groups probably had to conceal, as they were presented with the bread-and-jam they didn't want instead of the pennies which they did. No such insight ruffled the complacency with which I shared the joy of giving and the knowledge that my father could do these scriptural deeds because he was rich. His pay at that time was thirty-one shillings a week.

One day when I was about seven, a man came along the middle of the road playing a violin. Street musicians were frequent, and nearly always to be preferred to "singers"; the most exciting among their instruments being the barrel-organ—my rather old-fashioned father called it the hurdy-gurdy—and the most boring the concertina. Barrel-organ men were often accompanied by small chained-up monkeys whose function always seemed to me uncertain and their expression sad; and in the Seven Sisters Road you could see a man with a concertina and a chained bear, bigger than himself, which danced some lumbering steps whenever its master, judging that enough people might be looking their way, jogged it into action. The violinist was playing something which, to my infant mind, seemed quite tuneless and unplanned, and yet for some reason magical. I could hardly believe my ears. I became aware that my father, who was shaving at the time (I don't know what time of day it was), had suddenly gone to the front door and opened it. The playing stopped and it was as if some splendid light had gone out. Then the violinist and my father (his face still half-covered in shaving soap) went through to the kitchen. I hurried after them and stood in a corner to listen. Not only bread and jam this time: there

[1] Children and Young Persons Act 1933, section 4 (3); though I very much doubt whether, in 1933, this cynical use of children was still prevalent.

was also a mug of cocoa. And the man agreed to play again, for my special benefit, what he had been playing in the street. I suppose it's one of the most hackneyed pieces in the whole world of "popular classics", but I was transfixed. He must have been a competent player. When he had gone my father told me he'd been playing the Intermezzo from *Cavalleria Rusticana*, and then got out his flute and played it through to me again, with remnants of shaving soap still on his face. Nothing to this day can evoke in me such poignant nostalgia. My Uncle Bert was later brought into the discussion because he too played the violin (having, I remember, much trouble with his breathing while he was doing it; he held his breath as he arranged his fingering, and then breathed rapidly to make up for it as he plied the bow). He told me that the Intermezzo was far too difficult for him. It wasn't, but the assurance convinced me that the episode with the violinist had been a great adventure. And in its effect on my musical education, that's what it was.

Beginning at about this time, I was often taken to garden parties, fêtes, and open-air band performances at which my father played the flute and piccolo. Always he was called upon to play piccolo solos, which had names like *The Wren*, *Silver Birds*, and *Le Rossignol de l'Opéra*. They shrilled out among the surrounding trees and deck-chairs, the people applauded, my father executed little Japanese-style bows in all directions, and I nearly suffocated with pride and the effort of thinking up some way of showing the crowd that this magician was my own father. In due course I got to know the entire military band repertoire of the time, which in our case had to include *The Geisha* and *San Toy* because the then conductor of the City of London Police Band was Sidney Jones, the man who composed them—a musician, they said, to his finger-tips. Much more important, it also included what my father always impressively called "The Standard Overtures", delectable and unforgettable pieces which today you seldom hear anywhere, the almost forgotten minor work of composers like Rossini, Donizetti, Auber, Suppé, Wallace, Balfe, Herold, Adam, Offenbach, Verdi, Nicolai, Bizet, Gounod, and a host of others. Later I was allowed in the evenings to go to the practice

sessions of the bands and amateur orchestras in which my
father was playing or had played, to sit in a corner and listen
entranced while the shirtsleeved gladiators rehearsed the
things I loved. And occasionally the conductor would even
ask (I suppose because I had become a kind of mascot) if
there was something I would specially like—knowing in
advance that I should always choose an overture with spectacu-
lar passages for clarinets, or *Tannhaüser* for the trombones, or
Ruy Blas for its bassoons.

Opposite No. 101 Woodstock Road was a London County
Council "elementary school"; and facing our front door a
formidable iron gateway breached its long brick wall. Over
the gateway, in stone letters, was the word INFANTS; and it
was the first word I could ever read. As the fruits of prolonged
study from our front room window, I could even write this
word (or rather draw it, for I knew nothing of what the
individual letters meant) before I went to school, and I went
to school at the age of three. I believe I was considered pre-
cocious enough to begin at that age, and from long contem-
plation of the INFANTS in the playground (as seen from our
bedroom window) I knew exactly how, at play-time, you had
to rush about and scream, punch people, pull the girls' hair,
struggle about on the ground, and stand still when someone
rang a handbell. Moreover, for more than twelve months I
had been able to mount any kerbstone, having just crossed a
road, without first coming to a complete stop. Getting up
on to the pavement was now a continuous movement. (Incidentally, knowing what a climacteric this event must be for
all of us, I do not understand why it has always escaped the
attention of biographers, poets and those social psychologists
who can predict statesmanlike, holy, or criminal careers for
others if only they are allowed to watch them as children.)

Within a few months I was able to announce that I was
learning shorthand. My father was then teaching himself
Pitman's Shorthand and I had grown accustomed to seeing
its characters covering countless scraps of paper—even old
paper bags—with their spidery neatness. My parents tried to
explain that what I was learning was "pot-hooks and hangers",
that is to say the loops of longhand letters like h and y; but I

knew better, it was I who was now going to school, not they. Some years later I did learn shorthand at school, and by the time I was fourteen my father was not only very proficient but excited that there was now another shorthand writer in the family. He used to count up the words in a *Daily Telegraph* leading article, mark them off in hundreds, stand a clock on the kitchen table and get my mother to dictate the piece to both of us. My poor mother would read such selected passages for a couple of hours at a time, gradually increasing the speeds—until, at one period, my father and I could not only "get it down" at 130 words a minute but read it back. The time even came when I could beat him. I can remember a phrase from a Winston Churchill speech—it must have been about 1914. Churchill had referred in the Commons to "earnest, honest, incorruptible honourable members": I got it down and an hour later could read it back, or perhaps I should say guess what it was. My father's shorthand, incredibly, had failed him! It was another milestone. I would have said he was shorthand crazy if it hadn't lasted so many years. He was the only man I have ever known to possess his own little library of standard books printed in Pitman's Shorthand— *The Vicar of Wakefield, The Adventures of Sherlock Holmes, Huckleberry Finn* and, believe it or not, the complete King James Bible. (I read more copiously in that Shorthand Bible than in any other Bible before or since, and can still visualise the oriental neatness of its beautifully lithographed pages. I wonder if that particular—and surely eccentric—publishing venture paid off?)

I have been told that the teachers in my first school had sixty children in their classrooms and I can well believe it. Each teacher taught her class everything, from "Scripture" to drawing, from reading to "sums". The one in my first class, even though she had me and everyone else for a whole year, can't possibly have got to know us all, still less to "understand" us or find us interesting (if we were). Yet somehow or other that marvellous woman had taught me to read by the time I was four. Towards the end of that year she discovered what she'd done, and thereafter would sometimes depute me, last thing on a Friday afternoon, to read to the whole class from a simple version of the Greek myths about Hercules and the Gods. (I can remember thinking that Zeus was a silly way of spelling Jesus, rather like the deliberate mistakes they made in advertisements; and that Jesus must have been Hercules' daddy.) Nothing is more vivid in my recollection than the miserable embarrassment of that exercise, and my determination not to show it. Within a year after that the excitement had gone; and from then until the early end of my schooldays, for one reason and another, I hated and feared school as much as any child in Dickens. If there had been anything at home that could be called a nursery, Winston Churchill would have been speaking for me when he wrote:

> I was happy as a child with my toys in the nursery. I have been happier every year since I became a man. But this interlude of school makes a sombre grey patch upon the chart of my journey.

As it comes, I can consciously remember only two things (apart from how to read) that I learned at Woodstock Road LCC Elementary School, which I left when I was five. One is that "the fear of the Lord is the beginning of wisdom", which must have engraved itself merely because I liked the sound of it, for I certainly did not understand it. (I don't now.) The other, enunciated unforgettably by a very thin woman teacher who wore steel-rimmed glasses, is that uniquely exciting little jingle:

> Hark, hark, the dogs do bark,
> The beggars are coming to town.

Equipped with which knowledge I was translated to an exactly similar school at Montem Street, Finsbury Park, where my parents had moved to what seemed a finer abode (actually a tiny terrace house) at No. 122 Corbyn Street.

In those days, if you were getting on for six years old you were allowed to play in the street. There were public parks where you could play, but very few games you could play in them. Parks were for sitting in and looking at tulips, rhododendrons and ducks. And they had three other grave disadvantages:

they were so far off that you were not allowed to walk there, they were frequented by "strange men" to whom you must not talk, and they were patrolled by park-keepers who were paid to stop people enjoying themselves.

Accordingly, group juvenile enjoyment in the London streets of 1907 seems to have confined itself almost entirely to adult-baiting and wilful damage. Even when it took the form of lamp-post cricket, the only way to achieve a boundary hit was to drive the ball through a front parlour window— four if the window was open, six if it was closed and the ball went through. The trouble about a six-hit was that "stumps" had to be drawn immediately, both teams racing for the nearest street corner to get out of sight. For the rest, all was directly dependent upon grown-up wrath. My street mates and I, of both sexes, would hide behind the privet hedges by which the more decorous of the tiny front gardens held themselves aloof from the street, wait for a likely-looking passer-by, and throw down behind him a penny attached to a length of black thread. (Coins in those days made an absolutely distinctive jingle which, I sadly suppose, will never again be heard.) It would have disappeared before he could turn to pick it up, and then came the principal entertainment—the victim's anxious search, first for the vanished coin and then for any holes in pockets or handbags. How we kept quiet I do not know—he would be within a few feet of us and we were nearly bursting with glee. Sometimes we stuck the penny to the pavement with quick-setting fish-glue, stood round it until the glue was hard and the coin immovable, and then dispersed to watch. True, you could prise it up with a pocket-knife, but the moment we saw anyone go to his pocket for any kind of implement we dashed out, claimed the coin as ours, and innocently explained that, having accidentally fallen into some glue, it had then rolled out through the front garden gate. It was simpler, of course, to stick a penny stamp on the pavement, for people would spend a surprising amount of time picking at that with their finger-nails; but you lost the stamp, and it was better to have your fun for nothing.

For sheer enjoyment, it must be said, nothing approached "knocking down ginger", and in its most advanced form this involved tying a length of black cotton from one front-door knocker to another exactly opposite on the other side of the street. There then ensued a wait until a passer-by, perhaps a vehicle, broke the cotton and banged both knockers. One made sure, of course, that both houses were occupied and that all their occupants were indoors. (The advent of television must have made this game both easier and more rewarding?) Ecstatic, silent, wet-faced laughter is not to be had so cheaply by any other means. The malevolence of it, the dependency on the suffering of others, was the wanton cruelty of comedy and laughter throughout the ages; as always in such a context we credited our invisible victims with no human feeling other than rage and the will to retaliate dangerously. Juvenile delinquency had not yet been invented: the Children's Courts were still no more than a gleam in the eye of Sir Herbert Samuel at the Home Office. Nor, it is cogent to record, did any of our party come from a broken home, have parents who fought or copulated "in front of the children", or spend more than one evening a week at the cinema. We had, of course, no television to debauch our tender minds, though I can remember two households with magic lanterns.

Nor did knocking down ginger involve running away. You simply crouched and watched, until the angry householders had slammed their doors and gone in, when you came out and tied two more knockers together; or perhaps, on a specially daring evening, the same ones. What did involve running away was the riskier, and more deeply satisfying, adventure of tying the black cotton, at a carefully chosen moment, from a front-garden tree to a lamp-post at the level of a policeman's helmet. It shocks me now to recall that I did this many, many times, and that we all got away only because (a) the policeman had first to retrieve his rolling helmet and (b) we were wearing old plimsolls and he had to run in heavy boots. My disapproval of it began retrospectively when, years afterwards, I too had occasion to chase someone while wearing police uniform and heavy boots.

It was the world of the peg-top; the "winter warmer" for your hands (a few burning rags inside a perforated cocoa-tin); the peep-show made in a cardboard shoe-box with spy-holes at one end (one small marble, or "meggie", per peep). It was the world of the iron hoop, propelled by a "skimmer", the most satisfying of devices. At night I hung my beloved hoop on a nail in the kitchen, an object of as much pride and love as the smartest of souped-up sports models to modern man; and took the skimmer to bed with me, as a reminder that the hoop must still be hanging there, awaiting my pleasure and skill.

And among our multitudes of "traditional rhymes" I recall from 1907 one which Iona and Peter Opie, in their delectable book *The Lore and Language of Schoolchildren*,[1] could trace no farther back than the beginning of the First World War:

> Hark the jelly-babies sing
> Beechams' Pills are just the thing.
> They are gentle, meek and mild,
> Two for a man and one for a child.
> If you want to go to heaven
> You must take a dose of seven;
> If you want to go to Hell
> Take the blinking box as well.

It was sung as Christmas approached, to the tune of *Hark, the Herald Angels*. The last two lines had to be repeated, and the word blinking admitted a number of twin-syllabled variants for use when no girls were of the party. (Nowadays, would it matter if they were?) Never a good joiner-in at sing-songs, I sang this with an idiot and pop-eyed fervour, I remember, long after the parody had ceased to be funny.

It was at Montem Street School, at the age of eight, that I first became aware of injustice and the social defects of punishment. The whole of the story is too banal to bear repetition, but I was repeatedly caned, and made to sit during all my lessons at a desk pulled conspicuously apart from my schoolfellows, as someone unfit for their company because I had committed some petty offence and then persistently denied it. I was totally innocent of this offence, bewildered by the accusa-

[1] Oxford, Clarendon Press, 1959, p. 89.

Above, left: My mother, Edith Mary Hewitt (*née* Speed—died 1909)

Above: My father, Frederick Thompson Hewitt in 1901 (the year of my birth)

Left: My grandfather, John Hewitt [RSM, S. Wales Borderers] killed at Isandhlwana, Zulu War, 22 January 1879

1901, the year of my birth; and Cheapside, the centre of my policemanship twenty years later. A distribution of food to the poor to commemorate the accession of King Edward VII

tion, and appalled that grown-ups (they included the head-master) could be satisfied with such a low standard of proof. It's more than sixty years ago and I remember the whole thing with total clarity. The segregation went on for weeks, as did the community contempt and jeering which segregation, enforced or voluntary, always encourages. Unlike other children, I never had the guts to play truant; and went to school day after day knowing that the teacher calling the register, when he came to my name, would call out either "Liar" or "Ananias". (He was right for the wrong reason. I could lie resourcefully, but had lied to no one about this.) Eventually my parents realised that something was wrong and one evening the whole story came out. To my limitless embar-rassment my father stormed round to the school the next morning and "had it out with them". I was restored to a kind of reluctant favour and to my former seat in the classroom. And then a week later another boy owned up to the peccadillo, whatever it was, that had started the whole thing; and was *not* punished. From that time onwards I never had any faith in "justice"; and am quite certain that I acquired a kind of qualified contempt for "law and order" at the hands of one fatheaded and probably distracted schoolmaster.

I believe I regard this episode clinically rather than with self-pity, and I tell the story because I consciously connect it (not, I hope, fancifully) with a lifelong interest in punishment systems, "criminal investigation" and law reform. My first wife, who was at Christ's Hospital School for Girls, Hertford, at about the same time, had a similar experience which she too was totally unable to forget. Her initials were "A.M.B.", and someone else carved them on the wooden seat in the chapel organ-loft. (No one need doubt this story: unlike myself she was incapable of lying.) There was a ceremonial row, which got worse and worse as she indignantly and tearfully denied the offence. She was punished, and in addition the entire school sent her to Coventry for a whole term. . . . I don't suggest that either of us has spent a lifetime of smouldering resentment as a result of these penal idiocies, and I cannot speak for her in the matter of psychological consequences. But never once, in all the psychiatric and "social enquiry" reports that I have had to read in later years, have I found any sign that this kind of experience is even guessed at, let alone understood. "Children are remarkably resilient", people say if such an event *does* come to light. "They soon get over these things." Do they?

My mother Edith, less vivid in my recollection than the dominating, confident figure of my father, was nevertheless a spirited woman who could "give as good as she took". It has always been a surprise to me that I remember very little between her singing me to sleep when I was almost a baby, and the long, cruel illness that killed her when I was nine years old. It was her death from cancer which brought about my third change of domicile: my father took a house in Fulham (50 Gowan Avenue).

She had seemed to me to be always ill in bed, a state of affairs I accepted with a matter-of-factness that now seems to me inexpressibly shocking. Her sister Caroline, herself very recently widowed (how people died in those days!), had been staying with us as our substitute Mum. Auntie Carrie, as we called her, was one of the gentlest and most loving persons I have ever known, and at this point she justifies a digression.

Like all the Speed family and the Hewitts, Auntie Carrie was deeply religious, a follower of Moody and Sankey and of Torey Alexander, and an expert on all their rumty-tum hymns. Despite all that she lived through, including the defection of my father, my brothers and myself from the Methodist Church, and indeed any church, she retained to the end of her long life an unshaken faith in the simple Christian Gospel. She lived to be ninety-three, and in her last few years talked to me vividly about her early childhood. She remembered the Franco-Prussian War of 1870, and the "awful stories" about the besieged Parisians eating rats and dogs; 1870 was a sad year, she said, because Charles Dickens had died, and he seems to have been more important to the literate poor than any publicist has ever been since, despite all that the "media" can do. The Speed family had been great readers of Dickens's periodical *All the Year Round*, in which some of the Dickens novels had been serialised before or after publication as books. As a child, Carrie used to see Thomas Carlyle in the streets of Chelsea: he had been pointed out to her by some awe-stricken grown-up, and she had a hazy impression that he had somehow suppressed the French Revolution single-handed. He often spoke gently to children at play in the streets, but sternly disapproved of the absorption in hopscotch which commonly involved danger for passers-by.

The Speeds had lived at 82 Upper Ebury Street, Pimlico, and John Edward Speed, the father of the family, was a carpenter and joiner employed at the South Kensington Natural History Museum. He died in 1877 at the age of forty-six. Among his nephews were two who became famous artists: Harold Speed, who did portraits of King Edward VII, King Albert of Belgium, John Burns, Holman Hunt, Lilian Braithwaite and Mark Hambourg; and Lancelot Speed, who for many years drew for *Punch*. When John Edward Speed died it became necessary for the oldest daughter (Carrie, who became my stepmother) to earn money for the household. Accordingly at the age of thirteen she was making sleeves and bodices for women's wear shops, and button-holes for men's suits. A couple of years later Edith (my mother) joined her at Derry and Toms, and that is what she was doing when she first met my father.

Both Edith and Carrie told me many times, not complainingly but by way of pointing an interesting contrast, that throughout their childhood they never had a "shop-made" doll or toy. They made dolls out of rags, and they played with cotton-reels. Anyway, nearly all families, they said, had small babies which could be carefully used as dolls when necessary. She and her brothers and sisters seldom went in any kind of passenger vehicle. There were horse-buses, horse-trams, and hansom cabs, but no money. Any place that was beyond walking distance might as well have been across the English Channel. I know that my own mother carried me in her arms, a vast lump of a baby, from Marshalsea Road in Southwark to the People's Palace in Mile End Road, a good three miles, when we all went to the very first "bioscope", or movie, in 1902. (I disconcerted the family later by giving some account of the film we saw, a flickering affair in which bearded sailors ran round a capstan and hauled up an anchor. I remembered it quite clearly though I was but twelve or thirteen months old

B

when I saw it; but I think I never managed to convince them.)

Nursing her dying sister Edith through 1909 and most of 1910, Carrie lost her own husband in 1910 and we thus had two family funerals in quick succession. I can remember boasting about these at school, as if the loss of one's mother and uncle were something to be exploited for its prestige value. I do not know at what age common decency and humanity secured their first precarious foothold in my nature, but they had not yet appeared. Carrie swore to her sister that she would be a mother to us three boys, and if ever a promise was religiously fulfilled it was this.

I'm sure that we called her Mother almost from the day she took up residence with us. The Saturday morning on which my father married her had been heralded by some strange household developments, mainly in the larder. This had always contained a big McFarlane Lang biscuit tin which, since it had been known on rare occasions to contain ginger-nuts, played a large part in the furtive side of our lives. One day Harold made the shattering discovery that, instead of ginger-nuts, it contained a big iced cake. He kept this bewildering discovery to himself, but the next day the larder contained jellies and small basins of blanc-mange. Roland and I had discovered these for ourselves; and when he told us about the cake we all went into conference about the strange new ambience now subtly transfiguring the household. Harold was the first to come up with the answer. "I've got it!" he shouted. "Mother and Father are getting married!" And then, agreeably struck by the domestic comedy of the situation, he pulled Roland and me towards him and theatrically put his arms round our necks. "Poor little bastards," he said consolingly, "you'll be all right now." I felt that he had never said anything so shocking. The Saturday morning of the wedding is made memorable by an episode which I recall with shame, and with the special incredulity attaching to something which is impossible and which has nevertheless taken place. My father always sent us, and went himself, to German barbers. There was a popular English belief in those days, to which my father for some reason subscribed, that only a German barber knew how to cut hair. English ones were "botchers", bungling amateurs. Early on the morning of the wedding which was to give us a new mother, my brother Harold and I were accordingly dispatched to a German barber's at Walham Green, to be done. Harold must have said something to him about the wedding, and the delighted barber seized upon it as a challenge to his sense of *Gastlichkeit*. He spent a devoted hour distorting our dead-straight hair into semi-spherical clusters of tight little curls. I think we were both a bit appalled, taking comfort in the fact that it was a highly unusual kind of day and the belief that the curls would all disappear by Monday morning. (They didn't.) We hurried back to present ourselves for the wedding, to find that we were about an hour late.

My father was nearly beside himself. German hairdressing assumed a new position much lower down the scale of professional *savoir faire*. We were hurried into our new grey knickerbocker suits and told to keep our caps on as much as possible during the various parts of the day before us. We looked ridiculous, knew it, and disapproved, in consequence, of the entire proceedings. The episode prepared us to believe the appalling stories, so soon to fill the newspapers, of German "frightfulness" in the First World War.

I think it ought to be recorded that on the walk to the Congregational Church in Fulham Palace Road (there was no nonsense about cars or carriages), Harold, Roland and I found ourselves strolling unsupervised behind an unfamilar couple who were suitably dressed up for the occasion. The man, that is to say, was wearing a grey topper. I can't remember who they were: they must have been friends or rarely-seen relatives. Harold, to our horror, suddenly produced from his pocket an elastic catapult and a tightly-folded paper pellet— the V-shaped kind with which you pulled back the elastic and then let go. "Watch this," he said tersely. There was a thud and the grey topper slid forward on to the man's nose. When he turned angrily round the three of us were absorbed, with a botanical intensity none of us had ever shown or felt before, in the study of a miserable-looking shrub in one of the tiny front gardens lining the road. It can't have been very convincing, but perhaps the sanctity of the day interceded for us. Anyway I can't remember that there was any deserved sequel, and if there was I think its memory would have been effaced by the dislodgement of that grey topper. Grey toppers and catapults must have been invented by the same thoughtfully happy man.

I was now at an LCC "Central School" at Childerley Street, Fulham. This (I thought at the time) was because I had failed in what would now be called the 11-plus examination, was thought to be probably ineducable, and yet had to be sent somewhere. I'm sure now that the "failure" meant little to me at the time, though the consequences have since been starkly obvious. One day at the beginning of morning school, a teacher whose name and personality I completely forget, called upon eight boys to go and stand by his table. I was one of them. Having told the other seven that they had all passed the scholarship exam he turned last to me with a gentle smile to say "and not Hewitt". It would be fine and dramatic to be able to say that this almost unbelievable pronouncement came like the echoing clang of a cell-door, but it didn't. It came like one more awkward and unavoidable exposure to be explained at home, and a challenge to one's capacity to turn a palpable disgrace into an occasion for pity and head-patting. I forget what formula I evolved for this, but I did it. My brother Harold had passed his 11-plus three years before and was at the Latymer Foundation Upper School, Hammersmith. I was vicariously and intensely proud of this academic distinction in the family, and (far more than he ever knew) modelled my life upon his, using his school catch-phrases everywhere, though I seldom knew what they meant, learning his "poetry homework" by heart, memorising his school songs. I still know all the songs, they were always more exciting than anything at my own school:

> The old Black Monk stood still to hear
> Caerleon's bells go ringing clear.

Discipline at Childerley Street, its main preoccupation, was thought to be enhanced by the constant swishing of canes. My predominant recollection of that school is the whistle of a cane through the air as it was applied by some large and angry man to the hands or seat of some scholar who, miraculously, never seemed to think of hitting back. I was caned with clock-work regularity, even when I was fourteen and strong enough to have knocked some of the masters down and walked on them. But I never did. Instead, because I always turned white with pain and rage, I was sent out into the playground to recuperate in the fresh air—or perhaps to ensure some sort of interval, however short, in which I could not qualify for yet another caning. Significantly, I simply cannot remember what any of these canings was about; a fact which, I suppose, combines with the regularity of the caning to offer its own comment on the efficacy of punishment. Perhaps the masters felt better; though there were two of them, Boole and Snelling (they respectively taught shorthand and history), to whom it never seemed to occur. Perhaps it's a coincidence that, between them, they taught me more than any two men I have ever known.

School, therefore, from 1910 until the end of 1914, was a background to life as sombre and senseless as the war which then took over from 1914 until the end of 1918. An unreal and meaningless world, devoid of purpose, and to be escaped from only by way of countless books which intensified the sense of not belonging. The beginning of that period is con-fused in my memory with the death of my mother, my father's remarriage, and an enjoyably frightening period when he was coming home from the City each night to tell us about the Houndsditch murders, the Sydney Street Siege, Mauser automatic pistols, Dr Crippen and a fatal drug called hyoscine. I remember that on one of these nights my brother and myself, without quite knowing why, were afraid to go to bed. My private world seemed more and more remote and ever more desirable: the world of Scott's novels and Robert Louis Stevenson's, of Tom Sawyer and Huck Finn, Marryat and Ballantyne, Alexandre Dumas, the *Lays of Ancient Rome*, the uncountable books of the forgotten George Manville Fenn (I could recite a list of thirty or forty Fenn novels to this day; and yet I recently glanced through a few of them in wonder-ment that they could ever have been thought worth publishing); and of course the incomparable *Magnet* and the *Gem, Chums* and the *Boys' Friend Threepenny Library*, which offered long, complete stories (by "S. Clarke Hook") about Jack, Sam and Pete. Does anyone remember Jack, Sam and Pete? Jack and Sam were the white friends—almost, I think, hangers-on— of a gigantic American Negro, who was not only stronger than Samson but richer than Croesus. Pete picked up objectionable characters with one hand and dropped them into ponds, and if a railway company refused to put on a special train for him he bought the railway and ran it himself. With the exception of the *Magnet* and the *Gem*, all this literature had the *imprimatur*, though not always the active encouragement, of my father; which robbed it, unavoidably, of just a little of its glamour. Forbidden reading included anything you could call a "comic", of which I read a vast number, and elusively wicked books like Elinor Glyn's *Three Weeks*, Victoria Cross's *Five Nights*, and Boccaccio's *The Decameron*, all of which evoked a disappointment amounting to stupefaction; and all of which had to be read close to the bedroom window in the fading light of long sad summer evenings.

My books came from two sources. First, the Fulham public library, where their distinguishing characteristic was that they had black covers as thick as a drawing board and were printed on a kind of cartridge paper. Second, an elderly Sunday-school teacher (at Munster Park Congregational Church) called Mr Herbert. I was sent to Sunday school regularly, not just to get me out of the way while irreligious parents dozed in their chairs (as with so many of my fellow Sunday-scholars), but in the hope that Sunday school might succeed where day-school had failed in turning my eyes to the light. Far from being irreligious, my parents were regular church-goers (we called it chapel) and took their none-too-willing children to Sunday evening services for years. Mr Herbert at the Sunday school was a rebel against the system, which tolerated him uneasily because his Sunday-school class of potentially ill-behaved boys was always completely quiet and well behaved. And why? Because he read books to us: *Martin Rattler*, *The Settlers in Canada*, *The Fifth Form at St Dominic's*, *The Pickwick Papers* (so long as we promised not to laugh aloud). He even bought new books for the purpose—I remember listening to *The History of Mr Polly* and deciding, at the age of ten, that H. G. Wells must be the best writer the world had ever known.

But those years from 1910 to 1915 were also irradiated by family visits, almost every Friday evening, to the Putney Bridge Cinema, where the timeless Westerns, the Chaplin knockabouts and the cliff-hanging *Exploits of Elaine* were almost eclipsed by the joy of hearing a live "orchestra" accompany the soundless movies. Actually it comprised a violin, 'cello, flute and piano. My father would tell us that the flautist was using a Boehm concert flute and unorthodox fingering and we marvelled that he could tell. The orchestra didn't play all the time: it was the piano that got no rest. But the sound of that little ensemble tuning-up when it was about to begin the Overture to *Raymond* or the *William Tell* ballet music has lodged in my memory as more exciting than any music ever written, an ecstasy of anticipation which no performance in the world could have surpassed. The pianist, when alone, matched his music to the events on the screen, but not so the orchestra. That would go straight through the *Rosamunde* Overture, Luigini's *Ballet Egyptien*, or Alan Macbeth's *Love in Idleness* whether it matched the picture or not, with results that were sometimes comic to everyone but me. (I often defended it, afterwards, in tears of rage while everyone else was laughing. The members were anonymous heroes to me, never subsequently outshone even by Jack Hobbs, Bill Tilden, Toscanini or Kreisler.)

I always noticed that Westerns had a marked effect, in those days, on the deportment of grown-up men coming out of the cinema. You would see harmless-looking little fathers walking with their feet wide apart and their arms, which would normally be swinging, held stiffly so that their unclasped hands were about four inches from where their pistol-holsters ought to be. I did the same, of course, but it always wore off before one got home. It may perhaps be specially fortunate at these times that the British are not allowed to carry guns: for it is said by those who should know that after every motor-racing event the spectators, on their way home, drive like maniacs and have many crashes.

The one place out of bounds to me was the foreshore of the River Thames, and it was accordingly the place where I spent most of my time. I came to know every feature of the Putney foreshore (the Fulham one was almost impossible to get to and thick black mud when you got there) from Hammersmith to Barnes Bridge. I swam the river, naked, I don't know how many times, hiding my clothes in an abandoned punt that lay near the mouth of the Beverley Brook for years. I loafed around the famous boat-houses at Putney until, having been told repeatedly, eloquently and fruitlessly to go away, I finally got accepted as a kind of auxiliary and was allowed to help in carrying the racing skiffs to and from the water. Eventually I was permitted to take dinghies out to fetch things from boats anchored offshore; and once at least the great Bossy Phelps gave me hints about oarsmanship. Never could I mention these incredible adventures at home; and once, having fallen out of a dinghy, I sat through a long supper-time in my wet clothes and no one noticed that they were wet. I was Tom Sawyer on the Mississippi and it was a secret life.

It all came to an end with the war, with the distant and incredible boom of Zeppelin bombs, the sudden transformation of relatives into soldiers, the concert-parties in the Bishop's Park singing "Keep the Home Fires Burning" and "We Don't Want to Lose You, but We Think You Ought to Go". My father was promoted, given charge of a police division, and told he must move to the City. It was the biggest adventure of all. The City of London! It meant that I must leave my hated school for ever.

And yet I must not leave it here without acknowledging that it did rather more than inflict physical pain and fill me with a longing to be free of school for ever (though that's what it succeeded in doing). A form-master named Williams came to take an interest in my scribbling, and took me aside (when I could have been, and wanted to be, at football in the playground) to tell me how the "rules" could be broken if you knew when to do it. You *could*, after all (he almost whispered) begin sentences with "and" or "but". You could even end them with prepositions. You could split infinitives when that was less clumsy than an obvious avoidance. (For some reason I could not, then or ever, bring myself to do it.) You had to avoid purple passages until you were well enough established, like Dickens, to go in for them and deceive the multitude into the belief that they must be good writing. It was nearly forty years later that Robert Lynd told me the same thing, though no man ever used less purple than Lynd in the whole of his writing life.

Above all, the "Fulham Central School" at Childerley Street supplied me with a unique friend in one Harry Woolsey, a boy whose lugubrious manner, though it may have fitted his unusually thoughtful disposition, disguised a delectable sense of humour and a touching optimism about myself as a youth with dazzling prospects. This optimism sustained him until we were past middle age, though by that time he was tending to admit that the prospects seemed less dazzling as you got closer to them. As for him, he went to Stockton-on-Tees and turned into an Inspector of Taxes, may their tribe decrease; but atoned for it by siring a beautiful daughter, who in due course gave up being an air hostess to become a television producer called Jan Foster, while retaining her position as my favourite quasi-niece. The school can't have been all that bad.

Anyway, it taught me Pitman's Shorthand, something about English and History, and (through no fault of its own) absolutely nothing about mathematics in any of its forms. It nevertheless implanted in my mind the capacity to be saddened with envy, many years later, by Bertrand Russell's reminiscence in his *Autobiography*: "The sublimest statement I ever came across as a young man was that 'the square of the sums of two numbers is equal to the sum of their squares increased by twice their product'." If I do this little sum today, I still gaze at the neat and inevitable answer, wondering why I do not understand it and feeling like a man born without some vital faculty. My school tried to teach me some physics and chemistry, unconsciously laying a foundation of interest which I excavated thirty years later. It certainly taught me enough French to support, during my period in the police service, a masquerade of unparalleled and profitable impudence as a translator. And its scholars taught me in the playground what I later understood to be the facts of life, the most astounding feature of which was that one came into this world through one's mother's navel at the end of some kind of rope. Unlikely as this method of getting out seemed to me at the time, it was less bizarre than the reputed method of getting in, which, after a long period of scornful rejection, I accepted slowly and reluctantly.

I was fourteen, and school was over. I never went to another. But education was just beginning, the kind that Wells may have had in mind when he said that "human history becomes more and more a race between education and catastrophe". In my case, catastrophe never stood a chance.

Chapter 2

ADOLESCENCE

IN THE CITY of London, on the corner of Cloak Lane and College Hill, there stands a police station whose architect must have been restrained with difficulty from incorporating in its exterior masonry the invitation from Dante's *Inferno: Lasciate ogni speranza, voi ch'entrate*. It belonged to the Corporation of London, which not only ran its own police force (it still does) but even in 1916 rather wanted to pull the place down and build something less like a Victorian "house of correction". The Corporation manfully resisted this weakness, and even in March 1941 resented the help of the German Luftwaffe, for it later rebuilt the place as it was before. And yet on the first and second floors there was a large, rambling family apartment of solid and spacious comfort which today would fetch a rental of £100 a week. This was my home from 1916 until 1921.

My father was required to live there, as the Chief Inspector of a City of London Police division. This is not the place for a dissertation on the origins and survival value of this island police force as a separate entity, or on whether it was and is efficient in itself or an obstacle to the efficiency of the country's police system as a whole. (I may find myself coming back to this, for it was later to involve me in many controversies.) But the effect of living there was odd and lasting. It meant that at the age of fourteen I was thrown among bachelor policemen, at that time mostly middle-aged, slow-moving and solid, and living under barrack conditions in what was known as the "section house" or the "single men's quarters". (All the young bachelors were away at the war.) Remotely at the top of that building was a fine billiard room with two full-sized tables, and there those elderly and indulgent policemen taught me how to play. I was an objectionably successful pupil, and by the time I was seventeen I could match them all: they had helped me discover the only game at which I was ever to be any good. I think they had another effect on me which at the time was specially important: they made me realise that I was among a colony of men who, with rare exceptions, were the salt of the earth.

My father had proposed that I should go to the City of London School (as my younger brother did later). I was panic-stricken. I implored him not to send me to any more schools of any kind, anywhere; and after many argumentative sermons I think he came to believe that if he insisted on having his way I should leave home. In particular, he thought I would try to get into the Army by giving a false age, and indeed it was much in my mind. I probably looked about eighteen. And not only was I unhappily aware that people looked at me as though I must be a "slacker" (the current term for a draft-dodger), but I had always fancied myself as a soldier anyway. Countless boys felt the same in those pre-Passchendaele days. I had watched with the usual envy as my elder brother Harold, having enrolled under "Lord Derby's Scheme" as the law required, appeared one day in the uniform of the Honourable Artillery Company—the oldest regiment, he told me proudly, in the British Army. We had both been fearful that some Army doctor might reject him, though we couldn't imagine what for. He would jump up and down fifty times to test his heart; and then as we both pressed our hands to his chest we would look at each other in horror at the rate of his heart-beats—which then turned out to be the same as mine after fifty similar jumps, and the same as anyone's would be.

Accordingly, my father found me a job as a junior clerk in what was called the "Entering Room" (I think because we "entered" purchases in the day-books) of a firm of ladies' dress and coat manufacturers called Spreckley, White & Lewis, at 13/15 Cannon Street; an old, respectable, kindly "family" firm in a six-storey building on whose top floor there once had lived two or three dozen rag-trade apprentices like Wells's Mr Kipps. In the corner of a huge and dingy basement room, with glass "pavement lights" above my head, I sat in a ramshackle elevated desk which looked like a disused plywood pulpit. Hurrying men and women handed up to me the invoices representing sales just effected in the mysterious and glamorous "Departments" upstairs—Mantles, Skirts, Furs, Costumes, Children's; all of which were staffed by statuesque and nubile young women of whom I was very frightened. I "entered" the details of these sales in large, lettered daybooks; and if the customer was getting, say, three dozen child's mackintoshes instead of the women's fur coats he had ordered, I had to write on a "compliments form" the intimation "regret send best can do to your esteemed order from stock". I was always impressed by the fact that, whatever words might be omitted to achieve this pidgin-English apology, the word "esteemed" was always carefully preserved. For this I was paid £40 a year and I thought proudly of Goldsmith's parson in *The Deserted Village*: "a man he was to all the country dear, and passing rich with forty pounds a year". I was to discover that £40 a year meant fifteen shillings a week; and worse, when I produced my first fifteen shillings at home my congenitally frugal mother gave me back, in all innocence, a solitary sixpence for pocket money and took the rest! I was speechless. My father then appeared on the scene and said that I was to be given the whole fifteen shillings. My brothers were both at school and earning nothing, he said, and that was where I ought to be too. But he wasn't going to have me pay for the privilege of not going. I learned years later that he never ceased to reproach himself for allowing me to leave school, and never really felt happy about me until it began to seem likely that I should earn a living as a writer. That, he then supposed, had been God's will all the time. Certain it is that if I had gone to school and university I should have written little or nothing; which might have been a good thing.

As it was, I began writing at the expense of my first employers, Messrs Spreckley, White & Lewis. The "entering room" was a perpetually busy place, but after a few months, because I had carefully developed a neat and flowing copperplate handwriting and took a pride in it, I came under the notice of the Counting House, the summit of clerkly aristocracy. I was called to see its Chief Cashier, a man called Mr

Cosier, a tall, hunchbacked old man whose demeanour was so suave and dignified, like that of all his senior colleagues, as to suggest that all such functionaries were thwarted aspirants for the Diplomatic Service. The whole place was governed by tall, stooping old men, their suits immaculate, their voices very loud, their accents impeccable. They walked very slowly about the building with small pieces of paper held enquiringly between two fingers.

Mr Cosier told me I was to keep the Sales Analysis books in the Counting House. This turned out to be almost a sinecure. Indeed there wasn't enough to do in the Counting House, which must have been overstaffed. Among the junior clerks there was much nipping out to coffee shops in the morning to play dominoes. I did this once or twice under persuasion, but thought it was dishonest to the last degree: I was genuinely horrified, and was sinfully satisfied to have done it once or twice and not been discovered. It was then that I began, in the many slack periods, scribbling stories and articles, at first for my own amusement but after a few months for intended publication. So far as I can remember the first time I ever read my own words in print was in the *Daily Chronicle* in 1917. It was sent in the form of a letter to say that Dr Guillotine didn't invent the guillotine, the paper's diarist used it as a paragraph, and I was sent £1. The stimulus of that £1! I scribbled incessantly, both at home and on scrap-paper at the Counting House. Undoubtedly, and reprehensibly, I began to neglect my work so that I could write feature articles for magazines. Passing rich with my forty pounds a year, I bought an elderly Yöst typewriter. I could also buy a ticket for the Ideal Home Exhibition at Olympia, and wrote what I thought was a hilarious account of it for *Punch*. This came back, but not with a mere rejection slip. "Quite promising," wrote the Editor, Sir Owen Seaman, "and I shall be interested to see anything else you care to send me. Unfortunately we have already dealt with the Ideal Home Exhibition." Lesson No. 1: read the paper you are proposing to write for.

Lesson No. 2 was that if you are going to use your employers' time for freelance journalism you mustn't leave your discarded drafts in the office waste-paper baskets. "It's all very well,"

I heard the Chief Cashier saying to Mr White (one of the partners, and one of the most tolerant of men), "but if he hasn't enough to do he should tell *me* about it. This is all covered with his writing. I'm always finding sheets of screwed-up paper covered with his writing." In due course I was summoned to see Mr Cosier and mournfully sacked.

Then there was my father to negotiate. He was upset but not too reproachful: the job had not turned out as he had expected. One thing about it had caused him a great deal of worry. Every Friday I was sent to the Midland Bank in Thread-needle Street to cash a £1,500 cheque for staff wages. It seems incredible to me today, but as a somewhat gormless lad of fifteen I went on this mission alone. The large black leather bag, with round grip-handles, had been used for generations and everyone must have known it was a bank messenger's hold-all. No one (I gathered) had ever been robbed on the way back with the money. The bank cashier used to hand me two "bricks" of 500 one-pound notes, one of 500 ten-shilling notes, and some little bags of silver and copper coins. And every Friday I sauntered back with this fortune, a pushover for any observant gang of "wage-snatch bandits". For some reason my father didn't get to know of this for about six months. When he did he was horrified. He at once decided to see the principal of the firm, then changed his mind because he thought it might jeopardise my position there, and then detailed a detective constable always to walk with me from the Bank doorway back to the office. As soon as I had left the firm he told them what had been going on, and how criminally stupid it was to send *anyone*, let alone a boy, to collect such a sum of money single-handed. They made no change in the practice, except that the last time I heard about it they were sending a girl.

I went to the *Daily Chronicle* offices and sought a job as a junior reporter. I had already written for the *Daily Chronicle*, I pleaded, hoping not to be challenged on it; and I could write shorthand at 130 words a minute (which at that time, was a lie). There was no vacancy for me, they said. I don't think I could have been very impressive. I was shy, hesitant, and very spotty. (I've realised since that acne played a very large part in my life for the next three or four years; and that, if I can judge from my own experience, it may be a malign and formative influence in the lives of countless adolescents.) A *Daily Chronicle* news-desk man gave me a few parting hints. "Get some kind of a job," he said, "a bread and butter job, and do your writing in the evenings. Don't go living on your parents while you try and get a foothold in the writing world."

My father, whose forbearance in all this was little short of amazing, said the obvious solution was a clerical job with free evenings. He swept aside half-hearted pleas that I might work in a music-shop ("You can't even read music"), a publisher's ("Not with your schooling"), or a garage ("no future there, if your writing turns out to be no good"). Among the senior officers of the war-time Special Constabulary at Cloak Lane Police Station was a chartered accountant named Harold Sully. This good-hearted man, who in appearance got as close to being a Teddy bear as would be possible without actually dressing up, was induced to take me on as an audit clerk with the much-respected firm of J. & A. W. Sully & Co., Chartered Accountants, 19/21 Queen Victoria Street. I went to Mr Cosier for a testimonial. "Testimonial?" he said incredulously, peering at me over gold-rimmed glasses from between his permanently hunched-up shoulders. "For what sort of work?" I told him. "Chartered Accountants?" His shoulders came up so far that his head nearly disappeared. "Well, I suppose you know what you're doing, but I doubt if they do." The "testimonial" contented itself with the observation, surely generous in the circumstances, that the character of C. R. Hewitt "was very satisfactory in every way" and that "he left in consequence of the work not being suitable"; leaving possible readers to guess why it was unsuitable, and to whom.

J. & A. W. Sully & Co., a firm originating in Bridgwater, had a large clientele of religious and philanthropic societies. The partners were non-conformists, the senior one, A. W. Sully, being an active member of the Congregational Church at Lyndhurst Road, Hampstead. When I joined the firm, every day began with a prayer-meeting in his first-floor office overlooking Queen Victoria Street.[1] I never went to one of them. If you happened to be in the London office at that time of the morning, it was always possible to receive a timely phone call and keep it going. The two office typists, captive as they were, could never escape. But the Sully partners were a good firm, kindly and concerned and tolerant in a way that was sometimes brought under great strain by a staff of hard-drinking and hard-living, though when necessary hard-working cynics, some of whom were always in hot water (usually with bookmakers) and having to be rescued by the firm. But there were good companions in that oddly-assorted little community, and one of them, whose name was W. A. Shackleford, was a marvellous companion whom I shall always think of with affection. And if he ever reads these words, I hope he will feel as ashamed as I do about the hours we spent playing billiards when we should have been putting ticks in cash-books, bought ledgers, and bank passbooks. He could remember more happily our long evening walks from the office, through St James's and Hyde Park and across Barnes Common to Roehampton; where, in the King's Head, we were taught to play skittles by the gamekeepers from Richmond Park, and I played the piano while a barful of people sang Edwardian ballads with the excruciating tuneless-ness to be heard in English pubs and nowhere else on earth.

I spent the next two years ticking at places like the British and Foreign Bible Society, the Wesleyan Methodist Missionary Society, the Shaftesbury Society, the Church of England Temperance Society, and the World's Evangelical Alliance. These involved me in no worrying problems, since they were "major audits" and all important decisions and account-ancy took place far above my head. But soon I was on my own at smaller jobs in the provinces, staying at hotels for a week or two at a time, trying to agree "trial balances" after many days of ticking, and eventually being asked (by a victim who would be paying for my dubious services by the hour) how much longer I was going to be? I got frightened at my ignorance

[1] In the photograph facing page 128 you can see the whole building falling across the street as a German incendiary bomb obliterated one phase in my otherwise non-incendiary career.

and spent all my 'evenings either at accountancy classes or reading Cropper's *Bookkeeping and Accounts* and Spicer and Pegler's *Executorship Law*. These of course were books that you studied if you were an articled clerk, intending to qualify by examination as a chartered accountant; which I wasn't.

Having discovered this, my father bade me find out how a clerk became articled and prepared himself to enter the profession. I had no preliminary qualifications whatsoever from school; and I ascertained that, once I had overcome this handicap by way of a special examination, my "articles" would cost £500 and I should serve for five years without salary. My father whistled when I told him this, but a few days later I overheard him discussing with my mother, to my genuine horror and dismay, the possible surrender of his life-endowment policy as a means of putting up the £500. It was then that I announced I was going to join the Metropolitan Police. I was nineteen.

I can't now remember why I thought he might have been pleased. Of course, I should get twice as much money—£3.50 a week as compared with the £1.75 that I was getting as a ticking machine. I should have to live in a kind of barracks known as a "section house", and should no longer be a financial burden at home. I should be in a safe, pensionable job at a time of chronic unemployment (this was 1920). And in my off-duty hours I should be able to write. If in due time I found myself writing successfully I could resign and set up as a full-time journalist—it wasn't like the Army, where you were bound to complete your agreed term "with the Colours".

When he was really angry he had a bitter tongue. He upbraided me for idiocy, selfishness, fecklessness, obstinacy. I was a numskull, he added (a favourite word of his). He said I should never be able to endure the monotony, hardship, and lack of private life. (And oh, he was so nearly right; and I endured them only because he had said I wouldn't.) I was a fool if I supposed that my off-duty conditions would be conducive to spare-time journalism, and even if they were conducive it would be contrary to the Police Regulations. The discussion ended with my mother in tears and my father, for once, unable to say any more.

A week later he wrote a letter to the Commissioner of the Metropolitan Police supporting my application for admission. The Metropolitan Police Surgeon, having examined me, declared that I was "not robust enough" (I was about 6 feet tall and weighed 11½ stone) and turned me down. We discovered later that they were determined not to recruit men under the prescribed age (which was twenty), and I had nearly another year to go; and they were unwilling to offer needless offence to a Chief Inspector in a neighbouring force. It was my turn to be angry and his to keep quiet, which he did superbly. Very soon after that I announced that I was going to try the City Police. This was too much.

"You can't possibly do that while I'm still here!" he almost shouted. "Apart from the awkwardness for me, you'll be distrusted by everyone, you'll be on your own all the time, any sort of success or promotion you ever get will be put down to favouritism, the sergeants and inspectors won't know what the devil to do about you. Can't you see all that, you numskull?"

The City Police accepted me. My father bought me all the things I should need—a big cabin trunk for my belongings, a pair of hand-sewn boots costing three times as much as any footwear I have had since, a supply of shirts and underclothing. And then he resigned from the police service which I had so embarrassingly invaded. I tried in various ways, in later years, to repay him for what he had done for me and to redress the wrongs I had done to him. The account is far from squared. He watched me, as J. P. Marquand wrote somewhere, "across the gulf of years and pathos which always must divide a father from his son".

My brief experience of accountancy had given me, I suppose, some insight into a world where (as Baudelaire said) even honesty is a financial speculation. I should acknowledge this before I go on. But I never got to understand how the figures that balanced a draft Trading and Profit-and-Loss Account came to be accepted by the shareholders in the form they took for the published Balance Sheet. And although it was never really my world, accountancy had one tremendous and lasting consequence for which I must always hold it dear.

Among the places where I spent much ticking-time was the head office of a company called Welford's Dairies Ltd in Elgin Avenue, Maida Vale. (It has long since been swallowed up by the huge dairy combines.) Its managing director was a Mr Trotman; and the Trotman family was one of those fabulously lucky dynasties which possessed a freehold box at the Albert Hall. I became friendly with the son, Bert Trotman, a man so utterly devoted to music that he almost looked like a treble clef with ginger hair. Because the Trotman family were unable for various reasons to use their Albert Hall box, he sometimes let me have the ticket for months at a time. I must have gone to hundreds of performances in those few years, during which I seldom missed for example a Landon Ronald orchestral concert. I was always alone, and yet always much aware that listening to music is, on the whole, a gregarious enjoyment, never to be fully savoured unless with a companion. I heard all the operatic and concert virtuosi of the time— Cortot, Kreisler, Heifetz, Rachmaninov, Lotte Lehmann, Solomon, Melchior, Gigli, even Paderewski. I heard Vladimir de Pachman, in his eighties, give a long Chopin recital, played with dazzling and insolent carelessness, and with half a dozen brilliant encores. And then, as 6,000 people stood frantically clapping, a young woman approached to give him flowers. He stepped forward, dragged her to the piano stool, pulled her on to his knee, and began kissing her with great enthusiasm, while the clapping died away and the crowd contemplated this unexpected finale in startled silence. She seemed to offer no resistance but I remember that, when the old man had been finally induced to stop, she half tottered away wiping her mouth with the back of her hand.

I wasted many an evening watching professional billiards at Thurston's or at Burroughs' Hall. At Burroughs' Hall in Leicester Square there was a chance at the close of play in the evenings to win a brand-new billiard-cue and case. When the two great men had stopped for the day—Inman and Reece, Newman and Smith, Joe Davis and Lindrum—the three balls were removed from the table, their places were marked with chalk, and three other balls were put there so that members of the audience could compete for the biggest break. I tried this dozens of times and was always easily beaten, usually by someone of about sixteen with a very pale face, protruding eyes, and an unlighted cigarette hanging from a corner of his mouth. I wasn't nearly as good as I thought I was, and yet kept on thinking I was.

It would be an easy way of getting past an awkward patch to say here that, throughout these teenage years, I was totally untroubled by girls. It would fall a long way short of the truth. From fifteen to almost twenty I was, I should judge, about as repellent to girls as it was possible for nature to arrange, for my face was covered with acne spots and blotches. I must have looked like a thoughtful red-currant pudding. The fact that nothing whatsoever could be done about it was expensively demonstrated by a succession of doctors and skin specialists. Nor, I gather, would they be able to do anything about it now, even if they were given the chance. Nor again, would they be given the chance, for the simple solution available to pimpled young men today is to cover their faces and chins with hair, leaving small apertures for the eyes; under which matted concealment the pimples can be happily allowed to do what they like until it's time for them to go away.

But in those days, facial convention among teenagers being what it was, beards were not on; and acne took a powerful hand in pre-selecting the company in which its representatives were acceptable. This did not include girls or people like the late Lord Rosebery. "All my life," said Lord Rosebery, and he spoke for mankind, "I have loved a womanly woman and admired a manly man; what I never could stand was a boily boy." It is the comfortable standpoint, at once light-hearted and exclusive, of the non-boily. But I have never seen it anywhere acknowledged (though it is understandable, surely) that the boily boy is not *persona grata* among girls; and it is important—it decides the course of a young man's life at a unique period, perhaps irreversibly. It confines him to the company of boys, where no one cares about the spots except, occasionally, to rejoice that here is someone with more spots than he has himself. Nothing, however, could prevent me from losing my heart to a succession of girls, all of whom were effectively prevented, you will now understand, from losing theirs to me. The first was the telephonist at Spreckley, White & Lewis's, a provocative redhead about ten years older than I. She tolerated my admiration for a time because she found it amusing. She left the firm even before I did and I never saw her again. But I did hear from her about thirty years later, when I had begun regular broadcasting; she then sent me affectionately teasing postcards and letters in a handwriting she made no attempt to disguise though she gave no address and never signed them with her name. Another girl, this time of my own age (her name was Phyllis), provided me for about two years with that rose-tinted view of a transformed universe which, my brother Harold and I agreed, amounted to being in love. An odd feature of it, we decided (and he was an expert), was a "sinking feeling" which could not be dispelled by hot Bovril, and a sudden realisation that all the world was a stage and all the men and women amiably stupid nonentities playing expendable bit parts. But it came to nothing, and I doubt not that Phyllis was helped to its conclusion by the reassertion of a preference, natural in any girl, for boys without spots on. She was succeeded by a sixteen-year-old cousin of mine, Sophie Allder, who lived at Tooting and who reduced the world to rubble one day by telling me she was in love with me. She seemed to me very beautiful and likely to have dozens of youths at her beck and call; and I spent much time, some of it in front of the mirror, wondering why she should have selected me. I never solved this, and probably discouraged her by spending too much time in the attempt. But I was a very serious young man, determined to be sure of my ground before suggesting that she should marry me (I was seventeen); and this because I doubted my capacity to retain for a lifetime the devotion of someone so attractive. Furthermore, my parents (though not, I believe, hers) were thoroughly alarmed at the looming prospect of a cousin marriage, which they thought eugenically wrong. I looked up all the objections to cousin marriage and satisfied myself that they were ridiculous. (Many years afterwards at the Old Bailey, I saw so many children who were products of incestuous unions, and always found them so normal in every way, that I came to doubt the *bona fides* of the whole consanguinity taboo and especially the sanity of the law about incest; a line of thought much encouraged by Lord Raglan's famous book *Jocasta's Crime*, and by later discoveries about the breeding of thoroughbred horses and prize cattle.) I can't remember why I didn't marry the beautiful Sophie. It was probably because she married a commercial artist, went off to live in America, and was never heard of again. I still sometimes feel sad about her.

Forty years later I became involved in the management of a "Young People's Consultation Centre", which was endowed in London by a wealthy Dutch industrialist for the purpose of research into delinquency and maladjustment; and I often heard from our clinical interviewers that, among the boy resorting to it for help and advice, there were always a high proportion who were "terribly worried about their acne". If I know anything, it was a worry that isolated them, robbed them of self-confidence, kept them away from girls; in fact there were cases in which they had felt near to suicide. I don't know how they were comforted, if at all, for (since there was no cure) nothing could have been said at a young people's clinic that would have comforted me. The acne went away before I was twenty, but I think that by then it had done some pretty fell work. It had certainly given me a complex about girls, and I don't know when, if ever, this was outgrown.

Chapter 3

BEATSMAN

THERE IS AN untold story to be revealed about London police life which is barely credible; not because it is exciting, picaresque, sinister, but because much of it is so daft. I was one of a class of fifteen young men, "probationer constables", who in September 1921 sat daily in a large echoing room in the Central Criminal Court, Old Bailey, for four weeks of instruction in Police Duty. I think it had been intended by the architect as a room for jurors-in-waiting, but they never used it. Its marble floor and echoing walls prompted the thought that they could have been tempted in by turning it into a swimming bath. Our mentor was a gigantic sub-inspector named Sydney Goslin, who, it seemed to some of us, equated criminal law with the punishment of sexual aberration, and spent an enormous amount of time very slowly describing to us examples of rape, indecent assault, and erotic inventiveness. We were an odd lot. We included two merchant seamen, a scientific instrument maker, a Grenadier Guardsman, a plasterer, a barber's assistant and a milk roundsman. If we had a common denominator it was a state of mixed astonishment, fear and amusement at our own derring-do, a feeling such as you might find among fugitives from life serving in the French Foreign Legion.

For the first two weeks we were without uniform, and assembled daily in what were probably our best suits. Then we were put into uniform, and much time was spent in telling us how to wear it, particularly the helmet. This had to be worn with the peak almost touching the bridge of the nose, so that the eyes should early acquire the peering expression common to policemen and ferrets. The helmet seemed to add a cubit to your stature and, as you learned to hold it in place by dropping the lower jaw and thus tightening the chinstrap, gave you a little of the confidence that suddenly seemed so hard to come by. With the helmet on top, there was such a lot of head that ordinary people must, you hoped, see it as the repository of much wisdom and experience. And that was how it made us behave. Or some of us.

By a dispensation that was probably as merciful to the public as to the fledgling policeman, we spent our first three months on night duty. The first such night has never faded from my memory and is always invoked vividly, anywhere, by the smell of lamp-oil. For this was about a year before the City of London Corporation allowed itself to be persuaded that electric lamps were better than oil lamps; and as you prepared to parade for night duty at 9.45 p.m. you had to elbow your way into the lamp-room, and there join a crush of men equipping themselves for the night with smelly old bull's-eye lanterns.

A word ought to be offered here in praise of those lanterns. On a freezing winter's night (I can recall some with 20 degrees of frost) you could put on a cloth cape over your greatcoat, turn up the wick of your lamp so that, underneath the cape, it was generating much more heat than it was intended to, and suffuse the upper part of your body in comforting if malodorous warmth. The excess smoke from the protesting lamp issued round the neck-band of your cape like a smoke-ring of decayed incense, and surrounded your face and head with stupefying fumes. But you were warmer. Of course this burned away the lamp-oil at twice the normal rate; and in the depth of winter the truly enterprising constable carried with him a medicine bottle full of oil for its replenishment.

I was prepared to meet, occasionally on street corners, the conscientious, reliable, peering-in-all-directions Bobby I had always supposed to be guarding the citizen and his property at night. I knew he might have a furtive pipe in his mouth and be ready to "pass the time of night" with a colleague. What I was not prepared for was the groups of smoking policemen at corners where four "beats" converged, all as lively (in the small hours) as children at play, and all arguing at the tops of their voices about one of three unvarying topics: sex, sport and religion in the proportions of 60:30:10. I believed for a few months that I had arrived among the most sex-absorbed body of men in the country, but I was gradually led to understand that this naïve assessment could commend itself only to someone who had never served in the armed forces or the Merchant Navy. With such experience, no doubt, I should have been better prepared for an encounter, on my very first night's duty, with a party of office cleaners hurrying along Moorgate in the dark of a winter's morning at about five o'clock. (A marvellous regiment of women, those early morning cleaners; with little enough, God knows, to laugh about but always laughing.) "It's *very* cold this morning," I said to them sympathetically as they passed me. "That's all right, dear," shouted one of them, "pull your shirt down over it—mine's warm enough." And their shrieks of laughter could have been heard a mile away. I was learning my way about.

An extremely interesting phenomenon, which I have never seen referred to in all the social studies of policemen whereby modern sociologists beguile their left-over time, was that as the number in a gossiping group diminished, so the proportions I have given above would move into reverse. Sex was a group subject. It was rarely that *two* policemen would talk about it for long together, and if they did they were likely to be genuinely obsessed, not very intelligent, and in need of some kind of help. Two men would discuss sport, but not heatedly. But two men would often discuss religion with a fervour normally found only at revivalist meetings. Sometimes these nocturnal seminars, taking place on a deserted street corner in the deathly hush of the City of London at night, would be directly under the window of some resident caretaker's bedroom, high up on a sixth or seventh floor. Occasionally such a man would throw his window up and shout enraged instructions down to the meeting as to what it should do with itself. I can remember that, more rarely, he would suddenly pour down a bucketful of what we all anxiously hoped was water.

There should have been no discussion groups at all. Instead the men should have been regularly patrolling their beats, stopping frequently to look back, swivelling their eyes in all directions, shining their lamps into alleyways and dark corners, examining the whalebone "marks" they had tucked into door-cracks and window-sashes by way of discovering whether anyone had gone into a locked-up building—or come out. These whalebone marks, too antiquated now to rank any longer as an official secret, are worth a historical note. I think you could probably call it an obituary.

Every bobby had to provide himself with a quantity of black whalebone, of the kind used for stiffening women's corsets. There were shops where you could buy it in sticks about 2 feet long and a quarter of an inch wide. You cut this up into one-inch lengths and bent these into V-shaped springs. And on night duty you pushed the double end of such a spring into the door crack of every lock-up building on your beat. Sometimes there were hundreds, and it took a couple of hours to get them all in. Having accomplished this, you then examined all the doors as you passed and repassed them during the rest of the night, to see that all the whalebone marks were still in place. Sometimes one would have disappeared, and after a short search with your lamp, in which the frantic quality diminished as you got older, you found it lying on the ground. The first time I did this I was very excited, bracing myself for some kind of Ealing Studios roof-scramble after a gang of robbers. By the fifth or sixth time I knew that the explanation was nearly always one of the following:

> The door crack was too wide for the mark to keep in. You should have used a bigger one.
> The wind had rattled the door (or sometimes it was a late-night courting couple) and shaken the mark out.
> The bobby on the next beat, or a bored plain clothes man walking by, had taken it out in the hope of starting something.
> Your section sergeant had taken it out, to see whether you would report its absence.
> The tenant of the building had come back to the office, with a view to doing some late work.
> The tenant of the building had come back with a girl, but with no thought of doing any work at all.
> You'd forgotten to put one in.

There were other possibilities. But although my own experience may be unique, I never heard of any burglar or other unlawful intruder being caught by a whalebone mark. I still cannot see why this should be: you simply could not open one of those doors or windows without dislodging the mark, and you couldn't put it back again from inside. But so it was. What I did hear was that there were knowledgeable business men who, having worked (or something) in their offices until very late at night, would pick up the whalebone mark they dislodged on coming out, and obligingly put it back where it belonged.

There were other cunning ways of recording human behaviour by means of simple gadgetry. A low and easily-climbed wall was always a problem. You put a nail at each end and tied a length of black cotton to them. (Actually most of the nails had been in position since Queen Victoria was a little girl.) Then no one, it was fondly supposed, could shin over the wall without breaking the cotton. Stray cats gave many an infuriating demonstration that not even they could do it. If you tied this cotton tightly, a shower of rain would shrink and break it, starting all kinds of scares. If you tied it loosely, the wind would lift it over to the other side of the wall, so that it hung where you couldn't see it. You bought your own reels of 24 black cotton; or you took your wife's and hoped she wouldn't notice.

It seems likely that the men who first devised the "cotton mark" had not foreseen the possible uses of black cotton by the irresponsible. There are courtyards and passages in the ancient City of London which, from midnight until three or four in the morning, are as silent as the grave. They are even more boring than graves. Then suddenly they come to life as the shortest walk from, say, Liverpool Street Station to the General Post Office (for early postmen going on duty), or from Blackfriars Bridge to Smithfield Market (for meat porters unwilling to come in their cars). The arrival of the first few men in these cohorts was as punctual as the sun and the moon. You could, therefore, if you timed it well and began early enough, erect at some quiet corner on their route a vast structure of empty dustbins, milk-bottle crates, and other urban detritus, all delicately poised so that the breaking of a cotton length would bring the whole thing down with a terrifying and prolonged crash and reverberation. You selected, of course, a spot where the collapse would cause neither injury nor damage. All you wanted was noise. The number of hurrying and chattering early morning postmen who snapped this cotton with their innocent shins will never be known: but they always broke into a startled run (and who would not?) until one of their number, who had seen it all before, recovered himself and explained that it was "the bloody coppers—got nothing else to do". And somewhere nearby, hidden in dark doorways, the bloody coppers would be risking double hernia in their efforts to laugh silently. It fell to my lot to be instrumental in bringing this absurd pastime to an end. I was on plainclothes patrol duty one night, notionally looking for "suspicious persons", and was deputed to adjust the cotton trigger at the last moment. Not being in uniform, I was less restricted as to escape routes if anything went wrong. Something did. I had just concealed myself behind the "bostwick gate" of a nearby warehouse and settled to watch the fun when round the fatal corner came our patrolling inspector, a gigantic and slow-treading man whom we called Hindenburg. It was at an hour when all God-fearing inspectors would be inside their police stations, demonstrating with their feet up that they had total confidence in their sergeants and men outside. This one was a man whose sense of propriety greatly (and without difficulty) exceeded his sense of humour. His reaction to the appalling din of the booby trap was precisely that of the big man in the Chaplin comedies when Mr Chaplin hits him on the head with an armchair. He appeared to notice *something*; and then walked on. But there followed, at his instance, a searching enquiry by the sergeants, a great parade of unconvincing innocence and unpolicemanly lying. And an era was over.

Cripplegate Churchyard had a public footpath closed at each end at night by heavy iron gates. At some time in the 1850s a City policeman (the story went) had been found beheaded in this historic churchyard in the night. You couldn't leave the churchyard totally unpatrolled because its low railings gave access to the backs of numerous warehouses stacked with furs and valuables. For seventy years, however, it had been strictly ordained that no constable was ever to go in there alone, and you had to meet the man on the next beat and go in with him, unlocking the massive gates with a key that weighed you down as you walked, at 11 p.m., 1 a.m., 3 a.m. and 5 a.m. When I was there we had a young colleague of outstanding cockiness and self-assurance (I will call him Constable X) who had been deriding the custom with hearty contempt: it was, he said, something we should all be ashamed of, and ten-to-one the original story was poppycock anyway. No policeman had ever been beheaded. It was not the sort of thing that people did. One night I was to go in with a con-genital leg-puller named Sissons, at that time a seasoned constable, a handsome little man with a fierce moustache and a face of oriental inscrutability (and, by the way, he was known as Togo Sissons, after the Japanese admiral, because he was unusually short). We looked around first at all the backs of the warehouses, and then, as we tapped our pipes out on the base of Milton's statue, Togo said he had arranged for Con-stable X to relieve him for the next churchyard visit at 3 a.m., but that he was hoping nevertheless to be there himself, unobserved. I was not to be disturbed by anything that hap-pened. When Constable X and I were just about to leave the churchyard at 3.10 a.m. there was a ghastly, sepulchral scream from behind a large family tombstone, accompanied by the noisy rattling of a chain; and there appeared coming towards us an apparently headless, white-sheeted figure dragging a long chain behind it. Constable X clearly had no thought of waiting while I unlocked the churchyard gate (which always seemed to take a long time). He went over the top of the gate with the athleticism of terror, and disappeared. Togo Sissons, with no hint of a smile, removed his shroud (it was a house-decorator's sheet from the Station), unclipped the long string of handcuffs which had served him as a chain, tucked them all under his cape, and explained that he was then going off duty—"two hours off for duty done".

Decorators' and stonemasons' sheets have often served this kind of nocturnal purpose. In about 1927, a statue in the middle of the beautiful riverside lawn opposite King's Bench Walk in the Middle Temple was being repaired and cleaned; and at night, because the plaster or cement was still wet, it was left covered by a mason's white sheet. Then one day it was decided that the job could only be done indoors, and the statue was removed from its plinth and taken away. We had a zealous plain-clothes man who was so suspicious of everything that he would (they said) have liked to stop every passing pigeon to find out what it had in its crop. He took alarm that night at the disappearance of the statue and tried to get an all-stations phone message circulated. While he was doing this, the uniformed man patrolling the Middle Temple beat climbed on to the plinth, draped himself in the sheet, and stood motionless. When the plain-clothes man returned with a colleague, and was standing duly dumbfounded to find the statue back in place after all, it suddenly emitted a fearful howl and made a violent lunge at him with its shrouded arm. It is fair to the memory of the sleuth to admit that he didn't actually run away; and yet honest to record that, if he had, he would probably have been able to do so in dry trousers.

But no one could forget Togo Sissons on night duty. Another young constable had been boasting to a group of us that he was in training for the 220 yards at our annual sports meeting at Stamford Bridge and was certain to win it. Everyone was rather fed up with him. Togo and he were due at that moment to go to the Station for "refreshments" (the official euphemism for the huge plateful of bacon and eggs which, if you wanted it, you had to cook and eat in 30 minutes flat). "Right," said Togo, "I may be a lot older, but I'll beat you into the Station easily. You go the short route and I'll go round this way—best not to be running together, just in case anyone sees us. Get ready, one, two, three, off." And the 220-man set off at maniacal speed, carrying his helmet because it would have fallen off. Togo ran about 10 yards, and then came back to hear the finish of a story someone was telling. Inevitably, and half-way to the station, the 220-man nearly knocked over a startled inspector, who shouted "What the hell?" And (the story goes) the obsessed sprinter did no more than momentarily replace his helmet so that he could salute and gasp out, "Racing Togo into breakfast, sir!"

Togo Sissons had one peculiarity that puzzled a good many of us. In the mess-room, if you left your pipe lying anywhere near him while you went to replenish a teapot or snatch a forgotten piece of black toast from under the grill in the kitchen, he would deftly pull the pipe apart, insert a matchstick in the stem, put it together again and replace it exactly as found. When (with about three minutes left for a smoke) you had filled your pipe and were vainly trying to light it, he would watch your contortions impassively as he puffed away at his own. I never saw him laugh at this, or *seem* to enjoy it. Indeed he was seldom there to see the results of his odd ingenuity. I once asked him if he wasn't worried that he might break someone's pipe in unscrewing the mouthpiece, especially if it was hot. "What pipe?" he said.

All these things combined to suggest that the two worlds of active police duty and of theoretical "police duty instruction" were not merely separate planets but belonged in different solar systems. Indeed I was told by a succession of old sweats, as soon as I arrived at my Division for street duty, that "the best thing you can do about all that crap is to forget it". This had always been said, I know that it is still said, and it is unforgivably stupid. But oh, those poor instructors, of whom I was soon to be one! What *can* they really do to prepare a youth of twenty for the emergencies that may confront him in one week of duty? It would be boring to describe what they actually did, though I believe it has changed remarkably little and that, because so much more teaching is now crammed into so much more time, police training has probably evolved into the perfect vindication of Kingsley Amis's "more means worse". Let me recall four quite typical adventures of my own, making no pretence that they all happened in one week or even one year; and I should perhaps introduce them with the confession that no vestige of what I had been taught in training came into my mind at the relevant moments.

Adventure No. 1 was in fact the very first occasion on which a member of the public unsuspectingly called upon my untried services, and she was the woman attendant in charge of the ladies' lavatory in the subway at the Bank Underground Station; who, accordingly, was unknown to me. I suppose it was in November 1921 and about 10.30 at night. I was standing in front of the Royal Exchange, hoping nothing would happen, and she came hurrying towards me across the wide paved area so purposefully that I knew something had, and that I was about to go into action. Murder? A lost child? Robbery? She had picked up somebody's keys? Was there still another bus for Hackney, please? No, there was a young woman down in the lavatories who was very ill and in great pain. If you are a male police officer, do you go barging into such a sanctum? You do. I found the girl writhing on the floor, sweating with pain and trying to say something to anyone who would listen. She was about to have a baby, and it was pretty obvious that, even though I got an immediate message off to the ambulance service, she was going to have it before any ambulance could arrive. And she did. "Have you got children?" I asked the attendant. "I am not married," she answered rather primly and I remember thinking it was only half an answer. So we delivered the baby on the stone floor, and I held its gory little head to keep it from damage. The ambulance men arrived within another five minutes, and the clearing up they did, and the washing, and the cheerful, unfussy efficiency of it all made me want to give them a thousand pounds each, a temptation easily overcome. On the way to hospital that girl was actually giggling weakly about the whole thing, seemingly indifferent as to what happened next, far less emotionally disturbed than I, and absolutely resolute in her determination to tell me nothing whatsoever about herself, not even her name. I know no more about her. "You don't want to get all involved like that, lad," said my Sergeant as he took my scribbled report and initialled my pocket-book. "I had one of those jobs. Know what I did? Strapped my belt round her knees, very tight, and got her off to Bart's." The mindless cruelty of his story has haunted me ever since.

Adventure No. 2 occurred in a quiet City street called Aldermanbury. I had been on traffic duty at a road junction then called Addle Street–Wood Street. (This in the daytime was then an inferno of pair-horsed vans, Luton lorries, and articulated vehicles all manoeuvring for position in an area hardly big enough for two of them; and at night it was as quiet as the surface of the moon before the Americans got there, a place where you could smoke a pipe and watch for marauding sergeants through four points of the compass.)

Having finished duty for the day at about 5 p.m., I had returned to the police station at Moor Lane to "report off"—and then remembered that, like a fool, I had left my uniform cape hanging inside Carter Paterson's doorway in Wood Street. I hurried back to get it, and noticed uneasily on the way along Aldermanbury that a window-cleaner was standing on a parapet about 60 feet from the ground. I remember muttering to myself that the law which requires a London window-cleaner to wear a safety-belt at heights exceeding 6 feet (an LCC by-law) was applicable only if he was standing on a window-sill, and that if he was on a parapet the law didn't affect him. On my way back from Addle Street with my cape, I passed him again. This time he was lying on the ground, with a length of broken stone parapet near by; and it seemed to my shocked and inexperienced eye that his body was literally smashed, and prevented from spreading across the roadway only by his clothing. As it was, he was surrounded by small heaps of steaming and clotted blood. There was no doubt that he was dead, but this could never be assumed by the police without medical opinion, and you took even a decapitated body to hospital to get a certificate of "life extinct". Someone had already summoned the ambulance, so we covered the mess with sacking and awaited its arrival. Again I was astonished at the hard-bitten efficiency of the ambulance men as they cleared everything up; and off I went to Bart's Hospital with a job which added several hours to a day's duty that I had supposed was over. I was now taking instruction the hard way, a feature of this particular lesson being "don't forget your cape".

Adventure No. 3 occurred one very hot autumn evening in a huge block of offices called London Wall Buildings. The non-resident caretaker called me in and said that an office on the third floor, though locked from inside, was still lighted and apparently occupied, though he had never before known its occupant to be working late. It was 9.30 p.m. and he could get no reply when he banged on the locked door, which was bolted as well as locked. So I held my folded cape against the glass panel of the door and put my elbow through it. Then we went in to be horrified. A middle-aged, bald-headed, and very fat man in his shirtsleeves was sitting at a desk with his face on a once-blue blotting-pad that was soaked with blood. He had been shot through the side of the forehead, apparently with a small pistol which lay near his left hand; and blood was dripping rhythmically from a corner of the desk on to a piece of foolscap ruled paper on the floor. When I looked at this later I found that someone, and it may or may not have been himself, had typed on it:

> Who would fardels bear
> To grunt and sweat under a weary life
> But that the dread of something *after* death,
> The undiscovered country from whose bourn
> No traveller returns, puzzles the will,
> And makes us rather bear those ills we have
> Than fly to others that we know not of?

I suppose this alone would be enough to fix the scene in one's memory for life. But the recollection has two other aspects, both about equally memorable. The first is that at the coroner's inquest there was actually some controversy about the significance of the passage from the Hamlet soliloquy. When the coroner intimated that this pointed to suicide, a solicitor argued that, on the contrary, Hamlet was setting out the grounds *against* suicide, and so, therefore, was the poor man who had written out the quotation. I forget whether it was argued that the case must therefore have been one of murder; but the submission illustrated the sometimes fatuous lengths to which lawyers would go in resisting a verdict of suicide and its adverse life insurance consequences. The other memorable detail is the observation of one of the perspiring ambulance men who came to take the body away from London Wall Buildings. He wiped his face and neck as he studied the scene. "Too bloody 'ot for 'im," he said.

Adventure No. 4 was one in which I played only a secondary part, but it came nearer to the kind of thing that policemen are popularly expected to do, as contrasted with setting childish booby traps and holding street-corner meetings at night or collecting dead bodies by day. This one was at night, and the scene was again Wood Street. I had a particular pal named T. J. Davis, whom we all called Tom, though his family called him Jim. He was eight or ten years older than I, an infantry captain in the 1914 war, a man with a voracious appetite for books (he guided my own reading significantly), a Welsh love of music, a priceless sense of humour, and a prowess at cricket and running which I always miserably envied. More vividly memorable than anything else about him, he had a marvellous laugh, which made you feel happier even if you were the object of the merriment. He and I stood one very cold Sunday morning at about 2.30, with greatcoats and cloth capes on, smoking our surreptitious pipes in a dark Wood Street doorway and watching opposite lengths of the empty thoroughfare as we discussed the mutability of human affairs. Suddenly I saw a man on his hands and knees on the footway, about 150 yards from us. I whispered to Tom, who looked round. "He's come out of a basement," he whispered back, and we silently tapped our pipes out against the palms of our hands. Then Tom took off his helmet, cape and great-coat and put them on the floor in the doorway. I did the same, realising that there was going to be some running. (I suppose, in retrospect, that this was quite contrary to the Regulations and that we should have done our running fully accoutred.) By this time the figure had stood up and was walking away from us towards Cheapside, keeping close to the buildings. Suddenly, Tom was off like the wind, with me following less athletically. The man heard us at once, which can't have been difficult—we both weighed over 11 stone and had heavy boots on; and he ran too. We soon realised with dismay that he was wearing rubber shoes—though he may have been slightly handi-capped by the fact that he was carrying a raincoat. Tom was soon far ahead of me, but the fugitive was far ahead of him and gaining. Into empty Cheapside we went, west towards St Paul's Cathedral, round the silent churchyard, down Godliman Street to the broad slope of Queen Victoria Street. Tom and his man were now distant figures in a landscape which, so far, had included several mildly interested cats but no other human being, certainly not a policeman. There was no whistle-blowing because our whistles were on chains attached to our greatcoats, lying in that doorway back in Wood Street, now so terribly far away. By this time I was running, perhaps the right word is blundering, in such a state of exhaustion that I had my eyes nearly closed and would probably have fallen over a stray cat. When next I opened them I saw with surprise and glee that the fugitive himself had dropped from exhaustion and that Tom was sitting on him. When I arrived they were both still too breathless to talk. So was I. Motioning Tom to move over, I took my seat beside him and there was a long interval of heavy panting. When we all felt better we walked slowly back to Wood Street, the man firmly held between us, and there we asked him to show us which basement he had emerged from. He was too old a hand for that. So while Tom examined the nearby buildings for signs of entry or exit, I put the man down again and sat on his back. (I rather liked this means of restraint. It not only made sudden escape impossible, but it was restful.) It soon became apparent that the chap had come through the fanlight over the door of an Express Dairy Company's teashop; and we told him so. He rejected the accusation with a disturbingly convincing show of outrage. He had been walking from Liverpool Street to the Victoria Embankment to catch an all-night tram. No all-night trams on Sundays, we said. That just showed our bloody ignorance, he retorted: this was a "staff tram", for getting the Saturday night drivers and conductors home. Not at after three o'clock, we said; and each of us then took a turn at sitting on him while the other got dressed.

At the police station we had an unexpectedly surly reception from an acting station officer who (as was the crazy custom in those days) was busy compiling a vast pay-sheet for the next Divisional payday. This was always done at weekends by the night duty station officer, on the official assumption that he had nothing else to do. (He had much else to do.) When I came in due course to do that job myself I was astounded that some of the men involved had ever coped with it— they came from all walks of life and mostly from the armed forces, but few if any of them had even the smallest knowledge of accountancy or aptitude at casting figures. It came fairly easily to me as one of the very few things I was semi-skilled at, and the fact became known to certain station officers while I was still a constable. Accordingly I spent many a Saturday night, when I should have been out in the cold, compiling these vast pay sheets in pencil for subsequent inking-in by artful station officers who, whatever their deficiencies as accountants, knew how to deploy their man-power. There would have been a fearful row if it had become known at any higher level, but it was the beginning of my inglorious career as The Policeman Who Came in From the Cold.

Well, the distraught station officer to whom we told our tale of the man from the Express Dairy was unwilling to sacrifice any time to it. Did we actually see the man come out of the shop? No. Was there any sign of forcible entry or exit? No, but the fanlight was open. How did we dispose of the man's explanation that, when we saw him on his hands and knees, he had dropped a packet of cigarette papers and was groping for it in the dark? We hoped we could now dispose of it by searching him and finding no packet of cigarette papers. The angry station officer was just saying that no one had any power to search him when Tom Davis, who had been fumbling with the man's raincoat, allowed himself a beatific grin as he pulled from its pocket the Express Dairy Company's staff gratuity box. The man was charged, finger-printed, and put in the cells to have some sleep; and we went down to the empty mess-room to have some breakfast. Next day he was found to be an established practitioner, and many weeks later at the Old Bailey he asked for a large number of other thefts to be taken into consideration. It took Tom and me a long time to recover from the loss of sleep involved by our court attendances while on night duty. We felt experienced.

That thief owed his conviction to two circumstances in combination: first, that Tom and I had not been patrolling our beats conscientiously, in which event we should never have seen him; second that Tom was so good a runner. (I saw him once, in an open 440 at our Stamford Bridge Sports, lose one of his shoes, kick the other one off, finish the course in his socks and then come home third.) I rather hero-worshipped Tom, and must return to him.

Chapter 4

HOW I CAME IN FROM THE COLD

AFTER TWO OR three years of this kind of event, which must be understood to have punctuated at long intervals a life of extreme monotony, boredom, and physical tiredness, I should surely have begun to lose whatever esteem I had acquired among my colleagues. For I was more and more called upon to hide myself in quiet corners of the station and do clerical jobs that no one else seemed fitted or willing to do; in particular, the translation of documents from French police forces in extradition cases. And always when the word went out that I was wanted at the station, some harassed section-sergeant, already short of men, would have to find someone to relieve me; and more often than not the job from which I had to be relieved was a wet and windy one, directing traffic at some City street junction. (Automatic traffic signals did not arrive until, I think, 1930.) It happened so often that my colleagues could have been excused for regarding me as an unmitigated nuisance or worse, but they never seemed to show any ill feeling.

In fact they demonstrated an unimpaired goodwill by electing me their "Divisional Librarian". Each station had a lending library, maintained by a small compulsory levy on every member of the Division and, I must say, very much used by the men and their families. When I took it over I was appalled to find that it had always bought its books from booksellers at the retail price, less some small discount conceded to us because we were policemen. I began studying the "remainder" catalogues, made friends with Mudie's, W. H. Smith's and Harrods, and with the same money bought ten times the number of books from among the titles those libraries had "withdrawn from circulation" and replaced with new copies. The men read predominantly romantic novels ranging

from Ethel M. Dell and Maud Diver to Conrad and John
Buchan; all the current "Westerns" (at that period it was
Zane Grey, Rex Stout and Ridgewell Cullum); and surprisingly
few who-dun-its—there was a rather silly and intolerant
tendency to write these off as "tripe". On rare occasions there
was such a clamour for a particular book that, to keep the
peace, I had to buy in half a dozen copies: this happened
in 1925 with Ernest Raymond's *Tell England*, which had then
been out for about three years; and, most unexpectedly, with
the *Thinkers' Library* edition of Wynwood Reade's *The Martyrdom
of Man*—I had bought one copy experimentally, and within
a few weeks everyone wanted it.

To me, my sudden status as a linguist seemed both bewildering and ludicrous. In a force of men nearly 1,000 strong, could
I possibly be the only man able to translate French? At that,
it was a kind of school French then at least ten years dormant;
I had never been to France; I had painstakingly read (or
persuaded myself I had read) two books in French, Anatole
France's *La Révolte des Anges* and Alexandre Dumas' *Comte
de Monte Cristo* (which I knew almost by heart, anyway, in
English); I had never passed any such tests as those offered, for
example, by the Royal Society of Arts. And yet "Chief Office"
was always sending down papers for me to translate—the most
usual being a *Commission Rogatoire* from the Paris Sûreté.

I played all this up, I now confess, disgracefully. One
Commission Rogatoire was almost as much like another as one
passport is like another, only the names and the crimes being
different. But to keep the Hewitt superstition going (and keep
Hewitt off the boring streets), I resorted to subtle but semanti-
cally unimportant changes in each translation, using a small
library of tattered French dictionaries to which I was constantly
adding from the book-boxes outside secondhand shops. Sometimes I was called in to translate French magazines when a
bookseller or newsvendor was being prosecuted for obscenity
(or was it indecency?). I remember a luckless man who had
a little news-kiosk in King Street, Cheapside, and offered for
sale those mildly saucy publications, harmless even by the
standards of the twenties, *La Vie Parisienne, Le Régiment, Le
Sourire, Madame Sans-Gêne, Frou-Frou* and some others. A passing

citizen bought one and, in response to a small advertisement, wrote to Paris for some *photogravures intimes*. On their way these were intercepted by the British Customs Authorities, who sent them to the Home Office, who sent them to the Director of Public Prosecutions, who sent them to us "for action". I had about twenty magazines to translate from cover to cover and it took a couple of months. (A firm of translators would have done it in a week.) The man who had sent for the photographs, summoned as a most reluctant witness, made the mistake of posing thenceforward as an outraged citizen determined to bring this fearful trade to justice. In Court (it was at the Mansion House) he was easily, brutally and, I thought, needlessly deflated—it didn't matter what *his* motives were and he might as well have been allowed to credit himself with stuffy ones. But I came in for some rough treatment too. Was I a graduate in modern languages? No. What school did I go to? I needn't answer, said the Lord Mayor. Had I lived in France? No. Did I understand the French sense of humour? If it was very different from ours, no.

"I put it to you quite seriously," said the defending solicitor, "that wherever, in these translations, you have found yourself confronted with a choice of meanings, you have consistently chosen the worst, the most indecent?"

That might have been true, really. It's surprising how police-minded you can get, how prosecution-slanted. I said I thought it was bound to be a matter of opinion.

"Better answer the question," said the Lord Mayor.

"Thank you, my Lord. No," I said, "I didn't choose the worst, only what seemed to me the closest."

"Very well, we will just see, shall we? Let us look first at page 314 of your manuscript . . ."

But the Lord Mayor wasn't having this. He was supposed to be dealing with a shopkeeper who had advertised photographs you could get from France. He had seen these photographs and they weren't funny ones. Not even a Frenchman would laugh at them, whatever else he did, and however funny the magazine in which they were advertised. The fine would be £25.

Now that King Street newsagent was rather a buddy of

mine. He used to order the *New Statesman* for me; and when I was reading for promotion (which for some years was a chronic condition), he was good at getting copies of new Acts of Parliament and statutory regulations, for which I would otherwise have had to hang about at the Stationery Office (or Government Bookshop), then in Kingsway and then, as now, the slowest-moving bookshop in the world. So I was a little embarrassed about the prosecution.

"Not your fault," he said cheerfully, and he arranged the latest copies of *Le Sourire* and *Frou-Frou* on his display-racks. "It's the Customs people, I suppose. So here we go till next time!" We resumed our former relationship. But what an absurd prosecution! What a monumental waste of effort, including the two months it took me to produce a translation which was largely irrelevant and was probably wrong in a thousand places. (From the taxpayer's viewpoint it wasn't even cheap.)

I came to be used as a kind of clerical delegate, or tribal letter-writer, to a whole hierarchy of inspectors and lesser station officers. All they asked of me in addition was that I should keep out of sight, in case any of the Top Brass should happen along and enquire what I was doing. They slightly preferred that even their own co-equals in rank, who employed me in the same clandestine way, should if possible be kept in ignorance that they were doing it too. (It wasn't possible.) It was a situation made easy by two strange circumstances: first, there was then no such animal as a "divisional clerk", and a great deal of routine writing fell to the lot of the unfortunate station officer, whose mind should have been free for higher things like the hearing of charges against "suspected persons loitering" and the shouting down of disorderly drunks; and secondly, there was among the station officers a sulky and almost mutinous attitude to the Top Brass and the Commissioner which led them into all kinds of chicanery and column-dodging. A brief explanation of this will serve the added purpose of illustrating an important change that was coming over the police service at that time. It was, that is to say, intended to be important.

When I say "station officer" I mean either a sub-inspector

(the rank has since been abolished) or a sergeant who was "acting sub-inspector" to fill a temporary vacancy, and was behind the desk in the police station getting on with routine work. While so occupied he would be momently expecting the outer door to burst open and admit some struggling mass of humanity, from which would eventually emerge helmets, individuals, and a story of crime or passing sadness. Now at that time the government had recently introduced a new promotion system for the police, a feature of which was that all candidates, even those above the rank of sergeant, must pass an examination in what were called "educational subjects". And the station officers most affected by this were a large group of elderly sergeants who had done the job of "acting sub-inspector" throughout the First World War, and had been reasonably content to do it without the pay because they thought they saw certain promotion at the end of it all, when retirements were resumed. Most of them were competent, and all of them were experienced (which, admittedly, is not the same thing). Suddenly, after six years, they were told they must pass an educational exam before they could be promoted; and most of them, when they had conferred together, absolutely refused.

I don't know whether they thought the Commissioner would give way and promote them unexamined, in defiance of the new Regulations. But he decided that he couldn't; and seeing himself suddenly bereft of what had seemed a reliable supply of sub-inspectors and inspectors to replace those who had been waiting to retire as soon as the war was over, he hurriedly began the training up of a new generation of younger sergeants as station officers. These were pejoratively known as T.N.B.s, because the disgruntled men they were now to supplant had angrily christened them toffee-nosed bastards.

Now, why did these older men refuse to submit to an educational exam? It had much to do with the official concept of "education". The setting and marking of the papers was farmed out by the police authority (the Corporation of London) to the London Chamber of Commerce, which devised a syllabus of strangely academic irrelevance. There was some simple arithmetic, of the kind appropriate to children who were eleven or twelve years old and fairly backward. There was geography, of the sort which involved knowing not merely that the county town of Rutland was Oakham and that it stood on the River Wreake, but that to go by train from Southampton to Aberdeen you didn't need to go to London. When my turn came, I learned vast lists of railway routes, county towns, and Britain's off-shore islands (did you know there were more than 4,000 of these?), and probably knew more about trade winds, isobars and rainfall than the London Chamber of Commerce would ever have had the time to look up. And there was something called General Knowledge which, as the thing developed, came to include the origins and uses of gutta percha, ambergris, asbestos, the Corps of Commissionaires and the Heaviside Layer. The whole system foreshadowed the competitive fatuity of today's radio *Brain of Britain, University Challenge* and *Round Britain Quiz*. (I remember being asked *viva voce* if I knew what to call the shadow-throwing arm on a sundial. I did not. It was a gnomon, said the examiner gently.) The seasoned old station officers of the twenties would have none of it. Accordingly they never got promoted; and during the tapering-off period in which their services "behind the desk" had perforce to be called upon, they availed themselves of my artfully window-dressed abilities as much as they possibly could. It was fine for me, but sad for them.

I have always felt sorry for them, but their fancied need, and their desire to avenge themselves, combined to make my opportunity; and many a short story, many a dreamed-up feature article, was scribbled while I was tucked away in some kind of store-room (or sometimes an empty cell) awaiting the next job as secret Divisional Scribe. Few of these pieces, I may say, were ever submitted to anyone for publication. Of those that were, few were published. None, as a result of previous disaster, was ever torn up and left in a waste-paper basket for anyone to find. (No one, not even the closest of friends, knew what I was doing.) I rather think the first of these short pieces that appeared under my name was in the *Children's Newspaper* in about 1924 and it was signed C. H. Rolph, the not very skilful pseudonym by which I hoped to protect myself from the disciplinary proceedings that would normally have followed discovery. And this is a phenomenon which, in the light of subsequent knowledge, I may as well dispose of before going further.

The Police Discipline Code was a farrago of Thou Shalt Nots based on King's Regulations as they governed the regular army at the time of the Peninsular War, though they exuded also a faint flavour of Cromwell's Model Army. They forbade you to do almost anything, and in case they might have forgotten something they added that you must not do anything "likely to bring discredit on the reputation of the force or of the Police Service". The effect was that almost any kind of conduct, on or off duty, which was not compulsory was prohibited. But among the prohibitions was one which said (and still says):

> without proper authority communicates to the public press, or to any unauthorised person, any matter connected with the force.

At that time I was writing nothing about "matters connected with the force"; and even when, in 1935, I began writing a weekly legal page for the *Police Review* (which I'm still doing), they were "connected with the force" only in so far as the force might have found them instructive or worth reading. But the Commissioner could have ordered me to stop doing it; and thereupon I should have resigned, because that, primarily and no doubt reprehensibly, was precisely what I was there to do. The police service was the "bread and butter job" which was to make it all possible. I don't think my first Commissioner (Sir William Nott-Bower) knew anything about it, or even that I existed. He was succeeded in 1925 by Sir Hugh Turnbull; and although he soon *did* know about it, he left me alone for reasons which I will explain when, as in due course I must, I return to him.

Even thus early in my police career (it was 1926) I was chipping away at the more plodding absurdities of "police language", which sought to clothe the treacherous simplicity of everyday speech in a stifling pomposity borrowed from the semi-ecclesiastical ritual of the law courts. Policemen would never read a document: they perused it, because perusal was more dignified than reading. A wall could never be roughly 10 feet high: it was approximately about 10 feet high. If you were reporting a street accident involving a bus, you had to call it a motor metropolitan stage carriage. Why? Because it took longer and bus lacked dignity.

Not that you could always dispose of these elephantisms by ridicule. Now and again you found that they had a basis of reason. Example: it has always been a gift to the cartoonists, playwrights and novelists that policemen never go or come anywhere. They always proceed. But this is because the verbs "go" and "come" have a subjective flavour, indicating a spatial position on the part of the narrator. "Proceeding" has the olympian impartiality of one seeing the occasion from a great height, as in a helicopter. If you say in the witness-box that a vehicle was "coming" down Queen Victoria Street, and it was in fact going East, you will be asked:

"Now, constable, why do you say it was *coming* down Queen Victoria Street?"

"Well, that's what it was doing, sir."

"And if it was *coming*, that means it was moving towards you?"

"Yes."

"And where were you standing?"

"At the junction with Cannon Street."

"*Ah!* And which way was it *going*?"

"Towards the Mansion House."

"Did you happen to notice that Queen Victoria Street, all the way from Blackfriars Bridge to Cannon Street, *runs uphill*?"

"Yes."

"And yet you are telling the Court that the vehicle was *coming down* that hill?"

"I didn't say——"

"Oh, but didn't you? Let me remind you of what you said."

You can't win. Proceeding is always safer. Take no notice of that formidable team Sir Ernest Gowers and the subsequent Sir Bruce Fraser, when they say in *Plain Words*[1] that proceed means go. It doesn't. Similarly there is something perennially

[1] HMSO, London, 1972.

comic about the policeman who says in evidence that someone
was "proceeding in an Easterly direction". He will sometimes
be asked "You mean he was going East, don't you?" One
answer would be that he doesn't know the man was going
East, he didn't plot him with a compass, the chap was heading
for some point between ESE and ENE, etc. But the origin of
the "Easterly direction" business is that a police witness,
having committed himself to "going East", can then be made to
look a fool by: "Do you know that this short street in fact
runs almost due North?" Anything to shake his precarious
confidence.

If at the material moment you were just going on duty, you
had better say you were proceeding on duty. A man who said
"coming on duty" would be asking the world to believe that he
felt himself to be getting back to normal; homing, or escaping
from the unusual. A man "going" on duty would be one without
his heart in his job.

Every report to the Commissioner had to proclaim, on the
dotted lines in the margin, what it was going to be about. Then
it began: "With reference to subject named in margin, I beg
to report that . . ." If it was going to be a request for some
august favour, it begged respectfully. If it was going to be a
pack of exculpatory lies, it begged most respectfully. It was
the inherited language of unlettered men terrified of losing their
jobs and joining the ranks of the Victorian unemployed;
abject, adoptive, and no doubt semi-literate. I don't think it
happens very much now.

It held full sway in the wording of charges against offenders,
and if you ever had time to settle down and read the sixteenth-
century indictment against Ben Jonson for killing a man in
a duel you would see where much of that came from. It
reflected the danger that by leaving out a preposition or
even a comma, you would enable a villain to defy the law or the
Commissioner to reduce your pay for a year.

I got through my promotion examinations with no difficulty.
That is to say, by the time I was seated in the examination
room the difficulty was over, for I had applied myself to the
purely mechanical and unintelligent ingestion of "criminal
law and procedure", of "educational subjects", of "police

procedure and administration" with a frenzy of absorption that had established me as a kind of beetle-browed computer. The examiners had merely to feed me with a question and out vomited an entire section of an Act of Parliament, a statutory regulation, a Home Office circular to Chief Constables, or a written Parliamentary reply, with all the commas in their places and a line ruled neatly at the end. "Why do you swot like this?" asked one of my competitors in the race for sergeants' stripes. "Enjoy it?" Not much, I said. "Well, we all reckon it's because you're afraid of being promoted in front of someone else just because of your old pot-and-pan." And I knew he was right. My father's residual influence might have been stronger than I knew, even stronger than I uneasily suspected. Certainly there had in the past been no shortage of nepotism. I wanted to give the promotion board no real choice but to select me, and no reason to look for an excuse. In those days you could do this by scoring such fantastic marks in your written and *viva voce* exams that the Top Brass could do no other than recommend you to the Commissioner. He would see your marks anyway. If your name wasn't on the recommended list for promotion he would want to know why. "Oh," they might say, "he's not really quite suitable, sir." "Why not?" And they would try to think up something cogent. "Then why hasn't this been reported to me before? Why has he been granted his pay increments, his proficiency allowances?" They were sunk.

It was an absurd system. It promoted swots and theorists, parrots and computers, leaving many a good man to sweat out the whole of his service "in the ranks"—though he had passed the promotion exam with plenty to spare. And yet it was some sort of improvement on the racket which it supplanted, under which kissing went entirely by favour. . . .

I was determined to get over the first hurdle, the lift to sergeant, before I got married; and I wanted to marry, partly because that was the only escape from life in a police barracks— no unmarried man was ever allowed to live out.

I don't think I would have got through all the swotting alone. I had three swot-mates, all of whom achieved promotion; two of them in the end got more than I did; and I record with gratitude the names of Tom Davis (and how he hated study!),

Jesse Lucas and Albert Fuller, both of whom worked like beavers and had the unusual capacity that they would accept no legal principle until they knew *exactly* what it meant. I, on the other hand, could absorb anything like a fairly broad-minded parrot. But I had better, I suppose, acknowledge a lasting debt to what seemed at the time a rather fatuous accumulation of knowledge. I have never forgotten it all—solid verbatim chunks of the Larceny Act of 1916, of the so-called Criminal Law Consolidation Acts of 1861 (FitzJames Stephen's famous "criminal code"), of the numerous liquor licensing statutes, the Children and Young Persons Acts and the great jurists' definitions of every common law crime (as we used to say) from pitch-and-toss to manslaughter. And for forty-five years it has been, in my work as a journalist and broadcaster, the inexhaustible fount to which I could always return when editors either failed to suggest, or could not be persuaded, that I should write about something that seemed to me more exciting and imaginative.

1926 was the year in which they made me a sergeant. The three broad yellow stripes on each arm seemed to lift the elbows outwards as if by levitation, so that I walked like a man challenging everyone to fight. It was also the year in which Queen Elizabeth II was born, the General Strike was staged and flopped, and I bought some books which, though I had no time to read them just then, were going to affect my life more than all the recent years of swotting. There was an Eleventh Edition of the *Encyclopaedia Britannica*, which (with a gigantic Church Bible) I acquired for £4 from the then vicar of St Giles's Church, Cripplegate; and though I now have a modern one, I mourn that I ever parted with that "Eleventh", for it was incomparably *Britannica's* best. I also got copies of three brand new books: G. M. Trevelyan's *History of England*, R. H. Tawney's *Religion and the Rise of Capitalism*, and Beatrice Webb's *My Apprenticeship*; all of which came out in that year. And 1926 was the year in which Audrey Buttery, to her eventual and inevitable unhappiness, became my wife. This took place on 21 August.

Audrey and I had met on holiday in 1923, without taking much notice of each other, but later we corresponded and arranged to meet. She was a civil servant, an attractive brunette a little older than I; and the daughter of a linotype operator, George Buttery. He was a walking, perhaps one should say an ambling, repository of facts, a heavy, cheerful reference-book of a man who could probably have become one of the BBC's radio "Brains of Britain". A rather lovable man himself, he had absolutely no love for the police; nor, having worked in Fleet Street for twenty years, did he except the City of London Police (though it tended so to esteem itself) as a *corps d'élite*. My status with the family, accordingly, was never very high, though Audrey loyally and unshakably defended it, giving up a great deal in the process. I don't know whether they thought I was making a convenience of her, as a possible avenue of escape from what had become the intolerable bondage of barrack life. I myself was surprised that someone so marriageable, intelligent and (it seemed to me) sophisticated should be content to marry into the police service. She, for her part, wanted a home of her own, and was ready to face what are now called the "unsocial hours" of police life.

I came to realise that this was not the basis for a good marriage, and one day early in 1926 screwed up all my courage and told her so. She was initially rather shocked and quiet, then dismayed, resentful, and I think almost frightened. She would have preferred anyway that the announcement should come from her. She wrote and asked me to think again, and we met to talk it over. If ever I inflicted an irremediable wrong upon anyone, I did it by my weak-kneed agreement then to go through with the marriage after all. Both of us, at the ceremony, knew that we were making a mistake—and we confessed the fact long afterwards; but persuaded ourselves and each other, I believe, that a marriage was what you made it and that we would make this one good. We tried for nineteen years, no less, and it is not for me to say which of us tried the harder. I think she would have gone on trying all her life; she emerges from the story with more credit than I. But this at least is the place to say that the wife of almost any police officer, if she is a wife at all, is one of society's unsung heroines and that it is not—or certainly was not then—a life to be recommended to anyone.

We lived at New Cross, because I was required to live within three and a half miles of the City boundary—a requirement long since discontinued. We had a first-floor flat in Troutbeck Road, and our back window looked out over the playing field of Haberdashers' Aske's Hatcham Girls' School. By comparison with the slums in which most of my colleagues had perforce to live, it was an idyllic place and we were very lucky. And there, on 16 May 1930, was born our daughter Brenda, who is now a publisher's editor (whatever that means) in New York and is, despite her father and many other disadvantages, about the funniest and most Dorothy Parkerish young woman in all my acquaintance.

Chapter 5

COMPANIONS

I STILL CONTRIVED, at some risk of official disapproval, to keep in touch with a group of constables, old friends of mine, so unusual and almost eccentric in character and yet so important to me that my own story would be incomplete without some account of them. Most of them were much older than I, and they belonged to that solid phalanx of constables who—as policemen—never do anything much, never initiate anything at all, carry the uniform around in what they are pleased to call a preventive capacity, and are relatively happy to get paid for it. "You never know," they used to say, "whether the sight of you standing on some street corner has stopped a man knocking off something, or allowed a girl to go home unmolested." It seemed a great comfort to them and they never appeared to mind when, on account of it, they were called salaried scarecrows or told that their job could be done equally well by wax models.

There had been a police strike in 1918. It was not the first in police history—there were small ones in 1872 and 1890, followed by wholesale sackings, in the course of a long campaign for pensions and a weekly day off. The one in 1918, which was far more serious, was partly about pay but essentially about the right to confer. It was partially successful (the Police Federation was born of it); but although no one this time was sacked there remained for many years a "top brass" tendency to distrust and indeed to victimise men who, even if they were not actually known to have been among its more enthusiastic supporters, were believed to have left-wing views and had been seen with the *Daily Herald* or, what was much worse, *The Freethinker*. Even then the *Daily Herald* was not among the newspapers bought for police station mess-rooms and recreation rooms. They might also have been seen with

the *New Statesman*, but in those days this meant very little:
if you could understand what it was saying it was probably
subversive, but not more dangerously subversive than *Peer
Gynt, Widowers' Houses,* or the Sermon on the Mount.

The trouble was, Top Brass disapproval had imitators among
lesser ranks; diminishing in imagination on the way down,
but still powerful enough among the sergeants to make life
difficult for constables they disapproved of. For example,
on the quite unfounded assertion that they were not to be
trusted, these men got all the worst jobs—the fixed-point
duties where they could always be seen without having to
look for them, the traffic jobs where they would be splashed
with mud and half-choked with exhaust fumes, the all-night
posting to "watch premises" where something might (however
improbable) be amiss. Not for them, ever, the soft job in the
station, the quiet patrol, the eight-hour sit-down watching a
supposedly suicidal prisoner.

And yet they all had a Tommy Traddles kind of cheerful-
ness, the strange optimism which nourishes itself on a common
feeling of persecution. And I wouldn't myself say that persecution is too strong a word. They also shared an interest in
books and music which would have surprised many people
who thought they knew their policemen. Their *primus inter pares*
was a large, genial constable called Bob Turney, who was
one of the most widely-read men I have ever known. With
his huge domed forehead and a broad and flashing smile,
he shed a kind of aura round himself, redolent of secondhand
bookshops (he was known to most of the antiquarian booksellers in London), folk-lore, Marxism, natural history, anti-
clericalism, music and the English theatre. In 1972, when he
died after many years of retirement at the age of seventy-
seven, he had a country cottage at Chorley Wood containing
thousands of valuable collector's books, old prints, and gramophone records of music from Buxtehude to Aaron Copland.
When I knew them the Turneymen, as some of the sergeants
disapprovingly called his disciples, had found a shop in Shaftesbury Avenue where you could get discarded BBC records of the
classics at greatly reduced prices, and would club together to
buy (for example) the five "seventy-eights" which contained

the Brahms piano quintet in an album and which they played on hand-wound table gramophones. Once Bob told me he'd seen the *Enigma Variations* in this shop, and would I like them? (At that time he knew nothing about Elgar.) I commissioned him to get them; and then, playing them at home, he got so enthralled that he wouldn't part with them. I embarked on a programme of intimidation so ferocious, indignant and prolonged that he at last relinquished them, worn thin with constant playing. I always held it against him as an instance of Marxism at work.

The Turneymen once bought a season ticket for the Promenade Concerts (then at Queen's Hall), passing it from one to another on successive nights; and whenever this entailed changing duties with someone to get an evening off, waiting until there was a sympathetic station officer on duty to effect the change. They all read the *New Statesman*, passing each copy from one to another until it was many weeks old and falling to pieces. They read Proust and Spengler, Macaulay and Gibbon, Tom Paine and Cobbett, Hume and Herbert Spencer. They never missed a Harold Laski public lecture. They went in a solid phalanx to hear Shaw, Belloc and Chesterton debate at Kingsway Hall. And they formed an archaeological group to look for relics of Norman and Roman London whenever they happened to have freshly excavated building sites on their beats.

They were agnostics to a man, largely I think because of the formidable intelligence and patient dialectics of Bob Turney. I told him rudely once that he was a man without an original thought in his head: he was a gramophone, I said, an agreeable, kindly and inexhaustible gramophone. And it was true that if he quoted Huxley, Goethe or John Stuart Mill, he did so in a special voice put on for the occasion, and it combined with an occasional mispronunciation to emphasise the borrowed status of his erudition. The borrowing went on with such unremitting speed and concentration that he probably had little time to think, or to do more than mentally arrange what he had ingested. He was fully aware of this himself, fully prepared for my leg-pulling charge that his mind was a packed lumber-room of received ideas. He quoted Voltaire for his own comfort. "Originality," he would say, "is nothing but judicious imitation."

The Turneymen never sought promotion and would have been acutely unhappy in any higher rank. They were always mildly but discreetly amused at the semi-literacy and occasional fatheadedness of their masters. They reminded you of the kind of educated man (though they were not in the usual sense educated men) who enlists in the regular army to be shouted at by bull-necked sergeant-majors. If such a man joins the police service nowadays he doesn't stay very long, but at that time there were 2,000,000 unemployed and the inducement to put up with discomforts, inconveniences and even humiliations in a "safe" job was very strong. I do not know whether any such groups exist in the police today, but it seems unlikely that the necessary interest in books and the gramophone will have survived the cultural nihilism of television.

One characteristic that may have helped to earn them the uneasy disapproval of their immediate superiors was that, by and large, they were immune to the small corruptions which always beset the life of the constable. (The large ones belong to a world that such men seldom glimpse.) With one or two exceptions, they were not even mumpers; and the exceptions were always ready with another quip from Voltaire—"when it is a question of money, everybody is of the same religion". When I say that the incorruptibility of most of them, carried to the point of never even accepting a tip, earned them their sergeants' disapproval, I mean that it earned each of them an additional mark as "odd man out". It therefore intensified the distrust with which he would be regarded by men who were themselves the victims (however willing) of a conspiratorial system of small-time graft at least a century old. The system (I will fill in some details later) was so all-pervading that the police knew they must hang together or hang separately; and the odd-man-out was therefore so dangerous to the common weal that he might look in vain, at least among the intermediate ranks, for the goodwill and acceptance that helped a man towards promotion. This the Turneymen didn't mind in the least. Promotion was the last thing they wanted, and their contentedness gave them a collective strength which was the greater for being misunderstood and almost superstitiously over-rated. It was a source of endless amusement to them.

It is right to say at this point that my own odd career in the City Police sequestered me from all temptation. As a scribe I was also a pharisee, not as other men were. As I sat indoors scribbling, no one offered me a bribe to scribble something different. I *think* I would be too embarrassed to take a bribe or even a *pourboire*, but I think it with the more confidence because it would have been either too small to atone for the ignominy or too magnificent to be safe against eventual detection. My early introduction to the possibility is perhaps worth recalling. In Fountain Court, off Milk Street, there used to be a "Bodega" pub. It was below ground, a dive; and at the top of the stairs leading down to it there was a bostwick gate which was drawn across and padlocked during "closing hours". One Saturday I had been on "point duty" directing traffic, and when the afternoon came and the City was empty and silent for the weekend I was detailed for the rest of my day to patrol the Milk Street beat. At ten past three I stood at the still open entrance to the Bodega, looking down the stairs, wondering whether the occupants had gone home and forgotten to lock up, and quite unmindful that it was ten past three and that "closing time" was three o'clock. Suddenly a man, I suppose the licensee, ran up the stairs to me, slammed the gate and padlocked it, gasped out "Terribly sorry, officer, we were a bit late clearing up", pressed something into my hand, and hurried away. Was it a message of some kind? His holiday address in case we needed him? I looked at it curiously. It was a ten-shilling note; and after a surprised and chastening interval, I thoughtfully tucked it into my wallet. I did not feel corrupted. I merely felt an unexplained ten bob better off.

The Turneymen and their like must be seen as walking-on parts in a play whose leading characters were, for the most part, considerably less intelligent than they. It was their voluntary lot to be "bossed around" by men of a markedly inferior brainpower who, nonetheless, were better servants of the public. But there was another little enclave at each Division comprising men who, I should have thought under great difficulty, were leading strictly Christian lives. Quiet men, on the whole, not in any sense missionaries or evangelists, most of these too were outside the petty bribery system. Unlike the Turneymen, who rather despised them, they were active policemen; and occasionally one of them would precipitate a fiscal crisis by arresting the wrong street bookie and charging him under the Street Betting Act then in force. Accordingly these men, too, tended to be posted for duty where they "couldn't punch anything but their Bibles", but in all other contexts they were cherished as completely trustworthy and reliable, and were allotted the kind of jobs where a trustworthy and reliable delegate was balm to a worried sergeant's mind.

There was another group of men, again a handful at each Division, who puzzled me more than any. These were the blisterers, the summoning officers, the grim and vigorous law-enforcement men who allowed no breach of the law to go by. It was commonly said of them that they would prosecute their own grandmothers, this being apparently the acme of heartlessness even though some grandmothers may deserve it. They took every breach of the law as a personal affront, expiable only by punishment instigated by themselves. They embodied the law. I remember that one of them was talking to me in Fore Street, Moorgate, as a motor cyclist went by with a girl on the pillion. Her raincoat was hanging down and hiding the back number-plate. He saw it a moment too late. To my utter astonishment (for he was a friendly and normal man among the rest of us) he stepped out into the road and passionately shook his fist after the disappearing offenders. "Another one missed," he groaned; and it was as though God had turned away His face from the righteous.

Such men were always in the Magistrates' Courts: their cases seldom took them higher, for they prosecuted barrow-boys for obstruction, drunks for being disorderly, motorists for having defective silencers or dirty number-plates, street traders for not wearing their badges. But a few of them became pragmatic experts about legislation like the Motor Vehicles (Construction and Use) Regulations, and would prosecute outsize victims like London Transport or British Railways for technical defects in the actual *construction* of their fleets of road vehicles. Since these cases could involve the defendants in vehicle modifications costing thousands of pounds, they were strenuously defended, always by solicitor and counsel. The "blisterer" would always be on his own, prosecuting in person yet strictly (and no doubt mercifully) debarred from making opening or closing speeches. He would, however, cross-examine defence witnesses, including important-looking transport managers, road service engineers and vehicle designers; and these occasions were sometimes so richly comic that I would give much to possess tape-recordings of them. The comedy was not universally obvious, the defendants being among those who responded to it the least.

But the blisterers, like their opposites the Turneymen, were not promoted. To get through the examinations you had to be "good on paper"; and for some reason, despite all their practice in filling out summons forms and composing the necessary "statement of complainant", these men were seldom good on paper in the way that mattered.

It is nevertheless quite untrue to say, as is so often officially said, that promotion in the police service has nothing to do with the number of arrests or prosecutions initiated by the candidate. Suppose that two men are under consideration for promotion by a chief constable. One of them is a "blisterer", or a man with many arrests on his scalp-belt, and the other has never been heard of at headquarters before. They are in all other respects equal—identical exam marks, blameless characters, same length of service. Then suppose yourself to be the chief constable. Which man will you choose?

I have committed myself to statements in this chapter which necessitate a postscript. The "top brass", I have implied, were seldom philosophically-minded, seldom bookish men, certainly not "intellectuals". To this, as you might expect, there were a number of striking exceptions, and I think of their names as I write. And without question there were more exceptions in the CID, or as we called it in the City the Detective Department, than in the uniform branch. I have nevertheless a clear memory that, whatever may be the position today, the more vigorous and enquiring minds remained "in the ranks" and certainly did not rise above the rank of sergeant. Either something stopped them, some reluctance to assume police command, possibly a late-developing sense of the ridiculous; or they never intended to try at all.[1] But they squirmed sometimes when they heard a superior officer, in some radio news interview, delivering his heavy-booted officialese like Peter Sellers mimicking Peter Sellers impersonating a comic village constable. There were always some such men with the high-sounding title of Chief Superintendent Something-or-Other who, even when they ordered a drink, could sound as though they were reading from a dimly-understood printed form; and it seemed that the Fates, or the BBC, or an unholy combination of both, had an unerring gift for arranging that a police "spokesman" should usually be such a man. Bob Turney's attitude may have been that of many. "I don't want to order anyone about," he would say, "but I don't in the least mind having it done to me. In fact I like it. It saves such a lot of trouble. The whole of my working day is arranged for me, and yet if I had to do all the arranging myself I wouldn't get any more money."

In the twenties and early thirties we mixed very often with large detachments from the surrounding Metropolitan Police, because of the fascist marches and the mainly working-class reaction to them. Because the blackshirts were disciplined and marched with military precision, they seemed at first preferable to the shuffling and dreary rabble who opposed them, and who had neither the facilities nor the leaders for such organisation. In the City at least (where we had no Ridley Road speakers' corner and no traditional meeting places of any kind—even Tower Hill was just outside our boundary) Mosley's blackshirts provoked no trouble on the march. We had "approved routes" for processions, and would allow no deviations; and the fascists

[1] To judge from an article by Mr Peter Evans in *The Times* of 31 January 1971, this doesn't seem to have changed much. "The [Metropolitan] force contains people of much talent and character," wrote Mr Evans, "but this is still underdeveloped and under-represented in senior positions."

always complied. So did the "Kibbo Kift", a greenshirted lot who supported Major Douglas's Social Credit scheme, formed themselves into small marching groups, and at weekends strutted about in all directions with a marching step even quicker than the Rifle Brigade's. We were often accused in the press of being pro-fascist, but my recollection is that at first we thought the blackshirts slightly (and the greenshirts totally) daft. We had no love for them, because they messed up our weekly leaves and involved us in long extra hours of duty. Then some of us began to see, by the thirties, what fascism and the "corporate state" really would lead to: an exaggerated nationalism entirely obliterating individualism and humanity, and a complete destruction of all free cultural and intellectual discourse with other nations. But so would Communism, so far as we could understand it. So we hated them both; those of us who had political natures hating the fascists more than the communists because they gave us less excuse for policemanly shoving around. I remember once going up to the apparent leader of a blackshirt column on the march from Tower Hill to the West End, a tall and fiercely moustached man, and reminding him that they wouldn't be allowed to go along Cannon Street past St Paul's Cathedral but must go down Queen Victoria Street. Without looking at me he grimly and very slightly shook his head and stared straight in front of him, as if to say "You ought to know I can't speak to anyone whilst marching, and I am making a disgraceful concession to your stupidity by so much as shaking my head and I hope no one has noticed it." It was a bit like trying to strike up an acquaintance with some primitive kind of tank. Then I found Sir Oswald Mosley and told him. He was marching with equal rigidity, frowned at me, but responded with perfect courtesy that they would do what we required. Contemplating the fascists and the poor unemployed stragglers we so stupidly called communists, we were ready to call down a plague on both their houses but some of us hoped that, if it came down, it would turn out nastier for the fascists. In 1936 two important publications were warmly welcomed by those of us who felt as Bob Turney did. One was Salvemini's *Under the Axe of Fascism*, which I acquired as a member of the Left Book Club and passed round for the Turneymen to read. The other was the Public Order Act, by which Parliament at last put an end to the marches, to the political uniforms, and (in effect) to the ludicrous career of that brilliant but misguided man Sir Oswald Mosley.

Chapter 6

THE STATION OFFICER

I BELIEVE THAT the station officer is, and I am certain that he was, the mute inglorious Milton of the police service. He is the police system's only creative artist. During my own short period in this exacting role, I suppose three years at the most, I found the routine work stupefying, the telephone maddening, the Found Property fascinating, the duty parades faintly comic, the unlawful arrests a marvellous challenge to inventive lying, and the grape-shot of the criminal law highly dangerous.

People are always walking, and occasionally staggering, into police stations with things that they have found; sometimes because the things are not much good and there is little pain in parting with them, but quite often because the finder feels sorry for the loser. Remarkably few seem to know that if the found thing is unclaimed after a certain period (in our case it was three months, but why on earth is it not standardised?) they can have it back again: not strictly for keeps but until, if ever, the loser *does* come forward and claim it. Among the things I saw brought into City police stations, apart from the wallets and purses, keys and umbrellas, books and bags, were a live 12ft African cobra in a packing case, a brass sundial, a bust of Berlioz, a violin case containing an unopened packet of garden sticks, and a live goat. Well, I may as well confess that I took the goat in myself, and it was the first arrest I ever made: it was wandering past the Bank of England in Prince's Street at four o'clock on a Sunday morning, and although I was on my probationary three months' night duty, I was already experienced enough to know that this was irregular. It had come from the stables of a job-master in Finsbury called John Barley & Son; and it came to the station with me quietly enough, offering no more than two or three explanatory bleats on the way. It took me some time to live this episode down:

indeed for some months the opening salutation I got from almost every constable I met was what he probably imagined to be a goat-like greeting.

The reception and recording of found property, which in those days was done by the station officer himself but today is probably the marginal job of someone in a miniskirt, was on the whole less interesting than these examples may suggest. There was one instance in which it was maddening rather than interesting, and that was the reception and custody of dogs which had lost themselves and were unable to stop barking about it. A non-stop barking Baskerville is the heaviest cross a night-duty station officer can be called upon to bear, to say nothing of the single men who are trying to sleep. It sometimes seemed excusable to let the dog have another street airing (free from any police escort) in the hope that someone else would find it and some other police station acquire it. Late one evening at Bishopsgate station a man carried in to me a large collarless mongrel he had found lying in the middle of Liverpool Street. A vehicle had run over its head, and it was in great pain, he announced; you could tell because its right eye was sticking out. And, rather horribly, it was. There were no vets available so late at night, but there was an all-night chemist; and we were allowed by the regulations to summon a chemist to destroy an injured dog. This chemist said that on my authority (making it plain that it would not be on his) he could do the job with (I think) prussic acid. So the poor dog was put out of his misery, the chemist was paid his five shillings, and I got on with my pay-sheet. At 1 a.m. there was ushered in a little foreign-sounding man who said he lived in Aldgate High Street and had lost his dog. He gave a description of it that I listened to with mounting panic. When his own dismay at the news I had to give him was subsiding, I told him how the dog had been run over, and pointed to the evidence. "Zat dog's eye has stick out since he is a baby," he said excitedly, "and in the middle of all the roads all the time he is lying down. Oh dear, vot my vife's mother say?"

I was appalled. Self-preservation beginning to assert itself, I steered the conversation towards the severity of English law about dogs going around without collars. After a time he said thoughtfully that the dog was really rather too old, anyway, and would have had to be put down soon. Perhaps it *was* run over, yes? At home he would explain. It was very kind of me, thank you often. And I turned again to my pay-sheet.

I was always interested in the question of bail, and the fact that our legislators had invested relatively junior officers of police with the right to grant or withhold it in all cases of arrest without warrant. What an immense power, I used to think, to confer upon someone like me! It never occurred to me that it was a survival from the days when a parish constable could clap his prisoner in the stocks if he thought he might run away, or let him go home if not. And my very first experience of it involved, most awkwardly, granting bail to a prisoner to whom one of my colleagues had already refused it. I went on station duty one night and saw from the charge-book that a man was in the cells on a charge of "defacing a newspaper belonging to Cripplegate Public Library". He had clipped something out with scissors. I looked at his property and found that the clipping was from an article in *Nature* about eugenics. He was described in the charge-book as a "lavatory attendant, no fixed abode", which seemed odd because lavatory attendants usually live at home with their wives or mothers and are unlikely readers of *Nature*. I went out to the cells to see him. He turned out to be a laboratory attendant (the more modern pronunciation would have saved him), who was unable to give an address at that moment because he was moving to another part of London and didn't yet know where he would be living. The mistake was so obvious that I released him on bail, making my peace later with the station officer who had misheard him.

If as a constable you stood in the ranks parading for duty in the Muster Room, for some reason you never felt very odd; and your only emotion would be, perhaps, anxiety that the sergeants or the station officer might notice that you were wearing shoes (we were then required to wear boots). Actually they never seemed to notice very much. More than once I've seen single men, having dashed back to the station for

My brother Harold (seated) and myself; ages six and three. I was very
angry at having to be there, and felt a fool in the clothes

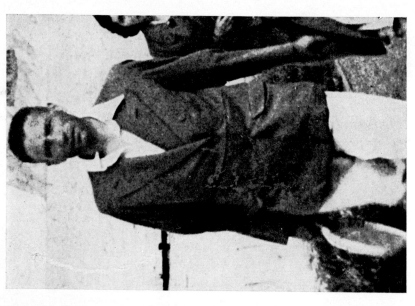

Myself in 1920

My cousin Sophie in 1917

night duty with insufficient time to get properly into uniform, parading in the rear rank with "civilian" trousers under their greatcoats; an essential part of this plan being that they should discover, immediately on marching out, that they wanted to go to the loo, where the trousers could be rapidly changed before any close inspection could take place. But once I had become a station officer, whose job it was to emerge from the office (with a pen behind his ear) and give the "Right Turn, Quick March" that sent the thirty or forty men out on duty, I could never see them without thinking of *The Pirates of Penzance*. On the command "First Section, Quick March" the rank nearest the exit would all stamp with their left feet, and then shuffle until they could get into motion. "Ta-ran-ta-ra", I used to say to myself in time with those feet.

> When the foeman bares his steel
> Tar*an*tar*a*, tar*an*tara!
> We uncomfortable feel
> Tarantara.

A policeman with an over-developed sense of the ridiculous is in the wrong job, even today. In those days, when the station officer had to "read the telephone book" to the parade before giving them the Quick March, his position was worse. He read out the registration numbers of cars recently stolen or "borrowed" on surrounding Divisions, long lists of them which no one could possibly memorise and of which no one could have taken notes. He would read out a long message about any burglary (though they weren't called burglaries then) which had just taken place on the Division—"Premises entered on this Division between 6 p.m. 15th and 9 a.m. 16th instant and quantity of furs supposed stolen." (They were only supposed stolen because the burglar might have been employed by their owner, with an insurance harvest to reap and share): "entry effected by thief or thieves concealing themselves in premises next door, ascending to roof under cover of darkness, breaking sky-light, removing property, and leaving by way of entry". The men knew it all by heart, and if you looked up as you read, like a vicar pausing at some salient point in the First Lesson, you could see the lips of some of them moving in

D

unison. You knew that as they left the station door on the way out they would be saying to one of their number: "That job was on your beat, mate, did you know? You want to get off your arse and start walking around a bit." I never got to understand why the message didn't *say* where the burglary was. There may have been some security reason that I was too naïve to imagine, but no one else seemed to know what it was, either.

The unlawful arrests were many and various, and the recognition that they were unlawful was usually an unpopular piece of pedantry. The law had neglected, no doubt by oversight, to provide that some kinds of offenders could be arrested without a warrant from a magistrate. Among them were people obtaining property by false pretences,[1] café customers getting a meal with no intention of paying,[1] and men committing what the law shudderingly called "acts of gross indecency". Few station officers seemed to bother themselves about this state of the law; and because fewer still had done so in the past, there had grown up a code of procedure, and a list of "specimen charges", which offered an alternative cover for errors of law which did violence to "civil liberty". If the alleged crime, and the resulting unauthorised arrest, had taken place indoors you added a charge under the 1824 Vagrancy Act of "being found in premises for an unlawful purpose". If it was out of doors, you added a charge (unless it seemed completely daft) of "insulting behaviour likely to cause a breach of the peace". Both of these rubber-stamp postscripts authorised "arrest without warrant", though the penalties attached to them were insignificant by comparison with the graver charges they artfully supported. Anyway they were ignored by the court and never read out to the defendant—the justices' clerk detachedly regarding them as a funny little police habit which did no harm and obviously in some way made the police feel better.

I soon found that this system, carefully exploited, gave the station officer an extraordinarily wide discretion. This was wide enough already in some ways, for it authorised and indeed

[1] Both of these have now been neatly provided for by the Criminal Law Act 1967 and the Theft Act 1968.

expected a quasi-magisterial enquiry which *could* end in the refusal of the charge and the liberation of the prisoner. When you did this you had to write a story about it in the Refused Charge Book; and this was studied with passionate interest by such superior officers as were spurred by native ill-will, devotion to duty, or self-preservation to look for trouble and stir up what they found. I am bound to confess that I developed a facility with the use of the Refused Charge Book which assured for me a kind of charmed life, though in fact it took longer to refuse a charge than to accept one. And I'm in no doubt that I sometimes grievously abused its intended purpose when it seemed to me that the lives of hapless men were going to be ruined by some trumpery charge of homosexual conduct in private (for an acquittal, though in these circumstances almost certain, would do them little less harm than a conviction), or of being "drunk and incapable" when they were clearly able to walk.

I did not understand homosexuality, and still don't. I was actually in the police service before I realised that it was a way of life, that its "criminality" was no more than the expression of an inherited stupidity (even that great lawgiver Justinian thought homosexuality was the cause of earthquakes), and, in the later words of the Wolfenden Report:[1]

> that it exists among all callings and at all levels of society; and that among homosexuals will be found not only those possessing a high degree of intelligence but also the dullest oafs.

But after a few years I had seen quiet family men brought to ruin by the law's cruel attitude to private physical acts which seemed to me totally harmless, even if inexplicable and unattractive. It was, I thought, a daft and ill-considered law; and except where some breach of it was openly and publicly offensive or children were at risk, I saw the quasi-magisterial "discretion" of the station officer as an opportunity in some cases to by-pass it. It was, of course, nothing of the sort. I was in the wrong and my police career would have been even shorter than it was if my bosses had realised what I was doing. The relative entries in the Refused Charge Book called for some

[1] Report of the Committee on Homosexual Offences and Prostitution 1957, HMSO.

literary imagination, since they had to exculpate the constable for bringing the case in as well as justifying myself in so disposing of it. It was probably a good thing for me that in 1930 I was appointed to run the City Police School of Instruction, then at Snow Hill; which removed me from the practical world of lost dogs, pay-sheets, refused charges and the Pirates of Penzance.

But as I leave the world of the station officer I want to record that never once in that capacity, or as an assistant to or a superior of anyone in that capacity, did I know of a case in which a prisoner in custody was knocked about or otherwise ill-treated. The fact that prisoners occasionally do get knocked about or ill-treated is known to anyone who can read a newspaper or turn the switch of a television set; and people thus gifted might be forgiven for supposing that a man helping the police with their enquiries is a man being shouted and sneered at, bullied, pushed into a chair, yanked out again, smacked round the head, belched at, tripped up, and worn down by the sweet-and-sour method of alternating questioners. I knew one or two detective constables who might have done this if they thought they could safely try, perhaps because they would have seen it done by gum-chewing film actors. But within my experience they never tried. The station officer alone held the key to the cell passage, and no one was supposed to see the occupant of a cell without his knowledge and permission. I can't answer for *all* my station officer colleagues, but no one went to see a prisoner in the cells, while I was responsible, unless I went too. I have reason to believe that CID men regarded this as a character-defect of some gravity.

By a strange and ancient custom, the sub-inspector in charge of the school was also held responsible for the policing of the courts at the Old Bailey (the Central Criminal Court). I had fifteen or twenty men in the school, brand-new recruits to be taught the theory of their coming job; and twenty-five or thirty senior constables at the Old Bailey. Two thoroughly reliable sergeants were on hand to deputise for me as I hopped, several times a day, from one responsibility to the other. In those days there were brief intervals between the monthly sessions at the Court (today it's almost a continuous perfor-

mance); and in those intervals I was able to give all my time
to the School and its usually bewildered scholars.

Despite all the criticism about using policemen as courtroom custodians in the magistrates' courts, where they may
well convey the undesirable impression that the whole show is
being run by the prosecution, few people seem to have bothered
about the City Police control at the Old Bailey. There are
occasional rumblings from the Greater London Council,
which has always wanted to take the thing over and run it as it
does the London Crown Courts; but the police survive. This
was lucky for me, for I learned a great deal (and made some
good and lasting friendships) in my seven years at the Old
Bailey.

Chapter 7

THE OLD BAILEY

NOT MUCH WRITING was going on at this time, except at the School of Instruction, whose syllabus I was allowed to reorganise completely—it had been sadly in need of a face-lift. Its pupils still sat copying ancient precepts into large notebooks which were to be their duty manuals. Among them, I recall, was a Home Office Circular headed "Infernal Machines" and signed Edward Troup. It told the police that they were to remove any infernal machine into the open air and then plunge it in a Bucket of Water. We all used to rub our eyes at this, especially those of us with any electrical knowledge: and though generations of embryo policemen had dutifully written it down, by great good fortune no one had ever plunged an electrically-operated bomb into a bucket of water. But now the school and the Old Bailey between them took up all my time; and I was interested enough in it all by this time to take work home—usually weekly test-papers compiled, in answer to my questions, by my hapless pupils in the School.

Facing page 129 is a photograph of one school which left my tutelage and was loosed upon the City of London in August 1933. The sergeant next to me is Frederick Bruty, a giant of a man who was formerly a Corporal-Major in the Life Guards: he combined a bark of carefully produced ferocity with a bite such as a lioness reserves for her cubs. I genuinely believe that, by reason of an iron devotion which gave him a kind of threatening pleasure, he would have protected my personal interests with his life. Behind him (fourth from the left in the back row) is Sandy Willison, who came to us at nineteen straight from Sedbergh School and is now, as Sir John Willison, Chief Constable of the West Mercia Constabulary. (His uncle, by the way, was Ernst Willison, business manager of the *New Statesman*, of whom I have written in my biography of Kingsley

Martin.) And on my left is Bill Niven, who came direct from Cambridge with his Honours B.A., his quizzical view of a world which didn't seem to want Honours B.A.s, and a capacity to take himself just seriously enough to become a Detective Inspector. I enjoyed some schoolmasterly crystal-gazing about such men, the enjoyment owing much to the fact that I was surprisingly often right.

For the first time I was, in fact, completely hooked, though I *never* got over the feeling that it was all strictly temporary and unusual and eccentric, like the strange things people find themselves doing in war-time. But even without this new turn of events, my journalistic adventures had led me very close to a trap from which I escaped only by the abruptest about-turn.

In 1929 I wrote a pseudonymous letter to the Editor of the *Daily News*. Something had goaded me into protest about the presentation of the police in fiction and on the stage. Stage bobbies kept their hats on and smoked in people's drawing-rooms, asked hundreds of silly questions, bent their knees when about to make weighty pronouncements, told the mistress of the house she could go for the moment but might be wanted in the drawing-room again, and were *never* turned out themselves for behaving like stupid boors and insufferable intruders. The Editor published it as a feature article, sent me three guineas, and invited me to lunch. I was on night duty, and going out to lunch with anyone who wasn't on night duty meant having about three hours in bed (which is a lot different from three hours' sleep). I arrived bleary-eyed at Bouverie Street and was introduced to the managing editor, to Mr Cadbury (whom I understood to be the proprietor, and who wore two pairs of glasses at the same time), to Mr Champion the News Editor, and to Mr R. J. Cruikshank, a man of great charm and erudition who was then Features Editor of the paper and later became editor of its successor, the *News Chronicle*. The outcome was that I was sent to a series of stage thrillers: Edgar Wallace's *The Ringer*, A. A. Milne's *The Fourth Wall*, Anthony Armstrong's *Ten-Minute Alibi*, and others; and wrote 500-word pieces about them from the police point of view. Then I was summoned to lunch with Mr Champion only. At what I guessed was a carefully chosen moment he said perhaps the time had come for us to have a more permanent arrangement? I could see what was coming and fended it off for a moment with a sickly grin. The newspaper world was fiercely competitive, he went on. You had to seize every possible chance of being one jump ahead of your rivals. "There must be times when you could give us a mere hint, the merest hint would do, about something in the news, some pending arrest, some detail no other paper could get. . . . We should be able to pay you fairly well, of course. Eh? What's the matter? Have another coffee? Brandy?"

I was standing up and feeling virtuous and ill-used. I remember asking him how long he supposed an arrangement like that would last, and whether he had really supposed I would fall for it. No, he said, but it wasn't his idea, he wasn't himself in favour of it but the proposition had been left in his hands. We parted amicably, but the honeymoon with the dear old *Daily News* was over, and when we came together again, seventeen years later, it had turned itself into the *News Chronicle*, its editor was Gerald Barry, and I was on the editorial staff of the *New Statesman*. I suppose I was nettled at the discovery, which a brighter man would have made at the outset, that the use of my theatre pieces had been a softening-up process. It didn't mean that they were any good; merely that they were not incurably illiterate and had, perhaps, the ephemeral Barnum-and-Bailey attraction which Dr Johnson had seen in women preaching and dogs walking on their hind legs. And yet, many years later, I nearly did it again. During the war I sent to the London *Evening Standard* a couple of articles on the etymology of the new war slang, and both were published. It was some time before I discovered that the *Evening Standard* had known at once who "C. H. Rolph" was and that he was at the City Police headquarters; and (I suppose) that he might be useful.

I got on well with the press men at the Old Bailey, a close-knit body of scribes who were nevertheless too watchful of each other to develop an *esprit de corps*. Admittedly I used to think their court behaviour sometimes unruly, until I saw the much worse antics of the newspapermen in American and Australian courts. But the fierce competitiveness of the newspaper world had certainly nourished in the minds of some reporters an illusion that the whole show was put on daily for the benefit of their papers or news agencies, and that any amount of bustling in and out, door-slamming, and unrestrained talking must be permissible to the gentlemen of the press. Certainly, still, they do things in court which no one else would be allowed to do. During the boring parts of a trial, and especially during the judge's summing up, they will sit and read newspapers, fill in football-pool coupons, study the racing tipsters, consult each other noisily over crossword puzzles. Few judges would ever stop them. But almost any judge, if appealed to, would stop anyone else, even members of the Bar, from doing these things. I was often asked by constables on duty in the courts whether it was permissible for non-press men to sit and take notes and make sketches, and could only reply that so far as I knew there was no law against it. There was a law against photography,[1] but none against sketching unless you could prove that the sketcher intended to publish his work (and how do you prove that?). If it rested with me, no one was ever prevented from taking notes or even from fairly discreet sketching. Anyway, some of the barristers sat sketching all the time.

So it was odd that, long after I had left the police service, I came to be prevented from taking notes in the Old Bailey myself. It was in 1960, and Penguin Books had commissioned me to write a paperback about their Old Bailey trial for publishing *Lady Chatterley's Lover*. I got the police inspector on duty to put me in the special seats in No. 1 Court always reserved for the City Lands Committee. (I wonder still, as I wondered when I was on duty there, why those seats were thus earmarked, by whose authority, and what special purpose of "open court" this restriction was supposed to serve?[2] I suppose the City Corporation's feeling was "well, we built the place and, apart from the judge and the prisoner, we're going to have the best seats". Not even the Festival Hall allowed its builders to do that.) I was making notes in a shorthand book when a friendly constable came to me (he didn't know me from Adam) and said he was sorry, it wasn't allowed. I showed

[1] Criminal Justice Act 1925, section 41.

[2] "The general rule is that all courts of justice are open to all so long as there is room" (*R. V. Lewes Prison Governor* (1971) 2 KB 254).

him my Press card and explained that the press bench was fully occupied. He replied that he had his orders, and they were that notes could be taken only in the press seats. I thought someone had got it wrong, but sadly gave in. Next day I did something far more heinous, though (so far as I know) still perfectly lawful: I took a small tape-recorder, and managed to use it, concealed, for the whole of the trial. I needn't have bothered, for when it was all over I was able to borrow a complete typewritten transcript of the five days' proceedings from one of the defending counsel. But why are people prevented from taking notes in court? Or taking their little tape-recorders (so long as they don't squeak)? Ear-trumpets are allowed. Only once have I seen an ear-trumpet provoke a court incident. Its owner was a woman called for jury service, and when the Judge saw it he asked the lady (through the trumpet) whether she would like to be excused? She would, she said eagerly: she was eighty-one and hard of hearing. She was advised to get her name removed from the jury list, but I don't think she heard because she was putting her ear-trumpet into a shopping-bag as she made gratefully for the exit. . . . But I digress.

It would be hard to forget some of the Old Bailey characters of the thirties, though in a small minority of cases it would be nice. The three who affected me daily were the three permanent Judges of the Court: Sir Ernest Wild, the Recorder of London, Sir Henry Dickens, the Common Serjeant, and Judge Holman Gregory, the Commissioner. Wild was a poseur and a mountebank, who might possibly have done better on the stage. He was much in demand as an after-dinner speaker, knew the Gilbert and Sullivan operas backwards (he brought members of the D'Oyly Carte Opera Company to sit on the bench with him), and published two books of truly awful verse. He was usually angry about something, and in the intervals when he was not angry he exuded a kind of odious and carefully projected charm. This worked best on the office-cleaners who came at 4.30 to start washing the marble floors and stairs, on the assumption (often mistaken) that the Courts would have risen at four o'clock. As he passed each one on his way out he stopped, took off his hat, bowed low, and beamed "Good night, ma'am". With one exception they would look up from their kneeling position in adoration. The exception was a quiet little woman called Jenny, who always looked to me too delicate to be charring, but it was only in appearance that she was delicate. Once when the learned Recorder had bent over her to pay his stately tribute, she grimly watched him go out of the swing doors as she wrung out her floorcloth into a bucket. "That man's a slimy bastard," Jenny announced. And the heavens stayed up.

Sir Henry Dickens was the novelist's son, and about eighty-five when I first knew him. He sat in Court No. 3, seemed to get all the dullest and longest cases to try, and listened to them with a hand cupped round his ear. His capacity to follow an involved company fraud, on which the Director of Public Prosecutions had perhaps been working for two or three years, was a miracle of sustained comprehension. And the Recorder saw to it that he got plenty of practice, picking out for himself all the cases offering human frailty at its most juicy and least boring. When Dickens made a note he did it with a long quill pen, which scratched and squeaked on the paper. He was the true embodiment of a Dickensian Judge, the very last of his kind; with some added peculiarities that even his minutely observant father might never have thought of. At 11.30 each morning he would fumble under his desk in a noisily-rustling paper bag and begin a ten-minute meal of biscuits, eating them with the toothless contortion of the aged and a superb absence of self-consciousness that always made me weak with envy. Often during the day he would push back his great chair and hurry off the bench to his private loo; and any young counsel who, not knowing of his habits, stopped speaking and looked at him enquiringly would receive an impatient command that he was to "get on, get on". Accordingly he got on in the Judge's absence, chastened no doubt to feel that his performance was so expendable, but playing for time and reserving some telling phrase or question for the return of a Common Serjeant refreshed. Sir Henry Dickens was a lovable old man, and much loved he was.

Judge Holman Gregory was not. I used to hope that someone, somewhere, liked him a little, because at that time I was that sort of man, but I don't think anyone did; certainly not anyone in court. His manner in speaking to counsel, court officials, and especially police witnesses made me long to throw soft fruit and eggs at him; which, when you come to think of it, would have made a unique scene, earning me a place in history just below Alfred and the Cakes. He always spoke through his nose. A friend of mine, a detective constable who was a good, simple and rather nervous man, once told him that the rag-trade area around Aldersgate Street in the City was much used for street bargaining "in the olden days". Judge Holman Gregory flung himself back in his chair. "What do you bead," he snapped, "by the olded days? Why are you allowed to cub here add talk such rubbish? *Wed* was it that street bargiddig was the custob?" Twenty years ago, perhaps, faltered my old friend, who was white to the lips and had no idea what was wrong with "the olden days". And you might have thought that was the end of it: but no, his Lordship went on and on, lashing himself into such an adenoidal fury that he ended by convincing himself that something was seriously wrong. He instructed me to report the incident to my Commissioner, making it clear that there were limits to the colloquialisms that could be heard from policemen in the witness-box; and I did so, deliberately and daringly making the occasion a comic one and adding the personal view that Judge Holman Gregory's strictures were wholly unjustified. "I agree," wrote the Commissioner tersely at the foot of this time-wasting document.

A man who used to talk to me in a specially friendly and unguarded way was Maurice Healy, Q.C., who sometimes got caught in one of those long waits for a jury considering its verdict after normal hours, when everyone stands around and gossips. It was a refreshment to hear him talk about anything, and simply to savour the superb Irishness of him; but I got him to talk about Swift and Gogarty and Yeats and Sean O'Casey. One didn't have to say much, but he listened attentively to what little one did say (an endearing quality). In Court he had the great gift of being able to lose his temper without looking ridiculous, and I never saw him lose it to better purpose than in a blackmail case he was defending before the Recorder, Sir Ernest Wild.

The prisoner was a Dutchman, who was said to have black-mailed two women, one of them his former wife. Throughout the first morning of the defence, Wild interrupted scores of times, sometimes with observations and queries so footling that he almost seemed to be provoking a row. (It's fair to say that he was not one of the more notorious judicial interrupters.) At length Maurice Healy had had enough. He turned to the Recorder and brandished his brief at arm's length. "If yer Lordship wishes to conduct this case himself ye can now get on with ut," he shouted, glaring over the tops of his spectacles. "I lave it intoirly to you, I withdraw from the case, I'll have nothin' more to do with ut." He flung the brief down on his desk and stalked out. We all watched as the double swing doors of No. 2 Court flopped to and fro behind him and then stopped. There was rather a long silence, and then the Recorder, his face very white and his mouth like a thin line drawn round the base of a cheese, looked up at the clock. "I think," he said, "this may be a convenient moment at which to adjourn for lunch."

When the Court resumed Mr Healy, to our great surprise, was back in his place. I believe there had been a lunch-time reconciliation. He stood up and called the prisoner to the witness-box by way of opening his defence. There had been a divorce at Reno, and Healy wanted to establish vindictiveness in the ex-wife who was prosecuting. What were the grounds for the divorce?

"Incompatibility of temperament," said the Dutchman.

The Recorder sat up. "Ah," he beamed at Maurice Healy, "wasn't that the ground for our divorce this morning?"

"Oh no, my Lord, there was no divorce. That was merely a judicial separation."

There was a roar of relieved laughter, Wild joining in un-restrainedly. I have always cherished the hope that this was all unrehearsed, but of course with these lawyers-cum-actors you never really know. All I know is that Healy was always capable of producing such a riposte on the spur of the moment; and that the case then proceeded amicably, with no more interruption from the Bench.

While they were in plain clothes, I used to sit my probationer constables in one of the Old Bailey courts on selected occasions to listen to a trial. Once during a trial which had strong political overtones the Clerk of the Peace thought there was likely to be an uproar, and probably a minor riot, in the public gallery. At his request I filled the gallery with my young bobbies, leaving no room for anyone else. They were spotted by the pressmen from their bench below, the story got into the papers, and there was a move to put a question down in the House of Commons about this outrage on the principles of "open court". I heard no more about it, but never suffered the smallest pang of conscience. These youngsters (I told myself) were members of the public, of rather more than the normal public gallery value: they were there to learn rather than to gloat.

Some of them learned an incredible amount of law in their short period of instruction. When Mrs Elvira Barney was charged with the murder of her lover by shooting, she was tried by Mr Justice Humphreys, who was a great authority on the common law, and defended by Sir Patrick Hastings, who was not. Sir Patrick planned his defence for a manslaughter verdict, and then the jury staggered him by declaring that Mrs Barney was not guilty of anything. The equally surprised Judge was about to discharge her when Sir Patrick, having recovered his breath and got to his feet, said:

"My Lord, there remains one matter which it would be desirable to clear up. My client still faces the comparatively minor charge of possessing a firearm without a police certificate. If your Lordship would be so considerate as to——"

"Now, Sir Patrick," said the Judge chidingly, "I think you had better take further instructions." And indeed his two juniors were tugging at his gown to get him back into his seat. When we all got back to the schoolroom I asked the class if any of them had spotted what was wrong. I should have thought this most unlikely, but I was mistaken. They knew, or at any rate one of them had known and told the others, that the offence of possessing a firearm without a certificate was not (then) an indictable offence, could not be dealt with at the Old Bailey, and must be disposed of (as in due course it was) by the magistrates. I omitted to tell the school that, as Sir Travers Humphreys had passed me in the Judges' Corridor on his way home after the trial, I heard him say to his clerk, "Apparently she should have been given a pat on the back? Most extraordinary."

Among all the High Court Judges who came to the Old Bailey in the thirties—the "regulars" seemed to be Avory, Roche, Finlay, McNaghten, Cassels, Rigby Swift, Wright, Hawke and Charles—the last two were by far the least popular. This was not difficult to understand in the case of Mr Justice Hawke, who was consistently rude and supercilious to everyone, but Charles seemed to me a big, bluff, belching boozer of the kind that gets accepted almost everywhere. Not a judicial figure, perhaps; built for a club bar background rather than for the Courts of Oyer and Terminer, less happy on the Bench than fishing from the pier at Deal. But he was very cordial to the police and other primitive forms of life, and we were all rather for him. He showed great composure, anyway, in one court episode that would have disconcerted most of his brethren.

He was trying a case in which Wal Hannington, of the National Unemployed Workers Movement, was charged with seditious conspiracy (or some kind of conspiracy—these unemployed people were always conspiring about something instead of manfully getting on with their unemployment). When the jury had duly said Guilty, Mr Justice Charles proceeded to deliver the "judicial homily" which most prisoners have to listen to before they know what has been wrapped up for them.

"People like you," he growled, "put themselves forward as the spokesmen of the working classes. You are nothing of the sort" (which at that time was fair enough, since Hannington spoke for the classes who hadn't got any work). "I know more about the working man than you will ever know. I live among working men, go fishing with them, share their fun and their anxieties." And so on for a little longer, culminating in the passing of a prison sentence. Watching from the privileged seats reserved for the City Lands Committee were two smartly dressed women, mother and daughter, who had prevailed upon me before the trial began to let them sit there. They both had considerable personal charm and knew what it was for. I had explained to them what august seats they would be sitting on, how nicely they would have to behave, and what trouble I should be in if their presence were challenged. The moment the Judge had passed sentence the younger woman leapt to her feet. "How *dare* you?" she shrieked at the astonished Mr Justice Charles, who looked at her with his mouth wide open. "Who do you think you are, to sit there and arrogate to yourself the right to speak for the working classes?" By this time a sergeant and myself were clambering over the leather-covered benches to get at her. "Just what kind of a man can you be?" she continued, and by this time she was in tears and really, I thought with a kind of mad detachment, looking rather beautiful. She drummed her clenched fists against her breast. "*I* speak for the working classes," she screamed, "and I can tell you this——" But she never did. I had a hand over her mouth and we were hustling her out, followed by her scarcely less distressed mother.

Outside in the marble-floored, echoing hall she proceeded to have hysterics, and I sent for a chair for her to have them on. When she had recovered we briefly ran through the conversation we had had when I allowed them into those seats. "This is a fine thing," I said; "after all that wheedling and all your disarming promises. And yet I might have known—there was something about the pair of you, and I don't only mean being women."

"Oh dear, I'm so dreadfully sorry," said the girl, who had by this time mopped up her face a little and was restoring its surface from her handbag. "Something came over me when I heard that awful man in his silly wig and robes talking about the working classes. You *must* forgive me."

I said it was the Judge's forgiveness she stood in need of. This was contempt of Court. True, it was the kind known as contempt "in face of the court", which although it seemed very shocking was often treated with surprising leniency. "Will I get leniency?" she asked. I said very severely that I thought she would probably cop it, but she must wait while I went to see the Judge and find out, and first I would want her name and address. Her name, she said, was Jane Featherstonehaugh, and she lived at Peasmarsh, in Sussex. Her father was a QC, practising in Toronto. (Why does one remember such details? It may be, in this instance, because I had always wondered how this surname was pronounced, and was ready to believe it was something like Foff. But no, she said, it was a four-syllable name, spoken exactly as written.) She was a member of the Independent Labour Party, and a group secretary (I think) of the National Unemployed Workers Movement. All of which I duly conveyed to the Judge in his room, by this time sitting in his shirt sleeves in front of a large whisky. "Good God," he said, abstractedly. "She was rather nice, wasn't she?" Did he want her detained and charged? "Eh? What for? Oh, Lord, no. Let her go, tick her off and let her go."

I went and told her how lucky she was. She thanked me in the voice she had used when we were arranging about the seats, moving her eyes in much the same way. And when she and her mother left in a taxi, it was followed by another taxi containing Chief Inspector Pasmore, of the Special Branch. I never heard how they got on.

Before I went to the Old Bailey I think I could have been classed as a fairly mild adherent of the punishing school, so long as (a) you were punishing the right man and (b) he knew what you were punishing him for. A few years in the courts, contemplating the stage army of offenders who crossed the scene again and again, to say nothing of the selective barbarity of the death penalty for murder, convinced me that we were on the wrong lines. I came to believe that socially the *ultimate* effect of hanging was wholly evil (as well as being ineffectual for its purpose), while the sole justification for imprisonment was as a means of containing the dangerous offender who could not otherwise be restrained. This I think it still is; and if I say that the civilised ideal should be the eventual abolition of imprisonment, I say it in the knowledge that this is probably unattainable but that one must, in such matters, consistently aim higher than target.

However, to hold these views in the police service was to belong to a very tiny and much-ridiculed minority. I can think of no more than half a dozen men, out of the hundreds I knew, who would think that murderers should be "kept alive at the public expense"; and even if it could be demonstrated that the killing of police officers was rather more likely in death-penalty countries, that would make no difference. Sex offenders of nearly every kind were similarly execrated, one exception being the boy-and-girl seduction case where the boy was just over and the girl just under the age of consent (and of these, anyway, only a minority came to court). The Old Bailey atmosphere was in this respect an unhealthy atmosphere. It was noticeable that, when the word got round the building that the jury in some much-publicised murder trial was coming back into court with its verdict, every seat was quickly filled and the rear of the courtroom was crammed with standing onlookers—some of them officers of the court to whom the death sentence must surely have been a common-place. I mentioned this once in a newspaper article and it was hotly repudiated in a letter from a court official who, no doubt, didn't want it to be true. But it was ineluctably true, and I watched its enactment dozens of times.

It was the final act in a lethal drama, the end of a blood-hunt; and the morbid excitement of it all was, I thought, against the "public interest". As Mr Roy Jenkins was to say in April 1973, in reply to a campaign to use a Criminal Justice Bill to get the death penalty restored, when it was in operation "it was the names of the men and women who were hanged—Bentley, Ruth Ellis, and Hanratty—which were most remembered: their victims were forgotten. Without capital punishment it is the other way round. And in the strange psychosis of criminality that cannot be without significance." It was no accident, I decided, that the three countries in which the detective novel flourished were all at that time death penalty countries—France, Great Britain and the United States; though they have all since ceased to kill their murderers, Great Britain by legislative decision and the other two by hesitation and default. Since the death penalty was abolished I have been in the Old Bailey during the closing stages of several murder trials. The drama is much reduced, the morbidity has been extracted, justice seems to have edged a little nearer to civilisation.

These considerations, strengthening in my mind from that time, in due course brought me to join the Howard League for Penal Reform, the Institute for the Study and Treatment of Delinquency, and the British Society of Criminology and to take part in a variety of specific campaigns to reform the law of punishment. And the obvious need, as I saw it, to supplement a prison system which was so manifest a failure turned my mind to the so-called "after care" of discharged prisoners. But that was not until I had decided to leave the police service.

The Old Bailey disenchanted me finally about two well-worn pillars of British justice: one was its mumbo-jumbo ritual, and the other was the jury system. Despite the best efforts of some of the kindlier judges and counsel, the serio-comic splendour of the wigs and gowns and the would-be awesome solemnity of the archaic official language seemed to me designed to instil fear (rather than respect) in ordinary people caught up in the proceedings. And as Don Quixote told Sancho Panza: "One of the effects of fear is to disturb the senses and cause things to appear other than what they are." The muttered incantations of the court ushers took on, once you were disillusioned about the fairness of the justice available, a quality of pompous mockery that I found intolerable. It would have been far better to leave them in Latin, or the law's own peculiar Norman-French; but they should never in any event be pronounced, as in those days they frequently were, by aged and sometimes half-tipsy men with crumpled gowns, stumbling diction and no teeth. "All persons oo 'ave anythink to do before my Lords the Queen's Justices of Oyer and Terminer and General Gaol Delivery for the jurisdiction of the Central Criminal Court, draw near and give your attendance." In Court No. 2 the police inspector's seat was just behind that of the usher, who was a rather lovable old man of (I should judge) about eighty, just about able to hear what was going on but certainly able to lift a pint mug with one hand in the Magpie and Stump across the road. I used to pass him sketches of the people in court, and under them he would shakily write insulting captions. Once I passed him a pencilled note asking him three questions. 1. What did he mean by Oyer and Terminer? 2. What was General Gaol Delivery? 3. How could you give your attendance without drawing near? His reply was unhesitating and all-embracing: "Mind your own bloody business." From his seat on the bench the Recorder used to watch him more closely than he realised. So far as I knew he was never actually caught out, but I remember that his eventual retirement seemed rather precipitate, though the word is difficult to associate with the speed at which he did everything else.

It worried me that the system of trial by jury, which had been virtually abolished in all civil proceedings, should still be the object of such veneration in criminal trials. I had to teach my probationer constables in the School that the result of the most carefully prepared of criminal prosecutions, however it might violate one's sense of justice and seem to discourage further effort, was no matter for the police. They were to be absolutely impartial, training themselves to contemplate unmoved the acquittal of obviously guilty villains, and smothering their uneasiness, if they felt any, about the conviction of the palpably innocent. Once or twice at the conclusion of a trial they came face to face, outside the courtroom, with a CID officer who, pop-eyed, white-faced and speechless, had just seen months of patient work destroyed by the acquittal of a professional crook. Was this the impartiality I was urging upon them, they wanted to know? I forget the answer.

But juries also convicted innocent men, or at the very least they convicted men they should have acquitted on the evidence. I would admit at once that the cases in which such convictions were upheld on appeal were not frequent; but the Appeal Court Judges, in their traditional reluctance to "interfere with the verdict of a jury", left me sometimes uneasy in cases where I knew the full story. The uneasiness was powerfully reinforced when I came to serve on a jury myself, many years later. While I was still at the Old Bailey I was much impressed by a passage from Sir James Fitzjames Stephen's *History of the Criminal Law of England*.[1]

The securities which can be taken for justice in the case of a trial by Judge without a jury are infinitely greater than those which

[1] Macmillan, London, 1883, Vol. I, 568.

can be taken for trial by a judge and jury. The judge is one known man, holding a conspicuous position before the public, open to censure and in extreme cases to punishment if he goes wrong: the jury are twelve unknown men. While the trial is proceeding they form a group just large enough to destroy even the appearance of individual responsibility. When the trial is over they sink back into the crowd from whence they came and cannot be distinguished from it. The most unjust verdict throws no discredit on any person who joined in it, for as soon as it is pronounced he returns to obscurity.

Juries give no reasons, but Judges do in some cases and ought to be made to do so formally in *all* cases if juries were dispensed with. . . . An appeal implies a judgement on the part of the Court, appealed from, and an argument to show that it decided wrongly, which cannot be unless the reasons for the decision are known.

And then came a passage which might have been written yesterday instead of in 1883:

In cases of strong prejudice juries are frequently unjust, and capable of erring on the side either of undue convictions or undue acquittals. They are also capable of being intimidated, as the experience of Ireland has abundantly shown. Intimidation has never been systematically practised in England in modern times, but I believe it would be just as easy and just as effective here as it has been shown to be in Ireland. Under the Plantagenets and down to the establishment of the Court of Star Chamber, trial by jury was so weak in England as to cause something like a general paralysis of the administration of justice. Under Charles II it was a blind and cruel system. During part of the reign of George III it was, to say the least, quite as severe as the severest judge without a jury could have been. The revolutionary tribunal during the Reign of Terror tried by jury.

If ever the criminal jury were abolished I should want to see it replaced by a judge and two assessors, the latter to be laymen appointed in much the same way as the Justices of the Peace. The *whole* of every such trial should be recorded on tape as well as by official shorthand writers. The judge should always give reasons for this Court's decisions, and if he did not give them in writing they should be taken down by a shorthand writer and then read, corrected and signed by the judge.

At the Old Bailey I used to talk to jurors about cases they had tried; or at least lend a willing ear when they talked to me. I do not know whether this was reprehensible or not, but I didn't much mind. (I never spoke to a juror during a trial.) Until *someone* finds out and collates what goes on in jury rooms, perhaps even startling a Parliamentary committee or a Royal Commission with tape-recordings of juries' deliberations, the truth will never be known or believed in the right quarters. After the conviction of Lord Kylsant, Chairman of the Royal Mail Steam Packet Company, for publishing a false company prospectus, one of the jurors told me he was quite unable to understand why Lord Kylsant's co-defendant on another charge, Mr Harold John Moreland, the auditor, had had to be acquitted. If one was guilty, surely both were? That juror can't have *begun* to understand Mr Justice Wright's directions or the summing-up. "But I wouldn't stand out against the others," he said. "Most of them seemed to know what they were doing." In those days, when only unanimous verdicts could (in criminal cases) be accepted, such a man could cause the whole weary case to be retried if he did decide to "stand out"; at a cost, probably, of another £100,000.

"Standing out" could, however, have its comic aspects; and one episode involving Mr Justice Rigby Swift and a defiant jury is worth recounting here because it has never, I believe, been told. The prisoner was indicted for what was then called embezzlement: he was the manager of a multiple wine shop and he was said to have been misappropriating goods delivered there. As soon as the last Crown witness had left the witness-box the Judge turned to Mr Eustace Fulton, who was prosecuting. "Is that your case, Mr Fulton?" he asked in his querulous high-pitched voice. Mr Fulton said it was. Mr Justice Rigby Swift closed his big note-book with a bang, and nearly everyone knew what was coming.

"Members of the jury," he said as he lifted himself round to face them, "you will please return a verdict of Not Guilty in this case, by my direction. There is no evidence upon which you can convict this man." (He did this rather a lot, and always with superb confidence.) The jury looked dumbly at him and waited for what was to happen next. This turned out to be a contribution from the Clerk of the Court, who had stood up to address them. "Members of the jury, are you agreed upon your verdict?" he said. "You find the prisoner Not Guilty on this indictment and that is the verdict of you all?"

They looked at each other first, and then glared at him with what seemed to me mounting suspicion. Then their foreman began a whispered colloquy with those nearest to him. This went on long enough to arouse the Judge; who, instead of peering over his glasses as most judges do, tilted his head back so that he could look under them, a far more intimidating and imperious manner of inspection. "Members of the jury," he said, "what are you discussing? There is nothing for you to discuss. I am directing you, if you like I'm ordering you, to acquit this defendant because it would not be safe to convict on the evidence which you have heard and which, we are told, is all you are going to hear. That is a matter of law and a matter for me to decide. Now will you please do as I say?"

But the foreman, a man of mettle, stood up. "My Lord," he began, "we don't think we *have* heard all the evidence. We would like to hear what the prisoner has to say. He hasn't said a word yet. If he was questioned he might—eh?"

The Clerk was gesturing to him that he was either to sit down, or shut up, or possibly both. The Judge spoke again. "If the case against the prisoner is not made out," he said with ominous patience, "you cannot call upon the prisoner to supply the deficiency. The case against him fails, do you understand? I cannot allow the trial to go on a moment longer. Now will you please respond to the learned Clerk's question?"

"Members of the jury," said the Clerk again, "are you agreed upon your verdict? Do you find—"

"No, I'm afraid we're not," said the foreman desperately. "The jury would like to retire."

"Retire?" almost roared the Judge. "What for? What do you want to talk about?"

A lady stood up in the back row of the jury, intrepid woman. "I think most of us are very worried," she said nervously. "We think he did it, we think he meant to keep all those bottles of wine and things so we're very sorry, but we would like to hear his explanation."

And she spoke for them all. Nothing would shake them. We were back in 1688 and the Trial of the Seven Bishops: I believe some of the jurors honestly felt that they might be making history, and that H. M. Bateman ought to be there to draw the pictures. In the end they were discharged from giving a verdict, chased out of the jury box, and told to go away. A fresh jury was empanelled from among waiting jurors sitting at the back of No. 1 Court (where you can occasionally hear something but can never see anything), and the whole procedure of "putting the prisoner in their charge" was solemnly gone through again: reading the indictment to the prisoner, taking his plea, swearing the jury, and telling them: "To this indictment the prisoner has pleaded Not Guilty, and it will be your charge, having heard the evidence, to say whether he be guilty or not." Then Mr Eustace Fulton told them they wouldn't be hearing any evidence at all, and sat down. The Judge told them they were to say "Not Guilty" because they had no grounds for saying anything else. "Members of the Jury," said the Clerk once again, "are you agreed upon your verdict? You find the prisoner . . . ", etc. (The necessity for all this was abolished in 1967 by a Criminal Justice Act.)

Fascinated, I watched their faces. It was all too good to be true. Couldn't there, please, be someone among them who would get up and say: "Sorry, we heard something about this chap while we were sitting at the back of the court. We think he ought to be tried." But no. The foreman did as he was told. "Not Guilty," he said; and "You are discharged," said Mr Justice Rigby Swift to the prisoner. It was over. "NOW can we get on?" asked the Judge wearily, and the next case was called.

"Difficult" jurors were rare, and the practice of committing them to prison had gone out with Judge Jeffreys (another Recorder of London) and the Bloody Assizes. They had, as a rule, to be humoured, though in those days I always thought they were treated with an astonishing lack of consideration (and at that time they got no expenses). I remember one "waiting juror" who, in No. 1 Court, was told by the jury-bailiff to sit with his colleagues behind the big dock, which seemed to have been carefully placed so as to prevent one from seeing anything except the ceiling. He decided to stand up instead of sitting, because thus he could see at least the heads of the jury and the Judge's wig. A constable told him he must sit down, and he refused. Well, you can't stage a rough-and-tumble in court during a trial, all because a juryman-in-waiting wants to stand up. So the constable came to find me and ask for instructions. I went to see the standing juror, and persuaded him that if he went to the back he could stand without being in anyone's way, and even see more because he would be higher up. I don't know whether he misunderstood me, but he went to the back row and stood on the seat; where he was soon spotted by Mr Justice Hawke, who ordained loudly that he was to get down. I went back to see him, and although he made the considerable concession of getting down off the seat, he still wouldn't sit on it. "What I think you'd better do," I said in the awful hush that was going on, "is let me find you a better place altogether. It's not much good here. Let's go round to the other side," and I led him, now docile and eager, out of the double swing doors into the hall. There I left him under the eye of a powerfully-built constable while I went in search of the jury-bailiff. And the jury-bailiff sent him home, cooking the books in some way to account for his disappearance. I present the story to any reluctant juror who would like to be sent home.

The picture of the Old Bailey that remains with me is that of Disraeli's "two nations" as an organised monthly tableau. Round the base of the domed ceiling on the first floor runs a legend which says "Defend the Children of the Poor and Punish the Wrongdoer". I never understood about the children of the poor. The Old Bailey was much more concerned about the children of the comfortably breeched, to say nothing of their parents; which was no more than you would expect, since the generality of men arraigned there for trial, as at any other criminal court, were poor-looking types who had failed in the simple business, even though it requires no rules, disciplines or concessions, of preying on their fellow-men. I used to watch the prison vans disgorging their human cargoes in what we called the prison yard, and marvel at the reappearance of the same old lined and stupid faces, time after time after time. They were like half-witted troops marching hand-cuffed into a gigantic washing machine which was not even designed to get them clean. The gulf between these wretched people and the men whose public school voices would speak about them for weary and platitudinous hours was as wide as ever. When, rarely, there was an educated man in the dock it was a matter for shocked judicial comment, as though it were the lack of "A" levels in biology, art, or mathematics that should get a man indicted. "Here are you," said a judge who is as famous as he is probably apocryphal, "a young man with all the advantages of a secondary school education, instead of which you go about the country stealing ducks." Yet it was only when an educated man was on trial, someone of effortless ease in the court atmosphere, like Lord Kylsant or Clarence Hatry or Compton Mackenzie,[1] that the proceedings came anywhere near the *Magna Carta* precept that a man must not be condemned "Except by lawful judgement of his peers"— i.e. his equals (*nisi per legale judicium parium suorum*). The presence of a jury never seemed to me to make any difference here. The true contrast was between a judge in his scarlet robes, the barristers with their wigs and witticisms and rhetoric, all about equally shop-soiled, and the little runt sitting between two prison officers in a big cage.

[1] Compton Mackenzie was fined £100 for revealing "official secrets" in a book about the First World War, called *Greek Memories*, a rather absurd prosecution. At his trial he seemed a tight-lipped and haughty-looking man, and treated the Judge and the whole court with a kind of scrupulously courteous disdain.

Chapter 8

WAR AND OTHER DUTIES

IN THE MIDDLE of 1934 I was found to be next on the list for promotion from sub-inspector to inspector; which, I saw only too plainly, would mean losing my nice interesting job at the School of Instruction and the Old Bailey, and being posted to "divisional duties" in place of someone retiring on pension. There was no escape from this process of being kicked upstairs, except by conduct which would qualify me for being kicked down. This was a calamity which revived all my longing to leave the police service and try to be a professional writer instead of an increasingly desultory part-timer. But then came an unforeseen development which, as my colleagues united in telling me, illustrated once more how the Devil looks after his own.

Most police forces have (or had) their own local "Instruction Book", setting out their Standing Orders, local Acts and By-laws with or without annotations, and various precepts on the attainment of good policemanship. Ours was dated 1894, and had never since then been revised. From among its exhortations to the constable, period pieces all, the following may be selected as typical:

If, at any Time, he requires immediate Assistance, and cannot in any other way obtain it, he must blow his Whistle or spring his Rattle; but this is to be done as seldom as possible, as such Alarm often creates Inconvenience by assembling a Crowd. He will be required to report to the Sergeant of his Section every Occasion for his using his Rattle or Whistle.

We had no rattles, only whistles (of which I never heard one blown in anger though there was much whistle-blowing at big fires, mainly I think by way of adding to the general din); and no one could remember a time when there had been rattles.

We needed a new Instruction Book. I don't think we should have got one but for the arrival of a new Assistant Commissioner in the person of Captain J. A. Davison, who came to us in 1936 from the War Department Constabulary. He at once embarked on a whirlwind programme of "new brooming" which, predictably, ended in an almighty row with the Commissioner, Sir Hugh Turnbull (who sooner or later rowed with everyone). Davison, as soon as he could, went off and became Chief Constable of Kent. But among his new broom items had been the proposal that I should write a new Instruction Book, a comprehensive one on an entirely new basis which would bring the man-on-the-beat completely up to date. To this ambitious proposal Sir Hugh Turnbull had agreed, Captain Davison not yet having fallen from favour. So I was once more, and this time officially, "struck off all duties", and embarked upon a vast, top-heavy and stifling tome which ran to nearly 350,000 words and kept me busy for about two years. I can claim, I think, that its language was a little less costive than that of its Victorian predecessor. It earned me some kudos, totally undeserved since I was doing the kind of thing I liked doing anyway (I didn't much care what I wrote so long as I was writing), and a "commendation" from the Commissioner for "great zeal and ability displayed in compiling the City of London Police Instruction Book issued in 1937". If you did anything in the police service that fell short of suicidal bravery and was yet thought to merit a recorded commendation, it was recorded that you did it with "great zeal and ability". It was our little language.

By the time the Instruction Book was fully launched we were well into 1938, and it looked as though war with Hitler's Germany, which had been looming since 1933, was now imminent. In July 1937 I had made the acquaintance of my future boss, Kingsley Martin,[1] editor of the *New Statesman*, for which I had been doing short unsigned book reviews; and he was encouraging me to write more, even if it meant leaving the police service and damning the consequences. I've often reproached myself for my lack of resolution in not doing as he

[1] See my *Kingsley: the Life, Letters and Diaries of Kingsley Martin*, Gollancz, London, 1973.

said, but in retrospect I can see that by dallying until the Munich "Settlement" and then the outbreak of war, when of course serving police officers were "frozen for duration", I probably got myself into the war-time job I was best fitted to do. I should have had to do something with war in it.

From 1937 onwards, indeed I think from the date of Guernica onwards (27 April), the confidential "circulars" from the Home Office to chief officers of police were heavy with the threat of war. In fact the war started for me in 1937. In a makeshift little office at headquarters in Old Jewry, I had already become a kind of one-man Legal Department; and once such a job is invented and established (and for my part it was actively fostered), then by Parkinson's Law it will justify itself very quickly and everyone will marvel that things ever got done without it. But the job certainly began in an atmosphere of war psychosis.

At frightening speed there developed a mass of "War Emergency Files", bulging with Home Office and War Office instructions about the evacuation of civilians, the control of animals, lighting, noise, fuel, food, clothing, motor vehicles. It became my job to "translate" these from officialese into language that ordinary bobbies might, only too soon, have to read and understand. Selected groups of senior officers were required to sit through lectures at Gresham College about the effect of mass bombing in the Spanish Civil War. The lecturers were members of the International Brigade, just back from Spain; of whom my friend Tom Davis drily observed that a right-wing government had to be very frightened before it would call upon such revolutionary desperadoes for help. One of the lecturers was reputed to be a man who had led the naval mutiny at Invergordon in 1931, and the senior police officers obviously felt that if they were now required to sit at the feet of a man like *that*, well, we had arrived at a point where anything might happen, and probably would. Later I was to meet (and to feel humble in their company) some of the real-life desperadoes, and to glimpse the genuine idealism that had led them to man this last bastion of European freedom: Tom Wintringham, whose very name, in police circles, had been like an incantation to the Devil, Giles Romilly who wrote

New Statesman reviews and was always borrowing money, T. C. Worsley, the literary editor, who probably lent it to him, Stephen Spender and many others. I've seen Right-wing attempts to decry these men, to impugn their motives; I dare say some British members of the International Brigade were mercenaries, and I'm certain that many of them were (or became) Communists. But I'm also certain that the majority of them, in their various ways, were fighting for something they believed in. Professor Hugh Thomas, in his book *The Spanish Civil War*[1] (p. 382), quotes from the unpublished diaries of Miles Tomalin: "Undoubtedly the great majority are here for the sake of an ideal, no matter what motive prompted them to seek one." The qualification, remarks Professor Thomas, is significant. To me at that time, the only ideals on offer were Christianity and Communism, which had not yet been classified as mutually exclusive. I had been reading the Webbs on *Soviet Communism: a New Civilisation?* and had developed a fairly naïve enthusiasm for the soviet system. It took even a monster like Stalin some years to kill this off, and indeed after the Stalin-Ribbentrop pact I was still, I suppose, a worried, solitary and certainly secret fellow-traveller. I wonder if anyone supposed that these dangerous thoughts were festering inside a British police headquarters?

In 1937 Tom Davis and I were allowed by our wives to go to Germany and have a look at National Socialism on its own soil. We travelled up and down the beautiful Rhine Valley, and stayed for a week or so with a Dr Post, the headmaster of a *gymnasium* at Kreuznach, near Bingen. He and his wife were the kindest of hosts (they were friends of Tom), but the political atmosphere in those Rhineland towns was heavy with fear, the streets were full of marching juveniles singing staccato songs, and everyone greeted everyone else with the daft compulsory salutation "Heil Hitler". The conductors on the crowded trams said it to every passenger getting on or off, for fear that someone would report them for not saying it. There was much empty threatening going on among the villagers and townspeople, usually threats of denunciation to the Gestapo,

[1] Penguin Books, 1971.

and some threatening which had blackmail as its ultimate purpose. Some of it was done as a joke, but by 1937 Germany had no longer any idea who might be joking and who might not. The sense of dread pervaded those mediaeval Rhineland streets as powerfully as did the smell of sauerkraut. One evening Frau Post took Tom and me aside and asked if we could possibly be so *very* kind as to give the Hitler salute when we were out walking with her husband and were greeted by his acquaintances? He was a very frightened man, she said. Everyone in Germany at that time was judged by his companions, and Dr Post believed himself to be in great danger because of the liberal opinions he had expressed in the days before it became criminal to have any. He had been a Captain in the German Army during the First World War, and Tom, who was a Captain in our Machine Gun Corps, discovered that for a long time they had been sitting in opposing trenches. The reason why this situation had remained static for so long, said Herr Doktor Post, was that the Germans were very short of ammunition. "I never noticed any shortage", said Tom, and they both roared with laughter and thumped each other's backs. I can remember no episode in all my life which showed me more poignantly the evil absurdity of war.

Tom and I, with the best will in the world, were very reluctant to say Heil Hitler to anyone. It was all so puerile and yet so nightmarish, and we loathed the very name of Hitler and all he stood for. But we compromised. When the occasion arose we extended our right arms in the salute and muttered "I'll tickle 'er", or "Mine's a bitter", or "I'm a stickler", and Dr Post beamed his thanks that we should be trying our poor best in a foreign tongue. Sometimes I wish I knew what happened to that good man, and sometimes, full of cowardly misgiving, I am glad not to know.

I think it was at about that time that I won the Queen's Gold Medal Essay Competition, without getting the gold medal. It was (and is) open to police of all ranks in any part of the Commonwealth and Mandated Territories, and the subject for that year was something like "Co-operation Between the

Police and the Public in the Prevention and Detection of Crime". The judging Committee gave me the £20 first prize, but decided to withhold the gold medal because "the entries this year were considered not to be of sufficiently high standard". On the day that this announcement was conveyed to the Press, the evening *Star* carried a short leader asking what was wrong with a judging committee that could give a chap the money and withhold the medal, and had I won the Competition or not? My runner-up was a Special Branch Sergeant in the Metropolitan Police called Arthur Cain. We arranged to meet and discuss the low standard of our essay-writing; and I remember thinking that if the Special Branch comprised men of Arthur Cain's intelligence, *savoir-faire*, and latitudinarianism, and if people knew it did, there would be a lot less fuss and anxiety about "Britain's Secret Police". I supposed that my essay had been the best of a poor lot; and the decision might have done a great deal of good in cutting me down to size (always a healthy operation) if it hadn't been for one thing. Among the three judges was none other than my Commissioner, Sir Hugh Turnbull, and of all the educated men I have ever known he was about the least qualified for such an exercise. What he was doing as judge in a literary competition I shall never know. Of course, he didn't know I was a competitor because we all had to use pseudonyms.

At about the time of the Munich crisis in 1938, it became known that the Government intended to establish a full-time auxiliary police service (to be known as the Police War Reserve, and to absorb for the time being the long-established Special Constabulary). We were to have about 400 of them, and the total in England and Wales eventually amounted to about 55,000. Incidentally, they all went straight out on police duty without a moment's theoretical instruction; and did it, so far as I ever discovered, with no ill-consequences. I can remember the wry amusement with which this made me look back upon all the work I had done in the instruction and training of "regulars". However, it seemed desirable that the new men should in some way be given a rudimentary idea of those police duties that lay outside purely war-time requirements (black-out, petrol rationing and so on). So the Commissioner

The end of 19/21 Queen Victoria Street (29 December 1940): see page 49

Bob Turney in 19

A school of trained recruits (August 1933), on the steps of the "Lord Mayor's Entrance" at the Old Bailey (see page 102)

sent for me one day and said I had better write a pocket manual of instruction for them, and do it as quickly as possible.

This put me in a quandary. Early in 1939 the Editor of the *Police Review*,[1] for whom I had then been writing a weekly law article for about five years, had foreseen the formation of something like the Police War Reserve and asked me to write a pocket *vade mecum* in the simplest possible language, about law and police duties, which could be sold to them for one shilling. I got on with this and it was published in June 1939 under the title *An ABC for Special Constables and Police War Reserves*. It had a prodigious sale for that kind of thing, county police authorities ordering bulk supplies of four or five thousand at a time; and of course I got a royalty. Now it seemed to me absurd that I should embark on the writing of something slightly different for our own local purposes, covering all the same ground, explaining away copyright difficulties without revealing that the copyright was mine, and yet disguising the book in some way that would conceal the identity of its author from my Commissioner, whose permission to write it I had not asked for because I knew I wouldn't get it.

"Well," I said shiftily, "as a matter of fact there *is* such a booklet on the market already, and I think it might serve our purpose without any further delay."

He said he would like to see a copy and I had better get one. I thought I might have one in my desk, and went and got it. There was a long silence while he looked through it, and then he looked up and said: "There's something rather familiar about the style of this?" I took the plunge and told him the story of it. After another silence which may not have been longer but certainly seemed it, he choked something back and said I had better requisition for 400 copies and get them issued immediately. I felt I had better get the question of royalties settled, and diffidently began to say that 400 copies would bring me in about——

"I don't want to discuss that at all," he said abruptly. "That's nothing to do with me."

It was, but I got out quickly. The booklet was revised several

[1] Rowland Harris, who became a great friend of mine.

times during the war, and with each revision a fresh issue was ordered and distributed. I should think a man could make quite a lot of money writing pocket manuals, especially if he timed their publication artfully. That little book earned me something over £1,000 without even the necessity, let alone the capacity, to be artful. I felt a little like Stanley Baldwin's "hard-faced men who have done well out of the war"; but not sufficiently to give away the royalties to a war charity.

My "one-man legal department" became a minute but solidly entrenched part of the national war effort. As hostilities hotted up after the first few months of "sitzkrieg", I got my family out of London, and myself slept at police headquarters in Old Jewry, where we had a shored-up basement, and (if we were lucky) sleeping-bags. My wife and ten-year-old daughter Brenda, and my parents, had been in a fairly comfortable house at Streatham Hill, which then stood empty for two or three years after their "evacuation" to Twyford in Berkshire, where we had managed to rent a tiny bungalow. (I put the Streatham house in the hands of an agent and asked him to let it rent free to any poor devils who had for some reason to stay in London. It was taken by a delightful family of Austrian Jewish refugees, who miraculously survived when it was destroyed by a flying bomb in 1944.) When the Germans had reduced their day-time bombing and taken to mass air raids at night, the "legal department" functioned like a man perpetually, though half unconsciously, expecting annihilation in mid-sentence. To work in the City in those days was to feel that personal survival was, on the whole, unlikely.

Other people's war experiences are never very interesting, but I recall three reflections which much occupied my mind during those crazy years and may evoke similar memories for others:

1. When air-raid warnings were in operation and we were all getting on with our work, as we tended to do after the opening scare period, I consciously worried that the building might be suddenly demolished before I had thought of the right ending to a paragraph. There might be no one left to read the paragraph, but I wanted it to be as good as possible.

2. Occasionally at night, the sleeping-bag on the concrete

floor of the basement actually swung a little to and fro like a hammock, as a bomb exploded nearby and shook the foundations. I could never understand how the subsoil and the building foundations of an entire street could move like this without total collapse. (And for that matter in 1968 in Western Australia, arriving in Perth a few hours after an earthquake, I was similarly perplexed to see how the furniture in offices on tenth and twelfth floors had slid from one side of a room to the other, while even in bungalows the pictures on the walls had swung out and turned themselves back to front.)

3. On the night of 29 December 1940 my old police division, comprising I suppose about 200 acres of close-packed warehouses and banks, was virtually wiped out by powerful incendiary bombs. In the small hours I went on to the roof at Old Jewry with George Hayes, our "superintendent and chief clerk", one of the best-loved men in the force. We looked around at an inferno that defied belief and language.[1] After a long and bewildered silence: "What the hell can we possibly do against that?" he said to me in a broken voice. "We can't possibly win. We shall have to give in." I remember saying, as anyone would to such a challenge, that Churchill's "we shall nevah surrendah" broadcast meant exactly that we should not give in. The Government wouldn't surrender, that is to say, even if it had to go and govern (as we all understood it might) from Canada. Any surrendering would remain to be done by the people left behind. And as to that, we had our secret instructions about collaborating with an occupying army to the extent necessary to maintain law and order. (I remember reading that document, with weary but popping eyes, a few days after M. Paul Reynaud had told the French people by radio that the French Forces "might not find themselves able to continue the struggle on land"; and I was overwhelmed by the certainty, not merely that invasion was imminent but that the war was lost. No one, I think, who went through June 1940 with any knowledge of this country's military help-

---

[1] The best compendious description of the London blitz that I have seen (it draws heavily on other books) is in Angus Calder's *The People's War*, Cape, London, 1969.

lessness after the colossal military disaster at Dunkirk will ever forget the dreamlike atmosphere of "England's last few days".)

Some good friends of mine were killed in air raids in the City. Having by now reached the rank of Chief Inspector I was on duty at regular intervals as "Control Officer" for 24 hours, and during an air raid this required one's constant presence in an underground control room equipped with an emergency duplicate switchboard for "incident" telephone messages. In its apparent but no doubt illusory safety I often thought guiltily of my colleagues out on the streets, though in the words of Angus Calder (and as many of them in fact cheerfully reminded me): "The luckiest, as well as the bravest, were those whose jobs took them out into the raids, where danger was visible and visibly limited."

Meanwhile I regularly wrote my *Police Review* weekly 1,200 words, reviewed books for the *New Statesman*, wrote "London Diary" notes for Kingsley Martin, read manuscripts for publishers (which, by the way, is the worst-paid work since the abolition of slavery), and drafted "Police Orders" based on instructions from the Home Office and the Ministry of Home Security. I find that the *Police Review* articles, all through the mounting anxieties of 1938 and most of 1939, give no hint whatsoever of the coming war; until on 15 September 1939, and in a pompous style whose authorship I should deny if I didn't know perfectly well whose it was, there appeared this opening paragraph:

The needs of topicality demand that a commentary of this nature should keep abreast of events,[1] however hateful may be the nature of those events and the avalanche of emergency legislation to which they give rise.[2] The very fact that this legislation has descended upon the police with such crushing suddenness evidences an advanced stage of preparation on the part of the legislators—

[1] If ever there was a completely circular observation, tautology beckoning people to come and look, I should have thought this was it.
[2] Few people, until this appeared, had ever heard of a rising avalanche.

many of the provisions now appearing must, it would seem, have been in draft form not for weeks or months but for years.

I learned long afterwards that some of them had been in draft form since 1925; which, it will be instructive to recall, was the year of the Treaty of Locarno guaranteeing the Franco-German and Belgo-German frontiers, swearing undying friendship between France, Germany, Poland and Czechoslovakia, and so exciting the British Government that 1 December was christened Locarno Day and all the schools had a holiday. A week later Hitler published *Mein Kampf*, his blueprint for genocide and the murder of human pity; and I don't believe Locarno Day, or the idea of a special one-day holiday, was ever heard of again. The *Police Review* article was heralding the Defence Regulations 1939, which even I recognised as the assumption of absolute power by the Government, the suspension of *habeas corpus*, and the formal declaration of "total war". The necessary blows struck at public liberty, I went on,

> go almost unnoticed and largely uncomprehended through sheer weight of numbers; and their acceptance by the public shows that a democracy on the defensive can deny its own principles without political upheaval.

From that date, much of my weekly outpouring was about war; about lighting offences and the use of hand torches in the black-out; the smuggling of currency; the use of identity cards; the control of noise; the rationing of petrol, clothing and food; "curfew" orders in danger areas; looting at bombed premises; alarmist rumour-mongering; road vehicles left unattended (and thus available for German parachute troops); the internment of aliens; the control of maps; the compulsory carrying of gas masks; the presumption of death after air raids; and the huge assortment of officially-approved windscreen labels which led an Oxford lady to equip her car with one that said "Just Me". Of course the capacity to write about all these matters for consumption by the police in their national weekly journal was greatly sustained by my daily diet of Home Office circulars and emergency legislation. But as the war dragged on, references to purely war-time law became less and less frequent and the *Police Review* of 11 May 1945, which might excusably have contained a reference to the surrender of Germany and the celebration of "V.E. Day" three days earlier, passes it over in silence, talking instead about the ethics and practice of "opposing bail".

During those years my job included the vetting of police applications for "process" against offenders who, for various reasons but mainly long usage, were not actually arrested and charged. In war or peace it always seemed to me that far too many people, anyway, were arrested and taken to police stations instead of being told they would receive summonses; and I think this is still true, though some police forces are worse at it than others. The dividing line was set by the available mode of trial: in indictable cases, i.e. those that could be tried by judge and jury whether in the end they were or not, there was nearly always an arrest. Exceptions were made, it always seemed to me, in respect of rich or important men, who could instruct their lawyers so much more easily if they were not sitting in Brixton Prison (and who, unlike the rest of us, would have been acting under solicitors' advice from the moment they heard that the police were enquiring about them). In most of the non-indictable cases, which we called "summary offences" because the magistrates could deal with them summarily, an arrest was thought unnecessary; which was rather a good thing, since otherwise every police division would require a building the size of the Albert Hall to accommodate its prisoners awaiting trial. There was always, in peace or war, a flow of motoring offences; but the war legislation, and especially the black-out rules and the petrol rationing regulations, added enormously to the volume of work and the number of potential wrongdoers. The machinery of British justice ploughed slowly through it all, turning up an occasional gem of the kind I will now describe. It's a story that ought to be told.

One day in 1943 a man on a two-days' holiday, a London bus-driver, was driving a small car from Woodford, in Essex, to Shepherd's Bush to attend a family funeral. Near St Paul's Cathedral he was stopped by a policeman who asked him what the purpose of his journey was. The Control of Fuel Order made it an offence to use petrol for a private car journey that could be made by public transport. The man said frankly that he was going to a funeral and the constable, reminding him that he could have made the journey by No. 11 bus, told him he would be prosecuted. I sent the "summons application" over to the Court, and a summons was duly served on the defendant.

When the case got before the magistrate at Guildhall the man pleaded guilty; but as soon as the police evidence had been given the magistrate's clerk, who was a stickler for procedure, wanted to know what evidence there was that No. 11 buses were running along that route on that day. They always did, he was told. Never mind what they always did: was there an official in Court from London Transport to say that one of its buses could have been used for this particular journey? (This enquiry was directed to the police inspector on Court duty.) Well, no: but if the Court felt that was essential, perhaps the magistrate would adjourn the case so that a bus official could be called? The magistrate would do no such thing. If the police came to court with a case only half-prepared they must expect it to go against them. Defendants were not to be messed about like that. And the summons was dismissed.

This was a smack in the eye for me. It was my job (as a kind of long-stop, for the application had been through many hands before it reached my desk) to see that every case *was* fully prepared. I foresaw a row with the Commissioner, to whom every "unsuccessful" prosecution was like a wet catherine-wheel to an eager child. Pre-emptively, I went to see him before he knew about it, told him the story, and urged that we ought to appeal to the High Court. Predictably and angrily, he was all for it, so I sent the case to the City Solicitor at Guildhall. A King's Bench Divisional Court declared, in due course, that the magistrate was wrong; he could have taken "judicial notice" of the fact that No. 11 buses went along Cannon Street to Shepherd's Bush, as in fact they often did and, at interminable intervals, still do. "Judicial notice" is the notice that judges and magistrates are expected to take, without formal evidence, of the obvious and well-known and changeless. Things like "the course of nature", the earth's going round the sun, the fact that there's a war on (if there is), standard almanacs, and the rule of the road—i.e. keep to the left. So the police appeal was allowed, and the case was sent back to the magistrate to be tried without unnecessary fuss. In due course the magistrate at the Guildhall obediently found the charge proved *without* formal evidence about No. 11 buses, and let the defendant go with a caution. Then the poor man, to his utter dismay, found himself called upon to pay the costs of the appeal to the High Court amounting to about £78—which as things went was fairly cheap. He came to see me.

"Why do I have to pay £78?" he demanded. "I didn't want all this fuss and appealing and that. I pleaded guilty, didn't I? Is this what they call justice?"

I said it was, and I took roughly the same view of it as he did. Justice having boobed, we must try and think of something fairer. . . . Who was his member of Parliament? He had no idea, he didn't think there was one. Where did he live? South Woodford. Winston Churchill! Didn't he know it was Churchill? Yes, perhaps it was, but he was running the war, like, wasn't he? Together we compiled a letter to the Prime Minister telling the bus-driver's tale. I got it typed on a piece of plain paper, he signed it, and off it went. We shook hands hopefully and he went away, looking quite different. A week later he was back with a brief reply from the PM's secretary saying that he was "having the matter looked into". And a few weeks after that he phoned me to say that the bill of costs had been paid. No, he didn't know who paid, but it had all been settled. Nor could I make any enquiries without some danger that my own complicity might be exposed. The High Court could easily have ordered, after all, that the magistrates should pay; but I don't think it did. People at about that time did pretty well anything that Mr Churchill wanted them to do; and the City Corporation, rich beyond the dreams of avarice, had its wealth tucked away in some oddly accessible baskets.

I still believed, all this time, that the pseudonym C. H. Rolph (used whenever an editor insisted on a signed piece) was protecting me from official discovery. I supposed, without undue apprehension, that discovery would have some disciplinary consequences. But I was artful enough to know that the Commissioner found me uniquely useful; that even if he didn't I should be unlikely, for other reasons, to get the sack; and that even if I got the sack there was probably a job for me at the *New Statesman*. Moreover, dear old George Hayes, Chief Clerk and my immediate superior, had had no alternative but to leave most of the war-time legislation to me; and even so, he gave some of us cause for worry in that he often seemed to be on the verge of a breakdown. He leaned very heavily on me throughout the war and I was glad of it. I learned long afterwards that the Commissioner had known for years who C. H. Rolph was, and had decided to leave him alone, no doubt watching with some attention what he wrote for public consumption. The Commissioner was especially keen on a monthly news-letter which, from March 1943 onwards, I sent to our men who had gone into the armed forces. Beginning as a means of giving them news about each other, this developed into a way of keeping them informed about their demobilisation prospects and the circumstances in which they would be resuming service with the City Police; and I must say that, in view of the high rank that many of them had attained in the armed forces, I was astounded at the stoicism with which most of them settled down again to the monotony and juniority of the jobs that had been kept open for them. This on its own would make many a story; and I remember one man, promoted to lieutenant-colonel just before coming back to us as a constable, who said to me: "It's not what you call stoicism, sir, whatever that is; it's just bloody despair. What else can I do?"

One of their problems was that they were coming back to a police life that would be made needlessly irksome by petty discipline and old-time persecution. Sir Hugh Turnbull, who was to remain there until 1950, was a tyrant, and I think I can say he was universally hated. I believe he caused more sorrow and despair, ruining more careers and blasting more hopes, than any man I have personally known. When he died in 1973 at the age of ninety, *The Times* said in an obituary notice:

Appointed in 1925, he was like many other police chiefs essentially a soldier with unbounded confidence in military methods, which

he applied with strict ideas of discipline to the small force he
took over.

And this is the point, I suppose, at which I should try to assess
the part played in my own life, largely through the part played
in the lives of my colleagues, by the boss whom I was so happy
to exchange in 1946 for Kingsley Martin of the *New Statesman*.
In the past twenty-five years I have written many obituary
notices for the public prints, most of them papering over
unseemly cracks with the conventional bits of prose. *De mortuis
nil nisi bonum* has always irked me, but I have complied,
recognising that a kind of decent interval must elapse before
the truth is told. How long? In my lifetime it grew shorter
and shorter. Somewhere I had read that the Rev. Samuel Parr,
a devoted Johnsonian, said when Dr Johnson died: "Now that
the old lion is dead, every ass thinks he may kick him." It was
my old friend Bob Turney, a devoted Voltairian, who used to
remind me of Voltaire's answer: "One owes respect to the
living. To the dead one owes nothing but the truth." About
the dead one owes the truth, sooner or later, to those they have
grievously wronged.

Turnbull was born in India, wearing a tiny pith helmet
and carrying a copy of Kipling's *Recessional*. His father was a
major-general in the Indian Medical Service and an honorary
surgeon to the King-Emperor. The year after I was born, my
future Commissioner was himself commissioned to the Indian
Army from Sandhurst, but after six years he came home for
reasons of health and joined the Royal Ulster Constabulary;
which in those days, it must be presumed, was healthier. Then
successively he was made Chief Constable of Argyll, commanded
a battalion of the Gordon Highlanders during the First World
War, and was Chief Constable of Cumberland and Westmor-
land until 1925, when (as the City Police were wont to recall)
we got him. On his appointment he was told by the Police
Committee of the Corporation of London that he would be
expected (and this he was good enough to tell me himself, many
years later) to "restore" the discipline of the City of London
Police and in particular to stamp out corruption. I'm not
absolutely sure what "corruption" meant, but I believe it was

any sort of supplementary income that is thought to disfigure the image of the honest man in the cloth cap. Turnbull weighed in at once as an enthusiastic stamper-out, sacking and punishing with the care-free abandon made possible by a pukka-sahib lineage and a depressed labour market, and displaying the infallible gift of the stamper-out for picking on the wrong kind of man. Let me select but one example, for it is typical of many.

On the first Christmas after his arrival he was walking along Cheapside when he saw one policeman speak to another in the middle of the road (the latter was on traffic duty) and press something into his hand. Turnbull was then barely known to any of the men he newly commanded, though he had had his photograph prominently displayed at all stations and the number of his car was universally required learning (I can remember it to this day—MK 2280). He crossed over, spoke to the two men, and found that what had passed between them was half a crown. Acting as prosecutor, judge and jury he proceeded to sack the donor and impose a heavy fine on the recipient, a man named Shackleton. I don't doubt that the former had been given five bob by someone as a Christmas box, and thought he should share it with Shackleton as the man on the spot. But Shackleton, who was a friend of mine, happened to be a man who was fanatically opposed to corruption or gratuities of any kind: in some ways he was a bit of a crank. And I *know* that at the vital moment he had no idea what the other man was giving him—he thought at first it was a key-ring found in the street. Many years later, in fact about 1943 during a prolonged air raid, I was sitting with the Commissioner in the Control Room waiting for things to happen and hoping they wouldn't, and he was talking sternly about discipline and corruption. I reminded him of this episode. The wife of the innocent man, Ruby Shackleton, a woman of great ability and charm, had meanwhile become the Deputy Commandant of our Women's Auxiliary Police Corps (an organisation born of the war) and had much impressed him.

"I think I may have made a mistake about that man," he said, rather like someone who had moved the wrong pawn. "I am sorry, for his wife's sake." I felt that he could afford to be a bit sorry for the man's sake too; since his totally unmerited punishment had had the unavoidable consequence that he was for ever disqualified for any promotion. But it had another consequence that the Commissioner could hardly have foreseen.

For many years all members of the City Police had received on New Year's Day from Rothschilds the bankers, and with official approval, presents for themselves and their children. I don't know that we ever did anything for the Rothschilds to merit this annual largesse, nor can I see what scope there was for doing anything. It may have been brought about by the rich man's conscience, much as the proverbial libertine has always been said to soothe his memory, on passing an orphanage, by throwing a handful of coins over the wall. But my two brothers and I, as a policeman's children, had always longed for "Rothschilds' toys" with aching anticipation—and we were allowed to say what we wanted, to the value of about £1 each.[1]

For the first five or six years of my police service, I recall, I received as my Rothschilds' New Year gift a Brumfit pipe and pouch and half a pound of tobacco. Immediately after Shackleton's unmerited punishment he was asked (as we always were) by a sergeant with a clip-board and a Divisional roll-call what he wanted "from Rothschilds" for himself and his children. He wanted absolutely nothing, he said; he had always disapproved of the whole thing, anyway, and now asked that his name be removed from the list. In some way this reached the ears of the Commissioner, and he took the opportunity to decide that the Rothschild gifts must be totally discontinued at once. A custom more than half a century old came to an abrupt end, no doubt bewildering and hurting the good-

[1] I remember that one year my brother Harold and I, impressed by the excellence of the toy motor vehicles you could see in Marks and Spencer's "Penny Bazaar", decided to pool our resources and have £2 worth of penny toys. On two successive days our protesting father staggered home with huge cartons packed tight with little tin lorries, limousines, buses, and models of the City Police ambulance. For months they were all over the house and garden, up the stairs, under the beds, in the bathroom, everywhere. To our parents and visitors they must have seemed like the Hamelin rats or the birds in Hitchcock's horror film. To us they were an important lesson about greed and the swamped disappointment of satiety.

natured Rothschild family but also saving them many thousands of pounds a year.

A few of us thought he was probably right, as a matter of principle. And certainly during his later years he had to face some nasty problems of mass "perks" and CID corruption. Some of these are familiar enough to any open-eyed citizen who knows how the rigid enforcement of the law—for example the law of highway obstruction at markets like Smithfield and Billingsgate—would bring legitimate business to a dead stop. But Turnbull, I came to realise, was oddly blinkered about this kind of thing. While it would be absurd and unfair to say that he was a "corrupt" man himself (he certainly could never be "bought") he had a concept of ancillary reward which divided the patrician from the pleb and took its origin from something like the Divine Right of Kings. When, for example, he travelled by rail to his Scottish home at Grantown-on-Spey, he travelled with a free ticket obtained for him by our Chief Clerk through the railway police department; and, at that, a first-class ticket. To this he had no semblance of entitlement. At his Regent's Park house he employed a servant whom he paid by including him or her (sometimes it was a girl) on the City Police "establishment" as a constable, a totally unauthorised procedure; and at the same time he kept a gimlet eye on any less privileged protégés on the pay-sheets. He always drew an allowance of £16 a month for something called "Cab Hire and Stabling", though he never stabled a horse and if he hired a cab he put it on his weekly expense sheet.

Among the senior officers there were I suppose half a dozen of us who would have to know that this was going on. Our complicity, guilty and craven complicity if you like, was essential not merely to its continuance but to our continuance. What he didn't know, and never in his divine rectitude came to guess, was that it was known to hundreds. You *cannot* do that kind of thing in a small, tightly organised body of gossips like the City of London Police and suppose that the knowledge of it will not become widespread. When I think of his duplicity, and what I remember of the man himself, I cannot but suppose that he genuinely saw the world as divided among two separate races, a large and inherently feckless peasantry serving and maintaining

a righteous élite. He occasionally acknowledged the righteousness of the élite (to the eloquent disgust of the peasantry)
by reading the lessons during divine service at St Columba's,
Pont Street; and in 1937 he suddenly announced that the
City Police would have an annual Church Parade and Service
at St Paul's Cathedral. This, he added for the purpose of
removing doubts, would be compulsory. It went on for many
years, though, diminishing in size and splendour as the initial
enthusiasm waned in even the Commissioner's mind, it moved
in later years to churches like St Botolph's, Bishopsgate, and
the City Temple on Holborn Viaduct. What it involved for the
men in loss of leisure and sleep and the imposition of "split
duties" (since the policing of the City had also to go on somehow) found one form of expression in the profane mental
mutiny of the 800 perspiring worshippers. I always managed
to dodge this sacred function. I forget how. I'm credibly told that
Bob Turney always dodged it too, and that was much cleverer.
For me, it was helpful that I had no uniform to wear; but not
decisive, because I remember hearing from the returning
worshippers how they had enjoyed seeing the senior CID
officers sitting in the nave with their hats on their knees, and
seeming by their attitude to be crouching in apprehension
rather than bowing their heads in devotion. Some of us knew
in our hearts that if Turnbull were the master of a ship somewhere on the high seas and we were his worthless crew, his
career would have ended one dark night in a comforting
splash, the crew having fought among themselves, or perhaps
drawn lots, for the right to participate in the ceremony by an
actual laying on of hands.

One Assistant Commissioner, a kindly man of great integrity
whom Turnbull treated with a disdain that was a cause of
dumb fury to the rest of us, once found himself faced with an
embarrassing problem while Turnbull was on an extended
trip abroad. The Chief Clerk placed before him, for his
signature as Acting Commissioner, the time-honoured expense
accounts for "Cab Hire and Stabling" and other things. He
absolutely refused to sign. The refusal raised a query which, as
these things will, snowballed despite some official efforts to
hush it up: and inevitably it reached the Home Office. On his

return, the Commissioner was asked for explanations and found himself in a very tight spot indeed. The sequel, which again can only be called a hushing-up, involved him in a sharp reduction of auxiliary income and the need to find a new Assistant Commissioner.

Now the recital of these facts requires, in my view, a more solid justification than the mere love of exposing something or the desire to sensationalise and sell a book of waspish memoirs. Truth to tell, I myself have come in recent years to believe that "the greater happiness" is not always to be served by the exposure of scandal, and I found my views epitomised by Mr Peregrine Worsthorne (who does not often speak for me) in the *Sunday Telegraph* of 12 August 1973. Writing in a vintage year for scandals in political and other public life, and heading his article "The Case for Silence on Scandal", he suggested that a generous measure of whitewash is indispensable to any stable political structure:

> All healthy societies require a widespread willingness to leave a great many stones unturned. The public interest is not best served by ceaseless exposure of all the odious slugs that take shelter underneath; or, for that matter, by prodding all the sleeping dogs into fractious barking and whining. . . . What has diminished radically is public appreciation of the truth that more harm can come through the exposure of scandalous acts than through their perpetration. . . . The good of the public weal can sometimes be served by maintaining illusions, by preserving myths: in particular the myth about the rectitude of public life. It may well be that those who serve this lie have done more to comfort the poor and console the weak than all those who so self-righteously set out to serve the truth.

A highly dangerous doctrine, no doubt; and it was primly disowned by an editorial in the same issue of the *Sunday Telegraph*—"in his usual stimulating, didactic and paradoxical manner Mr Peregrine Worsthorne argues on this page today the case for the concealment of evil, politically and socially. . . . It is because this newspaper believes passionately in the merits and duty of disclosure that it allows the contrary case to be put. We do not accept that case, nor do we believe that it can ever be accepted if there is to be any hope for democracy. . . . It is the covering up of truth which creates slaves."

On the other hand, I had seen two world wars in which not merely the covering up of the truth but the official propagation of deliberate lies had, in the end, liberated slaves by the million. Yes, of course it is a question of striking a balance. And the problem of police corruption seems to me of such importance that the truth about it should be told whenever the law of libel, the instrument we use mainly for suppressing the truth, happens to be powerless. In the case of Sir Hugh Turnbull and the 900 men he then commanded, any small likelihood of his "stamping out" corruption, the reception of gratuities, or the miserable danegeld levied on street traders, bookies, market salesmen and building contractors, vanished as soon as the notion (essentially untrue, as I have said) filtered down through the various ranks that the Commissioner himself was "bent". And this was partly why, just before and just after the war, he came to sack so many of his senior officers, or agree to their sudden and premature retirement, *pour encourager les autres*. He sowed and reaped a harvest of home-grown cynicism. "Do you know what Norman Douglas wrote about all this kind of thing?" Tom Davis asked me once. "Incorruptibility is the fetish of the half-civilised." As I write this, Mr Patrick Murphy, the New York Police Commissioner, has just announced an interesting innovation as a sequel to a devastating exposure of police corruption. In future, he says, if corruption is found in one of the seventy police precincts of the city, the precinct commander himself will be in trouble: it will be for him to prove that he did everything possible to prevent it.[1]

There may be more, but I know of only two bodies of public officials of whom one can say with total confidence: "Those people are absolutely incorruptible." They are the High Court Judges and (I still hope) the Civil Service; and the effect of that on the administration of the law and the integrity of public life is incalculably good. If any of those exemplars, merely a significant few of them, were believed to be "bent", the decline of this country would convict all our modern

[1] *The Times*, 30 March 1973.

Cassandras of half-hearted moderation. Sir Hugh Turnbull, in a way and to an extent that he never knew, was an exemplar of precisely the wrong kind.

The more so because he was both merciless and unjust in his punishments. In striking contrast to men like Field-Marshal Montgomery, he believed that you could and should run an army on hate and fear. And by storing up both in plenty, he destroyed in many a simple man the self-control and decency that are sustained by loyalty. So far as I can recall he never did me any personal injustice: my resentment is entirely vicarious, though I am disturbed to realise that it seems inextinguishable by the years. He was said by George Hayes to be "afraid" of me—"He fears you, boy, like the devil himself," George would say. I can but guess that he thought I should leave the Force, go on to a newspaper, and expose him. I think there is only one truly sad recollection of the police that I still have: and it is that there existed then a handful of sycophants who would have crept (I can hardly say sprung) to his defence, sworn on the New Testament to his innocence, and earned themselves a slightly less slippery foothold on the ladder.

He maintained his cruel and purblind little disciplines throughout the war, throughout the worst of the bombing, when men were getting home after a night of inferno to find their own homes destroyed and their families homeless. ("Old Jones lost his lot last night," we used to say.) Example: a constable was cycling home along Cheapside in the pitch darkness of a winter's morning, after a nerve-racking night among the flying bombs (the "doodle-bugs"), when his front wheel went into a small and invisible pot-hole and he was thrown. He was injured but managed to get home and get some sleep. When he submitted his doctor's report to explain his injury, the Commissioner had him carpeted for not having turned back at once to report the hole in the road; and inflicted a fine on him. The whole Force seethed with indignation, a number of powerful new epithets being added to the language. Such episodes were numberless.

An odd little story can be offered as his *ave-atque-vale*. When he was appointed Commissioner in 1925 he took to using green ink for minuting files and signing documents, so that you could distinguish who had written what. You might not have thought this in any way tied up with his diminutive stature (he was only 5' 8") and his sallow complexion, unless you were acquainted with a Milton Hayes musical monologue then popular—*The Green Eye of the Little Yellow God*. Turnbull's hated calligraphy became known to one and all as The Green Ink of the Little Yellow Sod.

I suppose one should recall such a thing uneasily and record it with self-reproach. I recall it almost happily, and reproach myself only that for all those years I held a candle to such a man, lacking the courage to challenge or denounce him and risk all the consequences. *Mea maxima culpa.*

Chapter 9

SQUARE-MILE CHAUVINISM

EXTRACT FROM THE Report of the Royal Commission on the Police in 1962:[1]

The City of London

228. To the stranger it must appear odd that a square mile in the centre of the vast Metropolitan area should be policed separately from the rest, with a distinct police authority—the Common Council of the City—a lower rate of police grant than elsewere, and a chief officer dignified by the title of Commissioner. The City of London has, however, an importance and position out of all relation to its size. In the field of policing its problems are unique and specialised. It has to contend with a daily influx of three-quarters of a million people; it has to protect some of the most valuable property in the world; and it has been forced to develop in a very high degree means of combating crime in technical fields, such as company frauds. We should hesitate to assert positively that these considerations necessarily call for a separate police authority or a separate police force. But all the evidence we have heard suggests that the arrangements for the policing of the City work well, and that there is entirely satisfactory co-operation with the Metropolitan Police. In the circumstances we make no recommendation for any change in these arrangements.

And even Dr A. L. Goodhart, who torpedoed the report with a long and powerful memorandum of dissent, seemed to agree with this part of it. "There should be a single police force for England and Wales," he wrote,[2] "to be entitled 'The Royal English and Welsh Police'. This should comprise all public police forces other than that of the City of London, which might be kept separate because its functions are unlike those of any other police force."

[1] HMSO, 1962, Cmnd 1728, p. 71.
[2] Ibid., p. 177.

How and why are they unlike those of any other? Daily the
City of London sucks in a vast number of workers from the
suburbs and nightly it spews them out again. But so do Manchester and Birmingham and Glasgow, Sydney and New York
and Tokyo. I suppose these numbers will decrease as commerce
"decentralises". . . . The City of London "has to protect some
of the most valuable property in the world". So does every big
city in the world; and the City's boundaries run right through
some of the valuable properties it protects, leaving half of them
(like the Crown Jewels in the Tower of London) to be protected
by the Metropolitan Police. . . . It has been "forced to develop
in a very high degree means of combating crime in technical
fields, such as company frauds". But it has no Company Law
Department, no company lawyers, no qualified accountants,
no taxation experts: instead it has detective officers with no
training in these fields, some of whom achieve prodigies of
self-education from a standing start, and they work as part of
the Metropolitan and City Police Company Fraud Branch.
Scotland Yard has an "Involved Fraud Squad" whose duties
constantly overlap with it and with which it should surely be
amalgamated. The case for a separate police force in the Square
Mile has really no other basis than square-mile chauvinism,
and yet any proposal to abolish it raises the kind of uproar
that would be touched off by a plan to abolish the MCC,
Stonehenge or the Monarchy.

But I'm not going on about this. I merely recall that in
my day, when you were patrolling a beat on the outskirts of
the City of London, you would occasionally come across a
smaller policeman, wearing a slightly less funny helmet, with
his duty armlet on the wrong sleeve,[1] his buttons made of

---

[1] One day the Rev. Mr Isaacs, the Vicar of St Giles, Cripplegate,
who used to talk to me about books, saw me gossiping with a
Metropolitan man on the corner of Fann Street. "Why is it," he
said, "that your armlet is red and white and his is blue and white?"
We all supposed it was because red and white were the City Corporation's colours. "And why are they both composed of stripes?"
he went on. We didn't know. "Well, I will tell you." And he proceeded to explain that in 430 BC, when Athens was threatened by
the Peloponnesian War, Pericles urged his countrymen to rely

some inferior white metal instead of brass, and—especially on a hot day—his chinstrap tucked up inside his helmet where it ought not to be. We liked to tuck ours away like that, to obviate the white chinstrap mark round a sunburned face which, we told ourselves, would betray our calling when we were out in plain clothes. But we were forbidden. Much was forbidden to us that seemed permissible for them, including chewing, leaning against the walls, smoking in uniform quite openly when off duty, and talking to girls. But because of the crowded City footways we were at least allowed, on emerging from the station for a day's duty, to straggle singly to our destinations. *They* had to march in single file, looking operatically comic. Ta-*ran*-ta-*ra*.

Of these boundary tales, one has been told so often that you would think it simply must be untrue, an ancient border myth. But it is true. On a dark evening you would stumble across a horizontal drunk, on or near your boundary with the Metropolitan Police District. You would pick him up, look carefully both ways, help him across the street, and lay him down again in the bordering jurisdiction. Then you would return to your bailiwick and go for another walk round. Getting back in due course to the same spot you would find the man lying on your beat again. Your perfidy might have been carefully watched by the Metropolitan man, possibly enjoying a quiet pipe in a doorway; and he had returned your drunk. Or he might have come across the drunk just as you did, and believed himself to be starting the proceedings. More carefully this time, you roused the drunk and took him back. It is certainly true that,

---

wholly on their sea power, disbanding the city's militia and using their staves to build a stockade in the City centre. They lost the war and Pericles died a year later, but the great circle of wooden staves stood for years as a reminder of his peaceful methods of government. "The stripes round your armlets," said the Vicar, "symbolise the pacific nature of your duties and perpetuate the memory of Pericles and his stockade. 'Polis' was the Greek word for the state, and you policemen carry the picture of the stockade on your sleeves. You don't believe a word of it, do you?" He went away laughing and I'm afraid we didn't. But I owe it to the memory of a delightful man to pray that I've got his story right.

by such a to-ing and fro-ing in the course of an evening, many
a drunk has been sufficiently restored to get up and go away,
saving himself the ignominy, and yourself the tedium and the
broken rest, entailed by a Court appearance. Of course it had
its dangers. The man might be ill, not drunk, and if so one was
taking an inexcusable risk with potentially disastrous consequences. But a man who is ill does not, as a rule, sing Nellie
Dean to himself or mumble the story of his life to passers-by.
The Metropolitan policeman's compensation came daily at
"closing time" for the pubs, for ours were open half an hour
longer and at the beginning of that half-hour the City sustained
a determined but unsteady invasion. Some of us (though I
think very few) used to see this alone as sufficient reason for
scrapping "the City" and all its obstinate traditions.

Another was the system by which the Lord Mayor and the
Aldermen, worthy and wealthy men all, sat as single magistrates
though not legally qualified. The few magistrates who could
do this outside the City were all "stipendiaries" and all therefore qualified lawyers; though there are still no more than 50 of
them beside the 21,000 lay justices in England and Wales. I
have nothing to say against a lay magistracy and much to
urge in its favour, so long as no such magistrate sits alone and
there is always a competent and legally qualified clerk. Happily
in the City of London the successive Justices' Clerks I knew
were extremely efficient, but the requirement that justice
should be seen to be done was ill served by the presence on the
Bench of one elderly man in a fur collar whose qualification
was known to be his membership of the Worshipful Company
of Fishmongers, Tallow Chandlers, or Wire Drawers.

For most of us the supreme symbol of parochial fatuity was,
of course, the Lord Mayor's Show, the day when the Lord-
Mayor-elect was borne to the Law Courts to swear his ancient
oath about the coming year; and yet I have to admit that, as
a festival, it always had some invincible attraction for me. I was
often taken to see the procession as a small boy; and can
remember how, as I was held aloft to see the Grenadier Guards
in their terrifying bearskins go by, the big drummer punctuating
Sousa's *Liberty Bell* seemed to be thumping so heavily on my
heart that I wondered if people ever died of it. My father, who

was never with us on that day because he would be doing about
sixteen hours' continuous duty, always enjoined us to watch
the Royal Marines detachment. The Royal Marines, he said,
"won the drill prize every year" and were the smartest troops
in the world. So when my turn came, as an Inspector of Police,
actually to marshal the procession for a year or two and march
with it to the Law Courts and back, I used to find the Royal
Marines band and, most of the way, march happily with them.
(I wonder how many people know today that their Musical
Director then was the incomparable Major F. J. Ricketts, who
under the name of Kenneth J. Alford wrote those splendid
marches *The Great Little Army*, *On the Quarter Deck*, *National
Emblem*, and *Colonel Bogey?*) Yet one never-to-be-forgotten
Lord Mayor's Day I found the impeccable, pith-helmeted
Marines doing precisely what I have so deplored in Chapter
1—marching on the wrong foot.

Not of course that they were marching to their own band.
The various regimental bands were always so close together
that at intervals they had to be careful (though they were not
always careful enough) not to play at the same time. This time
the Marines were about 100 yards behind the Coldstream
Guards, who were playing (beautifully) the German march
Old Comrades. I found to my horror that the Coldstreams and
everyone behind them, including the Marines, were on the
wrong foot. What on earth could a man do in such a dilemma?
I decided upon a deed of unparalleled impudence, daring, and
supererogation. Taking very long strides and probably looking
very funny, I caught up with the Marines' officer-in-charge
and *then* ostentatiously changed step. He saw me do it, and it
worked. Like an angry Stentor he ordered his detachment to do
likewise. Left-right-left, they danced quickly, and we were all
comfortable again. But not the Coldstreams. They stamped on
right-footedly to the bitter end of *Alte Cameraden*. I often wonder
whether they managed to live it down.

We all derided the Lord Mayor's Show. Weeks before the
day itself (always the 9th November in those days—it was some
King's birthday) the preparatory correspondence began to
flow—to and from the City Remembrancer's office, the City
Marshal, the various Livery Companies which were to display

their *raison d'être* by means of tableaux on lorries (the lorries were called "floats"), pretty maids and vegetables and machines and men dressed in twelfth-century garments to show how old it all was. A week before the day, on a quiet evening, I had to walk round the exact route to be taken by the procession, pushing before me a huge wooden wheel fitted with a crude sort of mileometer, to see how far they were all going to have to walk. The distance differed every year because it had to go through the City ward for which the new Lord Mayor was the elected Alderman. Early on the morning of the great day the various units began to assemble in carefully prescribed streets and alley-ways round the Guildhall—guardsmen and pikemen, hussars and gunners, the Yeomen of the Guard, the fishermen of England, the Dagenham Girl Pipers, brass bands from the North (why?), Boy Scouts, Girl Guides, sometimes—inscrutably —a pack of hounds; and once there were half a dozen Indian elephants. (On the Victoria Embankment these, I recall, were stampeded by the students of King's College, Strand, who had pinched, inherited, or otherwise acquired a huge red lion from outside a Red Lion pub and held it aloft with shrill cries as the hitherto well-behaved elephants came near. The frightened beasts broke ranks and charged the crowd, injuring many people—who must, I suppose, have been absolutely terrified. That episode involved me in many extra hours and endless writing, the essential basis of which was that it was all my fault and I had better think up a good story or else. I thought up a good story. Subsequent Lord Mayors got round without elephants.) Thinking of those early morning assemblies of waiting troops and bands and halberdiers, I sometimes wonder how and where my opposite number in Moscow marshals his outsize tanks and 60-foot guided missiles for the great parades. But at least he doesn't have to snatch a perpendicular lunch in some crowded little pub near the Law Courts, lifting a Life Guard's dripping plumes from his beer before he can drink.

For me the day always ended, or perhaps I should say the long evening began, with the Lord Mayor's Banquet in Guild-hall, when it was my duty to stand behind the Prime Minister's chair and see that nobody hit him. Once or twice I saw wisdom in this, since the Prime Minister then was Ramsay

MacDonald. From behind his chair I watched the epaulettes of his levée dress twitching as he told the glittering assembly in 1931 about "the fundamental pur-rinciples of wurrld economic unity", and something told me that, if there were such principles, he had long lost any hope of finding out what they were. But that year I got into trouble because someone on the *Evening Standard*, deploring the disruption of City traffic on a working day, wrote an article describing how the procession (whose theme that year had been agricultural) had "wound its tortuous way round unsuitable City streets like the funeral of a bankrupt greengrocer".[1] My Superintendent was quite certain that I had written it, and furiously he taxed me with it. Superintendent James Booth, although a northcountryman, had fiercely adopted the City of London and all its traditions: he was himself an ambulatory piece of the City, a rather large and very slow-moving piece, with heavy out-turned feet and a great walrus moustache. I knew nothing of it, I assured him. "Ah doan't believe you," he shouted unexpectedly. "Ah knaw your style, it's just what you *would* write." Which nettled me, and prepared the way for an admission I would otherwise have choked back. "Anyway," he continued irrationally, "if you didn't write it you agree with it." I fell for this. "Absolutely," I said, "except for its moderation." It stoked the fires and prolonged the interview unbearably. But in the end we forgave each other, and I can remember that we actually laughed in unison.

In the late thirties there had devolved upon me some of the duties formerly discharged by the Assistant Commissioner. In the person of Captain Davison, whom I liked very much (perhaps because he used to confide in me with a marvellous lack of discretion), we had acquired in 1936 a man who found himself on very unfamiliar territory. The tempo of events leading up to the war gave him little opportunity to learn his way about, and in 1939, having received scant help from Sir Hugh Turnbull, he applied for the Chief Constableship of

[1] This is still not a bad description, but the procession is now staged on Saturdays.

Kent and got it. One of the duties I had taken over from him was his *ex officio* membership of a Street Collections Advisory Committee, which met monthly at Scotland Yard to consider applications from charitable bodies for police permits to hold flag days. In the First World War, street collections had become a truly cynical racket, public anxiety and generosity being exploited by large numbers of rascals (as well as some worthy causes) outside the control of the police. Anyone could rattle a collecting-box in aid of the wildest schemes or no scheme at all, and in 1916 it was estimated that nearly a thousand such collections had been taken in London alone during the previous twelve months.

That was the year in which street collections first came under police registration and supervision; but in 1917 there were still nearly 400 legitimate and certificated collections in the course of a year. The job of the advisory committee was to whittle these down by requiring similar charities to share their flag-days—for the blind, for children, for the disabled, for animal welfare and so on. They all hated it, and us. But when their flag days had been reduced in London to no more than thirty-five in a whole year, they found that their takings had gone up instead of down because the citizenry were less fed-up with the sight of them. Then some of the more dubious ones, squeezed out of the business of actually collecting in the street, started collecting from door to door; and a particular feature of the late thirties was the spread of "hospitals waste collection schemes", by which householders crammed their discarded clothing into sacks left for collection, the collectors sold the clothing to dealers or rag merchants, and about two per cent of the proceeds went to some hospital. The hospitals didn't want this stopped or discouraged because even the two per cent could amount to a large sum of money. But in 1939 there came a House to House Collections Act which brought all this under control too.

Now it was largely because of this particular job that I became interested in the various voluntary services; of which, until then, I had known reprehensibly little. I began to find out what they did, about problems that were either special to each or common to them all. What was more important to me than the monthly meetings at the Yard was that, as the City of London's representative on the Committee, I received many personal visits from charity organisers who wanted to discuss City collecting strategy, or to get my signature to documents. I was regularly visited, for instance, by three ladies from the Convent of Poor Clares Colettines, whose dedication to "entire poverty" and to the alleviation of human misery I found infinitely humbling. So far as I could find out, they never did any proselytising; they simply got on with their work of mercy and let their nuns' uniform do any religious persuasion that was going to be done. They were always amused at the "Three Nuns" tobacco-tin on my desk. (We all wondered how that particular brand-name was born, and concluded that its purpose must be to suggest that smoking was not, after all, an evil thing. At times the label on my current tobacco-tin was "Parson's Pleasure", a name which they thought even more artful.) I've often wondered whether those three young women ever guessed the effect they had upon me, with their dazzling purity and the appearance of gliding, almost airborne serenity with which they entered and left my office. But I looked forward to seeing them and was always sad when they left. I suppose if the City hadn't been its own obstinate square mile I should never have seen them at all.

And thus, or similarly, I made the acquaintance of people working for the homeless, the blind, the spastic; for victims of disaster, for discharged prisoners and their families, for men and women disabled in war, for drug addicts and alcoholics. For, in fact, the whole appalling multitude of people whom John Freeman later described (when he was editing the *New Statesman* and I was working for him) as Rolph's Legion of the Damned.

Then in 1943 the Commissioner was asked by the Army Education Corps if I could do some lecturing for the London Regional Committee for Education among HM Forces. This was a welcome break in the routine, though the lectures usually had to be in the afternoon and the state of my office duties ensured that on such a day I must work all the evening to catch up. This didn't matter much, for during the air raids there was nothing else to do and nowhere to go. My audiences varied in size from 1,000 Servicemen and women in a vast echoing drill hall, where you had to bellow with extended lower jaw like a sergeant-major, to the eight men of a barrage balloon crew in a small Nissen hut, erected on a bomb-site in the odd belief that bombs, as lightning, never hit the same place twice. And the subjects varied in scope from civil liberties and the law of evidence to road traffic and (believe it or not) the factual reliability of the detective novel.

Now it was during and because of these lectures that I met Harry Ross, an "adult education" man, who was producing BBC radio feature programmes for the Forces Educational network. He invited me to write a documentary programme (I forget what about) and to read the narration myself. It was the beginning of a new phase for me, in which after a few years the BBC had become my principal source of income. There is no kind of journalism—I suppose one must call it that—which expands and flourishes as vigorously as radio script-writing, so long as you keep in touch with it, or withers and dies so swiftly if you withdraw from it for a year or so—for example to write a book. After one of the Forces lectures I found myself talking to Janet Dunbar, who was then editor of the BBC *Woman's Hour*. "Have you done any broadcasting?" she said. I told her of the little I had done and she said: "Come and do some talks on *Woman's Hour*." I think that was the real beginning; but its consequences belong to another chapter.

Chapter 10

FAMILY AFFAIRS

MEANWHILE[1] MY FAMILY circumstances had of course slowly changed; and they were to change drastically and rapidly in the near future. My parents had been living in retirement at Wimbledon since 1922, my father presenting the classic picture of a pensioned public servant in decline with absolutely nothing to do. He worried, ate too little, thought too much (like Cassius) and grew thin on hypochondria and doubt. Although he lived to be eighty-one, his last ten years were steeped in melancholy, relieved by flashes of sweet-natured and generous concern about my mother, my brothers and me. Harold and I, after his death, thought we had much to answer for in having argued him out of his none-too-confident religious faith. I have perceived since that we were thrashing second-hand arguments as if they were our own, the rationale of the writers we both enjoyed. Harold, treating these all his life with what seemed to me an exaggerated respect, was also to die an unbeliever. He had become a dissenter from all religions, and like Bertrand Russell he professed the hope that every kind of religious belief would die out. To me, as I contemplated lives as various as my mother's and Cardinal Newman's, C. S. Lewis's and St Augustine's, R. H. Tawney's and William Temple's, it seemed that religion must sometimes serve the imagination as a kind of vaccine, preserving it from

[1] This is a word much beloved of journalists. It means "I forgot to say . . ." or "here come the bits I haven't been able to find a place for". When it begins the last paragraph of a leading article it means either "No, we haven't got one-track minds" or "Now let's return to normal" (as in "Meanwhile, back on the ranch . . ."). Sometimes it is a means of introducing a paragraph totally irrelevant to anything that has gone before but, to the careless reader, making it seem relevant for long enough to get him interested.

absurd and dangerous beliefs; and I always thought it significant that some of my most vehemently anti-religious friends were the most cravenly superstitious. When Marx said that religion was the opium of the people he was saying, with Elbert Hubbard, that formal religion was organised for slaves, offering them a consolation which earth did not provide. But it's really the opium of the rich, whose ultimate need of it is the greater; not of the poor, for whom, as even Marx said in the same much quoted but always edited sentence, it is also "the sigh of the oppressed creature".

Harold, my brother and dearest friend, served out his whole working life at the London head offices of W. H. Smith & Sons. For something like twenty years he was the firm's head cashier; though what I thought he should have been, for all those twenty years and longer, was head of the book department—his knowledge of books was, in my experience, eclipsed only by old Bob Turney's. But when I came in later years to know some of the WHS pundits personally and acquired the impudence to chide them for having missed such an opportunity, they persuaded me gently that their top bookman needed to know what people would *buy*, not what my bookworm brother might enjoy urging upon them; and books were a diminishing proportion of what WHS customers would buy. WHS, however, were and are a magnificent firm to work for, and I was glad that I came to enjoy a relationship with them; at first second-hand and make-believe, as with the schooldays I had shared with Harold in imagination, and then first-hand when I found myself, many years later, a director of the *New Statesman*.

Roland, five years younger than I, went from school into the world of accident insurance and, I believe, hated his job from first to last. In a neatly ordered world it would have been he, not I, who eventually made his living as a writer. But it never seemed to occur to him to try; and, retiring early through ill-health, he proceeded to show me how retirement should be planned, lived, filled and enjoyed. The exhibition has now been going on for ten years.

You often hear people say how their marriages "broke up", which I take to be a way of extending the concept of marriage as an ocean-going vessel, lacking perhaps a rudder, a pilot, or a reliable chart; its difficulties being represented as a submerged reef of rocks. Marriages "on the rocks" are even refloated, sailing off into the sunset. But marriages do not break up, intransitively. People break them up. Sometimes it is a self-indulgent act of heartlessness, sometimes an act of despair, sometimes there is agreement. As Emerson said, it is not marriage that fails. It is the people that fail. All that marriage does is to show people up. Audrey would not, I think, have broken ours or agreed to its being broken, at least at that stage. She was probably no happier than I, and may even have seen our marriage, in its special circumstances, as what Stevenson called "no more than a sort of friendship recognised by the police". But during the war, as with so many couples, we saw much less of each other than we had been accustomed to; and both, I suppose, found the separation supportable, filling the blank with other matters. When the war was over I looked into the future and thought I saw an appalling vista of guarded toleration, recurrent misunderstanding and progressively divergent interests.

For me there was also going to be, now, the age-old problem of living a double life, a course of deception which would involve my sixteen-year-old daughter Brenda as well as Audrey; for my BBC work had brought me into regular contact with Jenifer Wayne, then a staff script-writer producer, and I soon knew only too well that this was no matter-of-fact relationship. There arrived in due course the moment for decision, never likely to recur and by far the most difficult decision I have ever confronted. It was then that, for a period of some weeks, I found myself carefully, and with growing determination, contemplating suicide. So many people have had such thoughts that I don't now, I hope, attach too much importance to this phase. But I knew that a direct consequence of my ill-considered marriage years before had been to inflict lasting unhappiness upon a number of undeserving people; and here I was, I thought, on the verge of doing something even worse, consigning Audrey to the socially difficult status of the "divorced woman", and involving my highly conventional and God-fearing parents and my much loved daughter Brenda in what they would all see as the stigma of divorce in the family. For the first time I saw why people killed themselves in the belief that there was no other solution to some intolerable private dilemma. My own sense of dilemma was appalling, lonely, and humiliating. I got as far as deciding upon a method of exit, and wrote letters to be left for Audrey, Jenifer, Brenda, my parents and both my brothers. I remember that these were carefully unsentimental and that, in their respective envelopes, they lay in my desk for two or three weeks before I destroyed them and, as most would-be suicides do, decided that I wouldn't be. But I should wish to emphasise that, although I have usually carried out a plan that I have set my mind to, I came to see suicide— in my particular circumstances—as an act of cowardice, not of courage. I knew only too well that I was following a familiar pattern. "I take it," wrote William James, "that no man is educated who has never dallied with the thought of suicide." As it was, the act of ending my marriage and staying alive was the only courageous act I have ever carried through. I came to see it as far more likely to redound to the ultimate happiness of all, and this, I now believe, is what it did.

I made every compensatory arrangement I could think of, or that lawyers on both sides could suggest, and went to live for a year with Harold and his family. My parents, who had been sharing the house, had no wish to stay there and went to live with my younger brother Roland and his wife Bunny, at the latter's generous suggestion. All this entailed a considerable change in the pattern of their several lives; and, in particular, I never concealed from myself that the drastic readjustment involved for Roland and Bunny was a vital part of the solution to a dilemma which, to put it mildly, was none of their making. The understanding and practical sympathy of my brothers and their wives were such as I shall never forget. I know now, though it would have been a genuine surprise to me then, that Audrey was unbearably distressed; and it was a discovery which convinced me, once and for all, of my abysmal incapacity to understand women. It was some years before I discovered that they don't understand themselves; and that, although it is commonly said that no two women are alike, the truth is that no one woman is alike. I thought her true interest had been weaned away from me by circumstances, that she was now showing a predictable and natural jealousy about Jenifer, and that she was making a token fuss. I was wrong. But in due course she remarried, this time happily and sensibly. I am quite certain that no such thought was in her mind when she agreed to divorce me. In doing so she was serving what she saw as my interests, not hers.

By a strange chance the man who heard her undefended divorce petition was Judge Henry Leon, then sitting as a special Commissioner in the Divorce Division; and Judge Leon, as author of the famous Henry Cecil books then beginning to appear, had already and unwittingly got me into trouble of quite another kind. I had been writing in *The Spectator* at the invitation of Wilson Harris, the editor, who was at the time Independent MP for Cambridge University. He gave me lunch at the House of Commons while we talked about what I was to do. Among other things I was to invent a new *nom-de-guerre*, and by a final twist to my names and initials I emerged as "R. H. Cecil" and began thus to appear regularly in *The Spectator*. (This seems so long ago now that, when I meet some-one who remembers R. H. Cecil, I want to prod him to see whether he is alive and real.) I expected that Kingsley Martin, who had first claim on my services for the *New Statesman*, would see through this disguise fairly soon and want a discussion about it; but I'm not sure that he did. What he did was to ask me rather testily whether, and why, I had adopted the name of Henry Cecil in order to write books about funny lawyers? I was flattered, to say the very least, and got more flattered as that incomparable spate of books developed.

One would need a far less perceptive Court than Judge Leon to be sure of an easy passage with a divorce. Audrey told me afterwards that it was "touch and go" and that I'd been very lucky. (She was lucky too in getting rid of me, but the realisa-tion of that was emotionally delayed.) Anyway, he relented, approved of the settlement, and granted Audrey the decree which she really didn't want. Years later, at literary parties and law lectures, he and I exhanged writers' felicitations with-out his becoming aware that I was one of his guilty men.

I was unable to leave the police service until September 1946, and did not remarry until January 1948. Writing now in the year of my silver wedding, I am disposed to inflict no more of this part of my story upon any of its leading and still living characters, to say nothing of readers neither involved nor interested; except to add that these twenty-five years have afforded, so far as I am concerned, a complete refutation of Dr Johnson's famous aphorism about a second marriage—"Alas! Another instance of the triumph of hope over experience." Perhaps the learned Doctor was speaking of bigamy, which is having one wife too many; he may even have been one of those who think the same of monogamy. But I am unwilling to leave the subject without recording my experience that divorce and remarriage entail an emotional strain which leaves indelible scars, and my belief that it is marriage, not divorce, which ought to be made more difficult of attainment. To quote again from Johnson, who held that it was commonly a weak man who married for love, it is possible that "marriages would in general be as happy, and often more so, if they were all made by the Lord Chancellor upon a due consideration of the characters and circumstances, without the parties having any choice in the matter." I don't know whether Johnson meant that people could be induced to fall in love with each other by arranging things for them, or that loving each other didn't matter. But as we contemplate those circles where choice of partner is usually restricted to the point of non-existence, as in royal families, we must believe either that the couples are brought together by some kind of marriage-broking providence or that they marry without love. If the latter, then this must be why adultery and concubinage are all right in the castle and morally outrageous in the cottage.

Certainly the moral outrage knows when to begin expressing itself on the way down from the one to the other, and a state built on Christian morality knows how to express its disapproval of "broken marriages" among the lesser fry. It did this, in my case, by confiscating the widow's pension to which my first wife should be entitled at my death, which she has certainly earned, and for which I paid compulsory weekly contributions for twenty-five years. Not that it becomes payable to my second wife: in the eyes of a Pensions Administration allied to an Established Church, she is no more than a concubine. In recognition of which, the whole thing is forfeited. Since I discovered this cynical anomaly in 1946 I have written about it to every successive Chancellor of the Exchequer, three of whom I came to know personally, urging that the pension should remain payable to the first wife, whether or not she is what the law regards as "the guilty party". They all expressed sympathy and concern, and promised to look into what (in the words of one of them) seemed "a very strange injustice". I suppose it was the mollifying answer reserved for elderly cranks who, if you could stall on the matter for a few more years, would be safely dead and forgotten, even if they spent those years chaining themselves to railings, hunger-striking outside the Department of Health and Social Security, or wearing sandwich-boards in Downing Street.

Many people seem to understand and accept that romantic love is a kind of technicolour gloss upon the primeval mating instinct, a product of the human intellect and the poetic imagination. But few have had the insight (perhaps because few have had his practice) recorded by Bertrand Russell in his autobiography[1] when writing about his grandmother's marriage to the man who was twice Prime Minister, Lord John Russell:

> It was obvious from her conversation that she never came anywhere near to knowing what it feels like to be in love. She told me once how relieved she was on her honeymoon when her mother joined her. On another occasion she lamented that so much poetry should be concerned with so trivial a subject as love. But she made my grandfather a devoted wife, and never, so far as I have been able to discover, failed to perform what her very exacting standards represented as her duty.

He was a wise man who said that love consists not in constantly gazing at each other but in looking outside together and in the same direction. I suppose my supreme unfavourite among philosophers (few of whom I have much loved) is Nietzsche; yet it was he who spoke the loudest to me about this—"It is

[1] *The Autobiography of Bertrand Russell (1872–1914)*, Allen & Unwin, London, 1967, p. 20.

not lack of love but lack of friendship that makes unhappy marriages." Some people get it both ways. I now have a friend who is always around, who is certified by the State as being my wife, and whom I have nevertheless loved as such for twenty-five years.

I have known many people who had no love for their parents, have cut adrift from them quite early in adult life, and in some cases (where I knew the parents) have seemed to me fully justified in doing so. Those who have not known, or do not remember, parental love or even parental anger are gravely handicapped people and generous allowance should be made for them. Parental love was a great influence in my own life, and so was paternal anger—often, though not always, with good cause. If I had had the wit it might have been I, not Mark Twain, who said: "When I was sixteen my old man was so stupid I could hardly stand having him around: and then when I got to be twenty-one it was amazing what that guy had picked up in the meantime." Going far beyond any duty of care, my father's main characteristic was a fondness and liking for my brothers and myself as people and companions, plus the constant readiness in emergencies to help any of us out when it was possible. I'm certain that we were conscious of no filial *duty* or obligation, only of gladly-assumed indebtedness. I don't see that any child owes his parents any gratitude for bringing him into the world while, as Jonathan Swift cynically observed, they were thinking of something else; but we all felt grateful that we came into it as the sons of our particular father. Speaking for myself, I can see that he laid the cultural foundation of my life, which was a rather strange compound of music, books, and military tradition (he obviously seemed to my boyhood companions rather like an NCO who was seldom off duty, and he always managed to take us to the Naval and Military Tournament at Olympia). There was also amateur astronomy, bird fancying, and the despairing support of Chelsea Football Club. But the oddest and least deliberate of his influences was in the matter of books.

Books, to him, meant encyclopaedias, dictionaries, reference tomes and "enquire within" books of all kinds, the importance of which, at this stage of my life, will perhaps excuse one more

backward glance at boyhood. Although he had five encyclopaedias, all second-hand and rather musty from long storage
somewhere, he at once subscribed to the *Children's Encyclopaedia* when it came out; and Harold and I almost fought for
the right to read each fortnightly number as it arrived. When
it was completed he had it bound in eight volumes; and not
only are they still on my shelves but they are still consulted
although my own children are no longer at home. Only once
did he acquire any hard-backed fiction: at an auction sale he
bought a tall, black book-case with glass doors, which, when he
saw it first, was crammed with books bearing the imprint of
the Religious Tract Society. I think he had little time to find
out what they all were and no time anyway for sorting and
rejecting. And thus we acquired all the novels of Talbot
Baines Reed; the Uncle Remus Tales of Brer Rabbit; Alcott's
Little Women; a long line of Henty books (from which my father
at once pressed upon me *With Buller in Natal* and *With Roberts
to Pretoria*); and all the Conan Doyle historical romances, which
I thought the best of the lot. There was also an aged and
mouldering calf-bound volume by James Janeway called
*Token for Children: being an Exact Account of the Conversion, Holy
and Exemplary Lives, and Joyful Deaths of Several Young Children,*
which, with *Sandford and Merton,* showed us what kids had to
read (if they could read at all) in the eighteenth century. I
devoured them all.

I forget how many times my anxious father successfully
implored me not to throw up my police job and take my chance
as a writer. He never influenced my thinking at all when he
held forth about the pension I should be sacrificing, the years
I should have wasted, the "competency" I had achieved (he
always spoke of a safe job as a competency), or the state of the
labour market—which throughout the twenties and thirties
kept thousands of malcontents reluctantly in the police. But he
was on firmer ground, and knew he was, when he asked me
to imagine what I might be doing to Audrey and Brenda.
"While you carry on where you are," he would say, "they are
safe." A ship in harbour is said to be safe, I would say to myself,
even though sitting in harbour is not what ships are for. But in
my lifetime the ships in some harbours had been blown up or

scuttled; and service under Sir Hugh Turnbull was a bit like an anchorage in one of those.

Turnbull was angry when I resigned. He had been looking forward to promoting me, he told George Hayes (characteristically he said nothing to me nor, when I left, did he say goodbye). But any promotion could only have robbed me of my uniquely autonomous little job and, what was worse, brought me into closer contact—and complicity—with Turnbull himself. I served out my last few weeks in a fever of anxiety lest something should go wrong. Nothing did, and I left for No. 10 Great Turnstile like a man coming out of Wormwood Scrubs but, untypically in such a man, knowing exactly where he was going. Quite literally, it was the beginning of a new life.

Jenifer and I had become involved in a long series of her BBC radio programmes called *This is the Law*, in which my own role was roughly the same peripheral one of tame "consultant" which I had been playing at the film studios of Metro-Goldwyn-Mayer. When she was at work on a radio programme, I recall, she liked to be surrounded by books on the subject of the programme. I knew where to find some of these, and I came to know that I could never provide her with too many, apart from such details as I could dredge up from memory. The programmes were wittily dramatised documentaries about "wrongdoers by fault or folly". I take the phrase from a publisher's announcement which, when some of them appeared in book form,[1] went on to say that "Miss Wayne has the gift of humorous true-to-life characterisation and an observant eye for the oddities of human nature". And, having watched these qualities at work for twenty-five years, I perceive that he could have said that again.

She had escaped into the BBC in 1941 from the reluctant teaching of English in a girls' high school, where her father would have preferred that she should stay. Philip Wayne was headmaster of St Marylebone Grammar School, a modern languages man, a lover of European literature, and a creative

---

[1] *This is the Law*, Sylvan Press, London, 1948.

writer manqué who nevertheless watched his daughter's BBC successes with undiluted pride and gratification. And he, more than anyone I had known since my adolescent friendship with Bert Trotman at Welford's Dairies,[1] was the personification of music; a good amateur 'cellist and a kind of walking *Grove's Dictionary*, who shared the wonder of Benedick in *Much Ado About Nothing*: "Is it not strange that sheep's guts should hale souls out of men's bodies?"

We were married on 10 January 1948 and went to live at Blackheath, where she was on her home ground.[2] It was a district then overhauling Hampstead and Chelsea as a kind of Nature Reserve for writers and artists. At first we had a minute apartment in a restored Georgian crescent known as The Paragon, with picture windows, a reproduction Adam fireplace and a kitchenette that would accommodate one person standing. And then, when children began to arrive, we found an adjacent bomb site (in Liskeard Gardens) whereon a new house was being built, and moved in before it was finished. Six years later we decided to live in the country, and found a cottage at Bramley, near Guildford; and there, from separate studies, we have both turned out books (including this one) in an intermittent stream. A cottage industry of considerable variety and infinitely pleasurable hard work. For me, it was all a new life indeed.

[1] See p. 52.
[2] See *Brown Bread and Butter in the Basement*, by Jenifer Wayne, Gollancz, London, 1973.

Part II

THE BETTER LIFE

Chapter 11

NEW JOB

By 1946 I had known Kingsley Martin and several of his *New Statesman* colleagues and contributors for about ten years. We had met almost weekly (except for the hottest period of the war) for lunch in pubs and cafés, and talked about the war, the law, the state of civil liberty, the people he had known, and the mushroom-shape of things to come. He gave me a special private lunch to welcome me to the paper, said he hoped to be able to "make a vacancy" for me,[1] and allotted me a small, empty office on the top floor, with matchwood walls, a flat lead roof, and a telephone. It had once been a resident housekeeper's spare bedroom, and was unused. I furnished it with some second-hand chairs and book-shelves and a huge leather-topped desk that my police colleagues had given me when I left them. By this time Kingsley had got over his early feeling that I was a kind of performing seal, but he was still inclined to see me as a boneless wonder and the

[1] Kingsley made a point of telling me that he had never done this before, and indeed it was a month or two before he finally made up his mind to do it for me. The occasion that helped him do it was a huge party at the Savoy Hotel to welcome Henry Wallace, former vice-president of the United States, as guest speaker at a series of *New Statesman* meetings to alert this country to the dangers of the cold war. It was all going very well, he felt expansive, and he told me there was a staff vacancy for me. Ten years earlier, making the worst "casting" error in his editorial career, he had allowed Michael Foot to slip through his fingers because "we have no vacancy—as I told him—but if I found God's own journalist, for co-operation over the Diary, etc., I should some time or other *make* a vacancy or rather appoint an additional man. I am in fact going on trying until I find such a man—if, which I doubt, he exists!" (See *Kingsley*, p. 291.) Finding no doubt that God did not supply journalists, he must have lowered his sights appreciably.

thought occurred to him that I might perform better with a structure of bone. He thought therefore that I should read for the Bar. It would be so much better, he said, if I could sign things as a barrister-at-law. What things, I asked him? Surely not *New Statesman* articles? Even if barristers were rarer than ten-a-penny, they didn't proclaim themselves barristers when they wrote articles. No, but he was often asked who "C. H. Rolph" was: the name wasn't in the Law List and people were mystified. I agreed to look into the idea.

First, the Council of Legal Education was asked on our behalf (by an eminent QC who was so cross at the outcome that I won't name him) whether it would be possible for me to be exempted from preliminary Latin for the Bar exams. No, it said coldly—though this had been done often enough before. I was well embarked on the process of learning about the division of All Gaul into Three Parts when I discovered that, surprisingly enough, qualification as a barrister would considerably restrict the occasions on which the BBC would employ me as a commentator on legal news and events. (It certainly wouldn't now, but that seemed to be the position then.) By this time the BBC was my main source of income, and so it was to remain for another fifteen years. I dropped the idea of the examinations as a total waste of time, read the kind of law I needed rather than what the law-crammers would have kept me to, and got on with earning the money I now needed rather urgently. The study of criminology and penology was obviously going to be of more value than that of Roman Law. And I believed at the time, quite mistakenly and rather too readily, that not being a lawyer had two advantages. I could attack and criticise the profession if I wanted to without feeling treacherous; and when, as a sequel to *New Statesman* articles, people with problems came to see me or wrote to me, I could proffer advice up to the point where I began to feel unsure of my ground, and then explain that I wasn't a lawyer and mustn't give advice as if I were. Far nicer than having to say, "Yes, I *am* a lawyer, but that's not the kind of law I know about."

From a police headquarters to the editorial office of the *New Statesman* ought to have been a fantastic change: they represented worlds so remote from each other and viewpoints so utterly conflicting (and both, I thought, so often wrong). It should have been a bit like creeping into the enemy trenches and hoping to stay there. But it was not. Perhaps because of some chameleon characteristic in myself, but more likely because of the amused sophistication of my new colleagues, I was able to settle in comfortably—and was occupationally happier than at any time in my life. There was, I learned, a difference between the Police and policemen. The latter, on the whole, were tolerable, sometimes useful, sometimes almost admirable. The former, the police as a whole, were the Home Office in heavy boots, the Establishment ponderously rampant. The Establishment was corrupt—all States were corrupt—and good men must not obey the law with never a question.

I had never been a political activist. My father used to say he was a Conservative but I don't remember that he ever voted, and he probably felt Conservative because he was colonially minded and disapproved of Lloyd George the pro-Boer. Like my brother Harold I always voted for Labour candidates, except once when I knew the Labour candidate to be a rogue; and then I voted for a Liberal. The difficulty about Socialism for me was that it involved a belief in two things which were absolutely different and perhaps even contradictory: freedom and organisation. The very few Socialists I had known in the police were cloth-cap Socialists, to whom their creed "meant little more" (as Orwell said in *The Road to Wigan Pier*) "than better wages and shorter hours and nobody bossing you about". The Socialists I was now meeting were more like the lady of whom Saki had said that "when she inveighed eloquently against the evils of capitalism at drawing-room meetings and Fabian conferences, she was conscious of a comfortable feeling that the system, with all its inequalities and iniquities, would probably last her time". And yet . . .

And yet if you wanted to see certain social reforms effected, as I did, it was to the political left that you must look most of the time. Tories were not reformers. Conservatism and reform were antonyms. By their very essence Tories (with rare exceptions to whom I make a public bow) were against change until it was forced upon them; and it was rare indeed, though

not entirely unknown, that it was forced upon them by other
Tories. So it was the desire to see changes that now rescued
me from the political eunuchism of the police service and got
me into the Labour Party. I saw that what the "ordinary man"
wanted was really liberalism with a small "L", and that when
the Tories and Socialists had done battle, this was what he
usually got. But opting out of the political scene altogether
had never seemed to me excusable or even sane: if you couldn't
choose the party you loved most and then vote for it, you should
choose the one you hated least and vote for that. But to vote
for none at all was like passively watching your house burning
down because you disapproved equally of the fire brigade and
the insurance company.

The social concerns I had inherited from my police experience
now found freer expression: I became an assiduous joiner. I
joined numerous societies for the prevention of this and the
encouragement of that; and after a time Kingsley encouraged
me to join others, the *New Statesman* sometimes paying my entry
fees, subscriptions, and incidental expenses. Kingsley thought it
was good for the paper that I should join them, and would
have had me go to a lot more weekend conferences and summer
schools than I wanted to. It's all right if your wife is dedicated
to all these reform movements and will come along too, but
Jenifer found me enough to get on with. Once when I went as
Chairman to a weekend school at Dovercourt (for the Institute
for the Study and Treatment of Delinquency) my youngest
daughter cried at the mention of "chairman" because she
thought I was so hard up that I had taken a seaside job as a
deckchair man. Kingsley, for his part, knew that my identi-
fication with predominantly Left-wing causes owed nothing
to any knowledge of Socialist theory and accused me of being
a Right-winger who had lost his way. In support of this he
complained that when we walked along a street, I always
edged him off the pavement to the right because I couldn't
walk straight. When I countered that it was he who edged me
to the Left he said he was merely protecting himself; and
referred me to an essay in which Hazlitt, writing of his "First
acquaintance with poets", complained of Coleridge's inability
to walk straight.

I suppose my main preoccupations were the abolition of the death penalty and corporal punishment, the treatment of psychopathic sex offenders (to say nothing of "treating" or punishing some kinds of sexual minorities at all), the problem of abortion, trial by jury, criminal procedure, legal aid, the treatment of arrested suspects, and the rehabilitation of offenders.

Since 1945 I had been a member of the executive committee of the Howard League for Penal Reform, and it was a contact which not only kept me informed of events in the world of penology but brought me into association with social workers, lawyers and politicians. Above all, as an influence on my life at that time, it was through the Howard League that I came under the spell of Margery Fry, who was then its vice-chairman and was for many years its secretary. She, more than any other reformer I ever knew, was more interested in people than in the many "causes" by which one seeks to improve their condition—world peace, education, social insurance, the China Campaign Committee, the problems of the aged, the abolition of the death penalty, penal reform generally. She wanted to see criminology established as a recognised academic study; and had she been twenty years younger she might perhaps have been appointed Director of the Institute of Criminology when it came to be established at Cambridge. When Cicely Craven retired in 1949 from the secretaryship of the Howard League for Penal Reform, Margery Fry invited me to dinner and asked me to take on the job. She was then just over seventy years of age, and still had that intense, enquiring expression which in a woman of her charm and erudition could suffuse the most ordinary face with beauty. You looked into her eyes and she was beautiful. She irradiated her surroundings in a way that made even the oddest and most eccentric details fall into pattern. I shall always remember my surprise on finding, in her comfortable and book-lined flat in Holland Park, hung with paintings by her famous brother, Roger Fry, that the dining-room, or rather alcove, was lit by a single naked electric light bulb hanging from the ceiling over the middle of the table. "I'm rather ashamed to say that we could only pay you £500 a year," she said, "but you could do some writing and earn a bit more; and of course you would get to know a great deal and be able to write from steadily increasing knowledge and experience. But don't decide now—think it over."

It was a great temptation, but alas I had to turn it down. It's a full-time job and an important one, and I should never have been able to meet my financial responsibilities. She was disappointed but characteristically kind; and almost certainly relieved when, in the end, the Howard League had the opportunity and the good fortune to appoint that remarkable man Hugh Klare. Margery and I afterwards worked together on several short-term projects, of which the most successful was her pilot scheme, some ten years later, for the compensation of people criminally injured. To bring that scheme to fruition, she spent much of her time and a great deal of her own money. The story is told by Enid Huws-Jones in an excellent biography[1] which touches on the controversy and frustration Margery had encountered while she was trying in vain to interest the Howard League in her plan to get victims of violence compensated not merely by their assailants (if they had the money) but also out of public funds. Written too topically for complete frankness, Mrs Huws-Jones's account made no mention of the fact that one distinguished member of the League's Committee was at that time in great distress because her own daughter had just had the terrible experience of killing someone while driving a motor vehicle. The committee's sympathies were in my view unduly affected by this isolated circumstance. Moreover (wrote Mrs Huws-Jones):

> Though they were used to Margery's perennial youth, some may have wondered how far a woman of eighty would be able to take her negotiations. It seemed also that she was interpreting "violence" in no narrow sense: she had mentioned the victims of heartless fraud. Not everyone could grasp the connexion, so clear to Margery's own mind, between the objects of the League and the philosophy of her scheme: to her it was part of the transition from wild vengeance to a constructive penology. She understood the objections but she was disappointed. At the next meeting of

[1] *Margery Fry, the Essential Amateur*, OUP, 1966.

the executive, C. R. Hewitt ("C. H. Rolph" of the *New Statesman*) promised to go with her all the way.

In fact I remember telling that meeting how its decision would be serving a policy of narrow obscurantism, safeguarding at all costs the field of penal reform by declining to reduce, through deterrent measures, the supply of offenders who could keep the problem of penal reform alive. Which was really rather unfair.

By 1950 I was writing regular paragraphs for Kingsley's "London Diary" as well as my signed articles, unsigned reviews and an occasional leader. There were some of us who found we could write a "London Diary" paragraph which was, so to speak, more like Kingsley than he was himself, and which he would publish unchanged.[1] It may well be that he changed mine less often than he would have wished, because they usually dealt with forensically technical things and, if I was not immediately available, he might fall into error and provoke unwelcome jeers from correspondents (I will come to these in a moment). This possibility was highlighted once when I had suggested that offenders of certain kinds on probation should be visited by psychiatric social workers (known throughout the social services as PSWs), and he had changed it to psychiatrists. I didn't see this until it was in print and when I mentioned it to him he said, "What's the difference then?" But whenever I could catch him in time, or whenever he actually sought my opinion about a paragraph that was already drafted (and this, in his case, meant already on galley-proof), he was most amenable to suggestion. During the war he showed me a paragraph about evacuee children "clutching" their cardboard gas-mask boxes. I suggested that clutching was a verb with only three uses: drowning men did it to straws, Victorian villains (the only literary figures with clutches) did it with maidens, and small children in news stories did it to

[1] When Secker & Warburg had published in 1960 an anthology of these famous paragraphs under the title *Critic's London Diary*, Kingsley was good enough to say in one of the last Diaries he ever wrote that among the many people who gave him paragraphs, Dick Crossman and I were the only two whose text he usually left alone.

everything, usually in hot little palms. He roared with laughter and changed it to holding. These little episodes were frequent, and he *never* took offence though my brief was merely to advise (when asked) about law, police, and social service matters. I suppose the oddest and yet most characteristic of these colloquies concerned a Diary paragraph on 6 September 1952. Kingsley had for some reason been talking to the second gravedigger in Highgate Cemetery, who was perplexed that the tourist public always asked for the tomb of Karl Marx, and not for those of better people like Holyoake, Herbert Spencer, George Eliot and the famous Victorian lady novelists. Kingsley showed me a draft Diary paragraph which began: "Marx and Spencer are buried next to each other in Highgate Cemetery." I asked if this might not disturb the stock market. Perhaps it might be better to begin "Spencer and Marx"? "I don't understand you," he said coldly. "Well," I said, "Marks and Spencer—do you see? If people get the idea that they've both suddenly died ——" He looked at me searchingly. "What are you trying to say?" I reminded him about the chain stores where people like me bought their underclothing, and he suddenly burst out: "Look, my dear fellow, it's nearly two o'clock and there's a boy waiting. Will you come to the point? This *is* about Marx and Spencer." I was just beginning again when he said: "Do you know, I sometimes think you and I don't speak the same language?" I knew when to stop, and said that I would be proud if he would just acknowledge that on the whole we *wrote* the same language. His face softened at once into the smile with which one disengages oneself from the village idiot. "Yes, Bill," he said, "yes of course we do. Let's go on trying to do that?" The paragraph remained unaltered, and appears on page 221 of the anthology I have referred to.

But he called upon me also for lighter notes, by way of relieving the gloom in some ghastly week's news and comment which had given full rein to the shrill grim Cassandra in him. I shall allow myself the indulgence of quoting just one of these fatuous paragraphs. It is from the "cold war" period; a silly season note recording, as journalists do every year, that there is no silly season any more. It appeared on 10 April 1954, and I recall that when I laid it before him it seemed to warm the

grey from his face and permit the short-lived appearance of a
wan little smile:

> Do you see any newspaper reports, this otherwise lovely Spring,
> that a Tooting typist is cycling non-stop to Tristan da Cunha?
> You do not. Is no man pushing a peanut with the tip of his nose
> from Maine to Seattle? Does no pole, in either hemisphere,
> support a marathon squatter? We are not told. The silly season
> has turned grave, or it may be waiting for the first cuckoo. I
> welcome, therefore, two items of news reaching me from unofficial
> sources that show the human spirit to be still as incalculable as ever.
> First, all postmen, when delivering letters, tie them with bits of
> string in bundles appropriate to streets or tenement buildings,
> and throw the bits away as they dispose of each bundle. Three
> ladies in a London suburb, finding letters to *The Times* ineffectual
> in stopping this iniquitous waste of string, are forming a society
> to collect the pieces, tie them all together, and sell them as
> "reclaimed balls" on behalf of sick animals. Second: one of our
> multiple chemists' shops has in one of its windows a special display
> of "slumber time sedatives", from malted drinks to pheno-
> barbitone, and in the adjacent window a pyramid of alarm clocks.
> The world may in many ways grow more frightening, but its
> occupants at least grow more interesting.

On most papers, Letters-to-the-Editor provide an inexhaustible flow of good copy; but few editors get the supply of
usable material that pours into the *New Statesman* office on
Monday and Tuesday mornings—cogent, highly literate,
opinionated, leg-pulling, often sneering and disagreeable and
sometimes downright bitchy. Looking through unused trayfuls
of these letters I used to wish, sometimes, that their writers
could all be herded into some secure compound, supplied
with typewriters, and left to type each other to death. But I was
alone in this. My editorial colleagues, more used to it all than I,
seemed unmoved by all the acrimony and indeed rather in
favour of it so long as the letter-writer had a good point to
make. And I must here confess that whenever I met one of
these correspondents in person I was usually surprised and
disarmed. Writers in person are nearly always strikingly,
sometimes shockingly, different from the image created by their
work, but seldom so different as in the case of *New Statesman*

letter-writers. I think it must have been the stress and anguish of the thirties that gave birth to the tradition that if you wanted to get a letter in the *New Statesman* you had better write it in acid. I have written very few letters to editors in my life, and they have usually had more lasting consequences than the mere seeing one's name in print or even ventilating some great truth. One of them, as I have related, led to my writing a series of articles for the old *Daily News* and had a rather sad denouement.[1] Another was in *The Times* in 1948, and its consequences were stranger still.

I was a committee member of the National Campaign for the Abolition of Capital Punishment whose Chairman was Victor Gollancz. The traditional picture of the police in support of the death penalty was getting plenty of publicity. It was commonly said that the police were "solidly" in favour of it. I knew that this was wrong, and that the minority who were against it, though very small and untypical, was made up of men who were not content to think with their bowels. My own position was (and still is) less idealistic than I would really like it to be, though I felt that the death penalty was probably a social evil. There were some kinds of murder for gain, some acts of political terrorism, some deeds of heartless evil which were not even murder, whose perpetrators I might have been willing to see officially killed—provided it could be done on the spot; at least as willing as in the case of those multitudes of innocent people then (and now) being killed in various parts of the world in the hope of making politicians change their minds. I thought the fuss so often made about the execution of some merciless thug was very odd when compared to the stoicism with which we heard daily tidings of all these innocent deaths, the timeless misery of invaded countries. But I knew by this time that the presence or absence of the death penalty made no significant difference to the murder rate, in any country; and that innocent men had been found guilty of murder, the prescribed punishment for which made no allowance for correcting mistakes. That was enough for me.

Gerald Gardiner, QC (later Lord Chancellor and at that

[1] See p. 103.

time a member of the Committee), suggested that it might be
a good thing, therefore, if I wrote a letter to *The Times*, in my
own name, countering the generally accepted assertion that
the police were *unanimously* in favour of capital punishment.
He himself, addressing a meeting of senior police officers in
the South of England, had taken a vote by show of hands before
he began speaking and another when he had finished. The
former was almost unanimous in favour of hanging, the latter
almost unanimous against it. Somewhat diffidently I wrote a
rather long letter to *The Times*, which published it as the first
letter of the day.[1]

The next morning I had a missive of enormous length from
John Lewis's of Oxford Street, signed John Spedan Lewis. It
was closely typed on sheets of foolscap paper and had sixty-two
numbered paragraphs; and I put it by for a quieter moment,
thinking it was some kind of circular. In due course I found that
it commended my *Times* letter and revealed that Mr Spedan
Lewis, who was chairman of the company (it was called a
profit-sharing partnership), was looking for someone to succeed
him as "general editor" of all the Partnership's "Journalism".
This comprised a *John Lewis Gazette* and several subsidiary
house journals. If I was interested, Mr Spedan Lewis would
receive me in his flat on the top floor of John Barnes & Co.
at Finchley (one of the John Lewis group of companies). I
went to see him, and arrived ten minutes late.

"You're very late," said Mr Spedan Lewis, a tall, stern-
looking old man, when I'd been ushered in. I said I hadn't
known about changing trains at St John's Wood station, and
had had to take a taxi. "It's all very plainly marked on the
station platforms," he said coldly, and told me to sit down.
Fresh from a job where there had been enough of this kind of
thing to last me for the rest of my days, I sat on a sofa and
contemplated him with growing disfavour, which was only
intensified by the fact that he was perfectly right. He embarked
on a discourse about the job I was being offered, looked at his
watch, announced that he was due at the Horticultural Exhibition at Vincent Square, and asked me to go with him so that

[1] 4 June 1948.

we could continue the conversation. We were swept there in a chauffeur-driven Rolls, and I followed him round like an attendant while he spent about £500 on shrubs and bulbs for the Partnership's sports ground. Then he said my salary would be £2,000 but that he would like me to spend three days at John Lewis's studying the various journals before I decided; and he hurried off.

Two days were enough. The *John Lewis Gazette*, typographically and in order of make-up, was a clumsy pastiche of the *New Statesman*, with a front-page leader, topical comments, a London Diary, feature articles and book reviews. Its prose was convoluted, repetitive, meandering, and strident. What all its items had in common was that every word of them was manifestly written by the author of the sixty-two-paragraph letter that had brought me along. Not only were they all about John Lewis's, but I could see that any man taking over the job and trying to write them would have JSL breathing constantly down his neck. I declined the job.

He was accustomed to picking his men from unlikely sources but not to meeting with any opposition once they were picked; and (I was told) he prided himself on his successes. He wrote and offered me £3,000. I gently declined again and he wrote to say, with some acerbity, that he would pay me £4,000, but that was as far as he would go. I replied that my objections were not of the kind that could be overcome by increased offers of money (I wonder how true that was?) and that, if he would prefer it, I would give him my candid reasons though I should really prefer not to be pressed about them. He wanted to know them in detail. His response when he got them, and it closed the episode, was that he had always known the *New Statesman* was written by cads for cads. I was sorry, for he was a man of enormous ability and had, I believe, a genuine concern for the employees of the business. He was an extreme autocrat of extreme benevolence, and very much wanted to feel elected and loved. But it would have taken much to tempt me away from the *New Statesman* and Kingsley. I told Mr Spedan Lewis that not even £40,000 would do it, which of course was very brave talk. I think what was decisive was the thought that, having started life unhappily in the rag trade thirty years before, at Spreckley, White & Lewis's, I would have been making a U-turn to finish up where I began; and what I wanted was a completely new career.

Well, I was installed, and the new career would be what I made it. When people asked me how I was getting on, they usually made it plain that they thought of me now as living abrasively in a community of "intellectuals"; but I had never really known what these were. Among a dozen conflicting dictionary meanings, the one I found easiest to comprehend was a "person of superior intellect or enlightenment (often used to suggest doubt as to practical sagacity)". I came to accept that an intellectual was a man too preoccupied with the exercise of his mind to do anything much with his body, and I felt uneasily identified with the ordinary man in W. H. Auden's verse:

> To the man-in-the-street, who, I'm sorry to say,
> Is a keen observer of life,
> The word "Intellectual" suggests straight away
> A man who's untrue to his wife.

However, one of the disadvantages of living by the dictionary, by comparison with those who seem to know the meanings of words by the light of nature, is that in any community like that of the *New Statesman*'s literary men you are bound to be a bit lonely. When it came to words, there were a good many Humpty Dumpties at the *New Statesman*, which is no doubt as it should be: a constantly developing language ought to develop in the best available laboratories. (All the reviewers, when they described a novel as "picaresque", gave that word a meaning of their own. I never discovered what it was, but certainly none of them ever meant anything about rogues and thieves, which was what all the dictionaries seemed to think the word meant. This kind of puzzle I had to give up.) Many of the poets, reviewers, and academics who used to drift in and out of the literary department came from a world I could only imagine. Some of them, with their long hair, thin beards, peering expression and gentle ways, were like perpetually startled Reginald Bunthornes, at once faun-like and clumsy. If they had been in and out of the *New Statesman* for less than, say, five years they would sometimes forget the way out, and come bursting into my little room instead. "Oh deah," they would cry, "this is wong,' and scramble out again. I came to like most of them very much, but always wondered why it was that among the succession of literary editors I worked under—Raymond Mortimer, V. S. Pritchett, T. C. Worsley, Walter Allen, Janet Adam Smith, Karl Miller, Nicholas Tomalin, Anthony Thwaite—there was not one who resembled in any way these chaps who were in the world but not of it, drifting along with armfuls of review copies, pushing open wrong doors, flapping their sandals as they went down the stone stairs of No. 11 Great Turnstile. The literary editors themselves looked much like anyone else, and seemed to think the eccentricity of their contributors and protégés was only what one should expect.

But once I had become an established part of the machinery I had the same experience as at the City Police headquarters: a new department gladly built itself up around me, this time a sort of amateur welfare office, a cross between the Samaritans and the Lonely Hearts department of a tabloid newspaper. I wrote, and was expected to write, not only about law reform and the victims of injustice but also about the victims of crime, homeless people, discharged prisoners and their families, unmarried mothers, disabled persons, epileptics, the hardships of tenants and even (occasionally) of landlords, and the plight of the aged. There began a flow of callers asking for me, sometimes rather desperate-looking characters who caused some uneasiness among the office staff. My visitors, because there was no name on my office door, would go looking for me in other people's offices, sometimes without knocking; and there is usually something about a man straight from prison that stamps him as an unlikely and potentially disturbing caller upon the literary editor, the advertising manager, or the secretary of the *New Statesman*. It was decided that I must have a name outside my door (this was when John Freeman suggested the inscription *Legion of the Damned*); and then it was ordained that, whether the name was there or not, my visitors must be chaperoned as far as my door and escorted from the territory (by me) when they left. Since I was on the third floor and we had no lift, no one liked this arrangement much; and the receptionist on the ground floor, at my entreaty, began a screening process which reduced the flow. She was very good at it.

The truth is that to run such a service (for that's what it really was) adequately, a weekly or daily paper needs a staff of fifty people—welfare workers, research assistants, typists, interviewers, people with a wide knowledge of the official and voluntary services available. What the *New Statesman* had was me, with a typewriter and a telephone and usually a deadline to meet with something I was writing. The editor always had two editorial secretaries who previously coped with such of these callers as they could, in the limited time they had; but once my position was established they happily referred all such problems to me. Even at the lowest level of expediency, no newspaper likes turning such people away, in case they have a story that should be told, but there had now been a marked increase of callers who either had no "story" or had one which was a self-evident pack of lies. Inevitably, a high proportion of them wanted to "borrow" money.

But I should like to record here that a great many of these people fought their way back to social acceptance with a courage that was literally humbling to watch. The names of dozens occur to me as I write, and I am still in touch with many. Whether they were fools or knaves, and some of them achieved the distinction of being both, I believe that if I myself had been in their situation I should have been among the high proportion who went to the devil. I'm in no doubt at all that a prison sentence spells social ruin for most men. And so, for vastly more people, does a stay in a mental hospital— the "after-care" service for discharged mental patients is still virtually non-existent, and their problem dwarfs the problem presented by the discharged prisoner, both in numbers and in poignancy. But you can't do everything, and the discharged prisoner was my chief concern, mainly (I suppose) because my experience had helped me to understand it.

It all built up rapidly after the formation of the New Bridge in 1956. This "Association of Friends of the Discharged Prisoner" came into being as a direct result of a 1953 Nuffield

Foundation enquiry into "the causes of crime". The enquiry was conducted by Lord Pakenham (now Lord Longford), with the expert assistance of Dr Max Grünhut, Oxford Reader in Criminology, Mr Frank Milton, the London magistrate (now Sir Frank Milton, Chief Magistrate at Bow Street), Dr David Stafford Clark of the York Clinic at Guy's Hospital, and Dr T. C. N. Gibbens of the Institute of Psychiatry at Maudsley Hospital, Denmark Hill. Lord Pakenham at the end of the enquiry was so depressed—as indeed I had been for some years—at the inadequacy of "after-care" arrangements for discharged prisoners that he called together a small group of people to discuss the formation of a new kind of after-care organisation. Among them were Hugh Klare, Stephen Spender, a couple of prison governors, Victor Gollancz and myself, and it was Victor who suggested that we should call the new organisation "The Bridge", because we sought to build a bridge from prison, over the chasm of post-prison vulnerability and despair, into a more receptive society. This was acclaimed as a good title until it was discovered that there was already an organisation called The Bridge which went in for collective yoga and used the back page of the *New Statesman* for a weekly "small ad" inviting others to come and join in. "All right," said Victor Gollancz, "call it the *New Bridge*." We did. We found as we went along that we were assumed to be a society advocating an alternative to the Channel Tunnel, a pressure group concerned to span the Thames at Greenwich, and a society for the propagation of some new variation on the Ely Culbertson method.[1] But we got into motion, and the process afforded me an experience of internecine hatred among the numerous organisations in the world of social science that I found positively frightening. We, in particular, met an astonishing barrage of ill-will, and were written off as "do-gooders" by many people already engaged in prisoners' after-care who, I supposed, did not want to be caught doing good.

Perhaps the phrase "do-gooders" took its origin from the *Book of Common Prayer*—"Eschew evil, and do good: seek peace,

[1] We were never "the New Bridge *Society*", but it was impossible to stop people calling us that; and the latest edition of the Government's *Guide to Voluntary Service* still gets it wrong.

and ensue it." What surprised me was its use by like-minded organisations about each other as an epithet of contempt. In 1956 there were in England and Wales thirty-three Discharged Prisoners' Aid Societies, each of which had at one time been associated with a particular prison. A lot of the prisons had been closed, leaving most of these voluntary societies without a territorial attachment, but they continued in being because they were needed.[1] With some striking exceptions they weren't very effective, or even (except in their optimistic annual reports) very human. But they didn't welcome the New Bridge, whose foundation was of course an implied criticism. I don't know how much good it did, or does, but in the form of case-histories I have plenty of evidence that it did much more good than harm (not always a foregone conclusion). I was its chairman for some years, and for me they were uneasy years because, giving me a synoptic view of the devoted work being done by its members, they kept me constantly aware of how little I did myself. For a time we held our monthly committee meetings in the *New Statesman*'s board-room, but then managed to get accommodated in the vestry at St Botolph's Church, Aldersgate.

I remembered that in 1921, when the Penal Reform League was amalgamated with the Howard Association to become the Howard League for Penal Reform, Margery Fry (who had really brought it about) remarked that it was "always satisfactory to see one reform movement growing where two had grown before". For years I thought this was right, but I came to think otherwise. I knew there were upper and lower limits, *practical* limits to diversification: I had seen the helplessness of government systems which gave scope for dozens of little political parties, and at the same time I distrusted the notion of "world government" (ideally attractive as it was) for fear that it might saddle mankind with a tyranny which nothing could overturn, no conceivable violence could ever bring down. There was some kind of "right size" for everything. And in the thirties the Russian writer Zamyatin, in a satirical novel called *We*, had denounced "the tyranny of uniformity" in terms that anticipated Solzhenitsyn by forty years.

[1] In 1966 they were all superseded by NACRO (the National Association for the Care and Resettlement of Offenders).

It was the New Bridge, then, that produced the heaviest flow of callers at my barely-accessible little *New Statesman* office. And once you embark on this kind of work there seems no end to the small jobs you can do, in this bureaucratic and form-filling age, for people who have lost their way in society and forgotten the regimented business of living. I will not go on about this: but on any one day in this country there are probably a million and a half ex-prisoners in our midst (the state of being an ex-prisoner goes on for a very long time), and if they are to be kept out of prison they are usually in need of someone not too holy whom they can, from time to time, confide in. Otherwise they will confide in other ex-prisoners, the only people who "understand" them, and their period of freedom will be brief. Lord Longford has two highly unusual qualifications for directing this kind of work. One is that, in his estimation, no human being who is not insane is incapable of redemption; he can accordingly say to someone whose crime has made him or her universally loathed and hated: "However bad they may say you are and however bad you may *think* you are, if you want to put it all behind you I'm your friend." The other is that public obloquy, of which he has attracted more than his share by reason of his anti-pornography campaign—and which, as a sensitive man, he minds about acutely—will never deflect him from a course he believes to be right until someone can satisfy him that it's wrong. I see no prospect that anyone will emerge to satisfy him (*a*) that he is wrong in befriending the friendless or (*b*) that what he sees as really bestial pornography is a good thing.

The after-care work involved me in an occasionally delicate relationship with the Metropolitan and other police forces, some of whom by this time were contemplating me without enthusiasm, tending to see a policeman-turned-penal-reformer as a sheep in sheep's clothing. And yet for many years at the *New Statesman* I was able to soften editorial references to the police, some of which in their draft form drew heavily on the belief that the police must always be wrong. I think I could fill a large volume with stories of anti-police paragraphs or articles which I was able to modify or "spike" because I, better than anyone there, could ascertain the facts. I had no desire to whitewash the police, and neither Kingsley Martin nor any of his successors in the editorial chair was sufficiently gullible, even if I had hoped to persuade him, to drink whitewash. I knew the police were sometimes wrong, sometimes disingenuous, usually fairly crafty, always (and naturally enough) suspicious of the *New Statesman*. I knew that they told lies, and that in this they took their cue from Whitehall, since "government by consent" cannot subsist on a diet of total truth for "the people". But I thought I could not only smell police falsehood when I came across it, but form a judgment as to when the deception might conceivably be in the public interest.

There is, however, a lesson to be learned, a lesson in police projection, from the fact that by having me on the staff the *New Statesman* was able to avoid at least a few of the commoner journalistic gaffes about police procedure and the countless shortcomings of the law. I don't mean that the police could plant their own apologists and propagandists in the offices of newspapers and journals of opinion, like agents of the Politburo: I mean that the facts of nearly every story of public interest could usefully be made more accessible to the Press. I think that in this context I must confine myself to two episodes, selected because one of them shows me to have been right and the other grievously wrong.

The first concerned an old thief named David Harris, who came to see me straight from prison because (he said) within a few hours of discharge he had had his pocket picked. He was Jewish, elderly, small, swarthy and glum. His indignation at this outrage was so anguished and eloquent, the tears in his eyes so natural, his obliviousness to poetic justice so funny, that I sat back and half enjoyed it for a time. Then I asked him why he didn't go to the police? "You've got to be joking, Mr Rolph," he pleaded, "they all know me, they'd just show me the door." What he wanted was a loan of a couple of pounds. "You've got it from the grape-vine that I'm a soft touch?" Not at all, he said eagerly: he had read all my articles about prison reform and rehabilitation and he knew I would help him. "You can really trust me with your money," he said. "I'm a hotel luggage thief, I'm not a con man." Something told me that he would come back with the money, and a week later he did. (Incidentally, the cheapest way to shake off a persistent sponger, if you are very busy, is to lend him ten bob: it leaves him with only one reason for coming back, and since that is too painful to be contemplated you never see him again.)

From that day onwards, Dave Harris would almost eat out of my hand. I got him a clerical job with a travel agency, to keep him going until the start of the flat-racing season—his real livelihood, he always explained, was that of a professional punter. And then a few years later he called in and told me he was on bail. Hotel luggage again? "I've done nothing, Mr Rolph," he said reproachfully. "Now you know me, don't you? Would I go thieving on a racecourse?" No, I said by way of keeping the thing going. Well, he had been arrested at Ascot by two Metropolitan CID men for stealing a raincoat from the cloakroom. He'd never seen the raincoat before: they threw it over his arm as they came up behind him, one on each side, and arrested him. "I'm a luggage thief, I never *touch* anything else," he said in tears again. "I don't mind being caught fair and square, but I've never pinched anything on a racecourse in my life—you can ask the Stewards at any course in this country and in Scotland too, they all know me, I'm trusted everywhere."

I was a bit worried about him because he had been out of trouble for quite a long time. I seemed to know in my bones that he had not stolen that raincoat; and anyway to accuse a long-established hotel luggage thief of racecourse pilfering was like accusing a Brahmin of being a Primitive Methodist. I took a long breath and wrote to the Commissioner, Sir John Nott-Bower, telling him the whole story and outlining my misgivings. His private secretary telephoned me the next day to say he was having it looked into. A month later Superintendent MacDougall came round from Scotland Yard to see me; a shrewd and kindly Scot, who told me bluntly (and unasked) that in my place he would have done exactly what I did, that the charge against Harris had been dropped, and that the two CID men had gone back into uniform and been transferred to another Division. It was a thought-provoking and far from happy episode.

The more so because a year later Dave Harris was caught coming out of a bedroom at the Strand Palace Hotel with someone else's suitcase. He optimistically gave my name as that of someone who might "speak for him" at his trial, and at London Sessions I was able to say (while he sat weeping copiously in the dock) that I had a half-promise of a clerical job for him in Tel-Aviv when he had completed whatever penalty the Court might impose. But I never saw him again,

The other episode was far more important and got me uncomfortably into the headlines. In 1959 I was doing some broadcast talks for a series in what was then called the BBC European Service—a weekly *Letter from Britain*; the subjects being suggested sometimes by the producer and sometimes by me. For one of them, a BBC messenger brought to the *New Statesman* office the law report from *The Times* and some other cuttings about a successful action against the police for wrongful arrest and unlawful imprisonment. On the face of it, the Press story suggested a pretty disquieting excess of zeal on the part of the police, to say the least of it; and the Press reports made no mention of the fact that a stay of execution had been granted by the Queen's Bench Divisional Court pending an appeal by the three CID men concerned. (When the appeal came on eighteen months later, the police were successful.) There was barely time to write a script for the recording, and I relied on the Press reports for the facts; the object of the talk being (I was advised) to illustrate to European listeners how the British police officer, unprotected by any *droit administratif*, could be taken into court like any other citizen and sued for damages. Alas, some of the details must have been wrong—I never did discover in what respect; and any comment on those facts might well have been defamatory. The broadcast went out at seven o'clock in the morning and was heard, in this country, by a retired judge living in the Inner Temple. He happened to know the facts of the case and rang up Scotland Yard to tell them what he had heard me saying. The sequel was a libel action against myself and the BBC jointly. The BBC decided to settle out of court. I think this was probably wise; from their position the case wasn't worth fighting, for in view of the odd system of awarding—or more often withholding—

the costs of a successful party, a settlement was likely to be cheaper than a victory. Moreover, and naturally enough, the BBC dislikes litigation and its attendant publicity; and almost from the very beginning in Savoy Hill days the newspapers have (again naturally enough) made a meal of every conceivable BBC embarrassment and difficulty. I was in no position to fight alone, the BBC having thrown in its mammoth weight against my doing so; and I agreed that the BBC's solicitors should settle on my behalf as well. The settlement was for £2,250, being £750 each for the three maligned policemen.

Now the BBC, in the terms of my contract, considered themselves entitled to call upon me for a proportion of this money. I was working under a seven-year Talks Contract which said that broadcasts must "not contain anything defamatory". There was no escape clause about accident or genuine mistake, no requirement as to malice or even recklessness. But no one broadcasting at that time seemed unduly disturbed about this, because it was generally supposed that the BBC, no less than any newspaper or the smallest of weekly journals, would pay the bill and either drop the culprit or ask him to be a bit more careful next time. It is in fact standard practice. Instead the BBC told me I must pay ten per cent of the settlement figure, i.e. £225, and in due course I had a letter from the solicitors acting for the Metropolitan Police demanding the money.

Now why was the BBC, usually the most considerate of employers, suddenly behaving like this? My journalist friends found it incomprehensible, old hands in radio work assuring me that it was without precedent. Someone, they said, was putting pressure on the BBC. For my part, I believed (and still believe) that the BBC is utterly impervious to most kinds of outside "pressure", and makes up its own mind. But a clue was then supplied by the behaviour of Mr MacDonald Baker, of the Solicitors' Department at New Scotland Yard, a man of great charm and much experience with whom I had had a happy relationship for many years. He had been infuriated when he saw the script of the broadcast, called me on the telephone to say so, and added that I could regard our friendly relationship as a thing of the past. Apart from the writs for

Above: Audrey, my
first wife, in 1937

Above, left: My
brother Roland in
1959

Left: My brother
Harold in 1971

At the *New Statesman* office in 1950

defamation, he added darkly, he was considering what other action might be taken against me. For a former police officer to say such things about serving police officers was like dog eating dog. And there were, he implied, bigger and hungrier dogs who might not care what kind of thing they ate.

I hadn't got £225, but a Court order has to be obeyed, and the plaintiffs' solicitors agreed to accept ten post-dated cheques to spread it over a period. A week later I had a telephone call from Sir Alan Herbert, whom I had got to know in circumstances I will describe in the next chapter. "What the hell's all this?" he almost shouted into the phone. "Tell me the story quickly." I told him. "Absolutely monstrous," he said. "The BBC can't get away with that kind of thing." The story got round among regular broadcasters and journalists whose contracts exposed them all to the same risk. APH called together a small committee and sent a letter of protest to *The Times*, the *Daily Telegraph*, the *Manchester Guardian*, the *Spectator*, the *New Statesman* and some of the provincial papers. It was signed by APH himself, Lord Francis-Williams, Norman St John-Stevas, Benn Levy and (I think for the National Union of Journalists) Hannen Swaffer. It said (in effect) that if the BBC, with its immense libel insurance cover, now proposed to leave its individual contributors to hold even a portion of the baby in such cases, then none of us would be safe; an alarming precedent was being established, the terms of the standard Talks Contract must be amended, and anyone who felt disposed to help in paying off the £225 demanded from me could send his contribution to Norman St John-Stevas, who had agreed to act as treasurer. The *Manchester Guardian* published a leader-page article on the story, and in the *Spectator* Bernard Levin made it the occasion for one of his three-column block-busters.

Meanwhile APH came to see me. What about *The Times*, he said? If one of its Law Reports was wrong it ought to come to the aid of anyone it had got into trouble. Had I written to Haley? Sir William Haley was not only Editor of *The Times* and a former managing director of the *Manchester Guardian*—he had also been Director-General of the BBC. What he didn't know about newspaper libels and the way to treat contributors would hardly be worth knowing; and he might

G

feel some concern about the behaviour of the BBC. I wrote to him, and he didn't.

A member of the BBC's General Advisory Council, Sir Hugh Linstead (Tory MP for Putney) telephoned me to say that some members of the Council were deeply concerned about the case and the bad publicity the BBC was attracting. Would I send him all the papers? I did, and the eventual outcome was an amendment to the standard "Talks Contract". With the aid of a powerful microscope, this can now be seen to declare that although your talk must not "contain anything which is calculated to bring the BBC into disrepute or which is defamatory", you will not be held liable "in respect of any defamatory material which, in the opinion of the BBC, was included in the contribution without negligence or malice on your part". A satisfactory outcome; but what was even better (for me) was the response to the Press appeal of Sir Alan Herbert and his co-signatories. The cheques simply poured in, and they came from all over the world—largely, and significantly, from BBC "resident correspondents" in various far-distant capitals. "What the hell's the Old Lady up to now?" wrote one of them to me. "Good God, if I'm to send my dispatches on those sort of terms I'm getting out." The two first and biggest cheques (and I hope their generous donors will not object to my revealing this) were from Marghanita Laski, who was and is a frequent broadcaster, and Charles Wheeler, at that time BBC correspondent in New Delhi (he is now in Brussels). Norman St John-Stevas duly sent me all the money received—about £300 more than was needed to pay the bill. And when I wrote to thank all the donors I suggested that, unless they dissented, I would pay the surplus to the Committee for World Refugee Year. No one objected and the treasurer of that fund, acknowledging the £300, told me it was the strangest windfall he had had from any quarter. It was in fact a very strange episode altogether, reflecting little credit on me, less (I think) on the Solicitors' Department at the Yard, and none at all on the handful of BBC executives who (to the shame of all the other BBC people I knew) had allowed themselves to be manipulated as stooges in a rather silly and self-defeating police vendetta. It was self-defeating, of course, because it dragged the whole story from the obscurity of the BBC's European Service, where it would have done minimal damage, on to the front pages of British newspapers. And I have little doubt that it was my old friend MacDonald Baker, now my most aggrieved enemy, who had successfully insisted that I must be made to smart.

It had two other consequences, one of which will conveniently round off this chapter, while the other can more suitably usher in a new one and a new phase. The first concerned the rather odd and mixed attitude, until at least half-way through the story, of Kingsley Martin.

When I told him that the Metropolitan Police were suing me for libel he was most amused. So that we might be able to laugh together, I asked him to explain the joke. "My dear fellow," he said, "of *course* they will try to silence you. I've had plenty of this." I said that they had never tried to silence me about anything, and that in this instance if the facts of the broadcast were wrong they were entitled to have them publicly corrected. The police, for once in a way, were defending themselves. Diderot, I reminded him, had said the wittiest thing about such dangerous people:

> Cet animal est tres méchant:
> Quand on l'attaque, il se defend.

I should have been more careful in Kingsley's company. He knew more about Diderot and his world than most men. That little couplet, he assured me, was not Diderot's and no one knew whose it was: the trouble with people like me was that anything both witty and French had to be either Diderot's or Voltaire's. (I never found out whose it was.) Anyway I was not to worry—I'd made a genuine mistake and the BBC would stand by me.

A month later I was able to tell him of the BBC's decision. "Oh NO!" he shouted, this time simply incredulous. He immediately rang up two or three BBC pundits, who were regretfully unable to help. He became thoughtful, and then a great idea struck him. "If you refused to pay this money," he said, "you could go to prison instead? That might be very useful. First-hand knowledge of prison conditions? We've never had even a police officer on the staff before, but to have an ex-prisoner as well, both in the same person?..."

One-sidedly, the situation was resuming its funny aspect. I reminded him that you couldn't evade a High Court order for damages by electing to go to prison instead. "They will come and take my piano and gramophone, lawn-mower and typewriter, ox and ass, and whatever else will make up the £225." He didn't believe it. Scandal sheets like *The Week*, he said, little magazines with plenty of venom but no assets or money, had always been able to defy the libel laws. . . . Suddenly it was my turn to have a bright idea. The *New Statesman* was at that time threatened by the Government of Portugal with a libel action that promised to put it out of business completely, and I knew that Kingsley was worried stiff about it.[1] If we lost that case, I said, how about letting the Editor go to prison instead of paying? We could probably carry on in his absence; and when (or if) he came back, we would actually have an Editor who was an ex-prisoner. What an immense advantage *that* would be? He brought the conversation sharply back to my own problem.

"You can pay all right," he said unexpectedly. "It's not a ruinous sum, after all?"

[1] See *Kingsley: The Life, Letters and Diaries of Kingsley Martin*, Gollancz, 1973, p. 369.

Chapter 12

COUNTER-ATTRACTIONS

SHORTLY BEFORE THE BBC libel episode there had been two rows with Kingsley; or perhaps it would be apter to call them solemn discussions in voices half an octave higher than usual. The first was when he finally discovered that I was writing for the *Spectator* as "R. H. Cecil", and I told him that if I was not to be allowed to do that I must find some other way of supplementing what he paid me. He said he would have his secretary send me a list of the publications for which, because they were all to some extent in competition with the *New Statesman*, I must undertake not to write. He forgot about this, and I forbore to remind him, but there was no more *Spectator*.

Then I had a telephone call from Bill Connor, better known as the incomparable "Cassandra" of the *Daily Mirror* (he later allowed himself to become Sir William Connor but remained unscathed). The *Daily Mirror*, he said, had bought the weekly magazine *Public Opinion*—which had been trying, in its last few years of life, to become some kind of a rival to *Exchange & Mart*. They were going to turn it into a literary-cum-political journal for the middlebrow, with himself as Editor. He would like me to write for it, and would I go and see him? I found him in a noisy little office off Fetter Lane, sitting and waiting for me with open shirt collar, red braces and a green eye-shade that clipped over his ears. I said I had always wanted one of those, and he instantly took it off and gave it to me. He spoke American (though he wasn't American) but varied it with some very odd pronunciations. For example: "Now let's see," he said, "your line is sockiology?" We arranged that I should start with twelve articles about "British Justice at Work". How should they be signed? I couldn't use C. H. Rolph, and R. H. Cecil was in bad odour. How about something like "Forensis"—I had used that before? "I don't want any made-up Latinisms," he said. "You godda name of your own?" So it was arranged that the articles should be signed "C. R. Hewitt"; and we started.

When the first one had appeared, Kingsley called me into his office and told me to sit down. I saw at once that on his side of the desk lay a copy of the new *Public Opinion*. He threw it across to me. "I'd like to know what you think of that?" he said. I had of course read most of it, but I put up a show of examining it closely. It was a perfect mock-up of the *New Statesman*—if you saw the two papers from a few yards' distance you would hardly know one from the other. "Looks a bit like us, doesn't it?" I said carefully.

"A bit like us?" he almost shrieked. "The mast-head is the same, the type-face, the layout, the contents—leaders, comments, diary, reviews, arts, competition, half of my best writers and now *you*." I thought that last line was unhappily arranged, but I said yes, and waited. "Well, we've talked about this before," he went on. (And nothing came of it, thought I.) "This simply can't go on." I said I had signed a contract to complete the series. "Then you'd better complete them, and do no more," he said. This was the moment I had seen coming for some years. "I'm afraid the truth is, Kingsley, that I can't live on what you pay me." He then wanted to know what the *New Statesman* did pay me, and I said in the course of a year it wasn't coming to much more than £200. "I simply don't believe it," he said, and rang for his secretary. "Get me Bill Hewitt's figures for last year," he commanded. She came back and said £180, and he looked at me genuinely aghast. "It's chicken-feed," he said. "I'd never have believed it." I sat there looking poor. Luckily he was too appalled to investigate. He would have found that I'd written very little for the paper that year; and further enquiry might have established that, with an office and a telephone provided by the paper, I was working largely for the BBC. "This simply won't do," he said, meaning the money. "I shall make you an offer, and I shall attach to it the names of the papers I don't want you to work for. I'll write you a letter."

The letter announced a magnificent rise, and a contract for

signature which set out a list of proscribed periodicals. For the purpose of removing doubts, as the legislators say, it also set out the names of some papers I could write for, among them being my beloved mainstay, the *News Chronicle*—which at that time was paying me six times what I got from the *New Statesman*.

In 1956 I was offered the editorship of *The Author*, the quarterly journal of the Society of Authors, a part-time job which would require my attendance at its Chelsea offices on perhaps one or two days a week. "You are piling an awful lot on your plate," Kingsley warned me, and I remember that the gastronomical image made me feel gross and greedy-eyed. But it proved to be manageable and in two respects it was a salutary experience. First it taught me that the writers of books (as distinct from the writers of newspapers) are about the lowest-paid workers in the whole national economy. Their earnings at that time averaged about £600 a year, and if you left out the Somerset Maughams, the Compton Mackenzies, and the Agatha Christies the average would fall to about £200. Why on earth did people write books? "Every man," I was once told by Sir Stanley Unwin, "has one good book in him." Yes, but must it come out? Suppose that every man got his book published? The billions of books that no one could buy and no one could even shelve: the great and ever-growing repositories with books piled from floor to ceiling! "Of making many books there is no end," wrote King Solomon,[1] bewailing the worthlessness and vanity of human life. And that was 3,000 years ago.

I had always been abashed at the paucity of my reading. I had to put the thought from my mind whenever I sought an excuse for earning a living as a writer. I needed to remind myself constantly that as a young man I had read somewhere of De Quincey's belief: "It is one of the misfortunes of life that one must read thousands of books to discover that one need not have read them." To be a member of the Society of Authors you had to be the author of at least one book; and I once heard

[1] Ecclesiastes 12 : 12.

John Strachey say in mock despair, when he was Chairman
of the Society's Committee of Management, that it might not
be a bad thing to require that a member should resign if he
proposed to write a second.

In my five years at the Society of Authors I met a great number of famous writers and got to know the ways of the publishing world. They happened to be the years in which the so-called
"censorship laws" of the country were changed, largely at the
instance of the Society itself. That story has been so often told
that it needs only the briefest reference here. It is in any case
a continuing story and may even prove to be a cycle, leading
us all back to prudery; and I have already, I suppose, covered
some acres of print on its many aspects, usually the funnier ones.

In 1954 five of the most respected British publishers were
prosecuted for publishing "obscene" books. Two of them were
convicted (one having pleaded guilty to save time and money)
and the other three were acquitted. It was widely believed at
the time that this was a "campaign", reflecting a Home Office
determination to clean up publishing. I think the Home
Office had absolutely nothing to do with it: the sole function
of that Department of State being its time-honoured one of
attracting all the abuse which in this case, if it had to fall
anywhere, should have been showered upon the Director of
Public Prosecutions, Sir Theobald Matthew. These five books,
none of which today would bring a blush to the cheek of a
sewage farm manager, were among a selection shown to
Lord Goddard, LCJ, by a man named Reiter who was appealing against his conviction for publishing erotic paper-backs.
"What about these?" demanded Mr Reiter. "Nothing I've
published is worse than these. Why pick on the little man?"
Lord Goddard said the appeal court judges could not possibly
discuss any other books, but "No doubt the Director of Public
Prosecutions could look into it?" He did, and the five prosecutions followed. I sat in Court throughout all five, reporting
the proceedings for the *New Statesman* and other papers. I
concluded at the time that in these "obscenity" trials, as in no
other kind of trial that ever takes place, the personality, moral
philosophy and social awareness of the Judge matter supremely.
If only, in each case, a tape-recording of his summing-up to

the jury could have been available for the Court of Criminal Appeal! In each case his prejudice and subjectivity would have shown through the judicial phrases which look fairly detached and impartial on paper: "You may think, members of the jury"; "Well, of course, it's a matter for you"; "Fortunately, perhaps, that is not a decision that I have to make"; "Did *that* strike you as being a good answer?—it's a matter entirely for you." And so on.

There was consternation in the writing and publishing world. The Society of Authors decided to form an action committee to get the law clarified and the literary imagination freed from the threat of prosecution. The Publishers Association "could not see its way clear" to being officially associated with the campaign, but a number of individual publishers could, and they joined the action committee under the chairmanship of Sir Alan Herbert—the vice-chairman being Sir Gerald Barry. Its members were Walter Allen, H. E. Bates, David Carver (secretary of the PEN Club), Professor Guy Chapman, W. B. Clowes the printer, W. A. R. Collins the publisher, Joseph Compton of the National Book League, Rupert Hart-Davis, Roy Jenkins, MP, A. D. Peters the literary agent, V. S. Pritchett, John Pudney, Sir Herbert Read, Denys Kilham Roberts (secretary of the Society of Authors), Norman St John-Stevas (who was not then an MP but had written a recent—and still the best—book on the subject)[1] and Sir William Emrys Williams. *Ex officio*, as editor of *The Author* and what was called "Consulting Secretary" of the Society of Authors, I found myself in the position of honorary secretary.

We drafted a Parliamentary Bill, which tried to give more substance to the "tendency to deprave and corrupt" principle, by substituting the need to consider whether "the general character and dominant effect of a book" was corrupting. It had always been difficult to *prove* the mere "tendency" envisaged by the famous *Hicklin* judgment in 1864. How were we going to prove "general character and dominant effect"? We proposed to *allow* evidence of actually corrupting effect if such evidence was forthcoming (which we thought unlikely)

---

[1] *Obscenity and the Law*, Secker and Warburg, London, 1956.

and to *require* evidence either that this was the author's intention or that he was indifferent or careless about what effect his book might have. And the court would be required to consider "expert evidence" about "medical, legal, political, religious or scientific character or importance". The word obscene would include "any matter which, whether or not related to any sexual context, unduly exploits horror, cruelty or violence, whether pictorially or otherwise". The House of Commons sponsors of the Bill were Roy Jenkins, Sir John Foster, QC, Michael Foot, Angus Maude, Mrs Eirene White (now Baroness White of Rhymney), Nigel Nicolson, Kenneth Robinson, and Jocelyn Simon (now Lord Justice Simon). Roy Jenkins introduced the Bill under the ten-minute rule in March 1955. He got no further, but he had "waved the flag"; and the Home Office, showing a cautious desire to co-operate, offered suggestions for "improvement". The next version, presented in November of the same year, was "talked out". And at all these various stages I was writing progress reports for circulation to the Committee and others.

We thought we were doing reasonably well: and then the Government suddenly bowed to a storm of protest about imported American "horror comics", and brought in a Bill of its own to ban them specifically. This duly became the Children and Young Persons (Harmful Publications) Act 1955, and the Home Office had stolen our thunder; or at least may well have made our own Bill seem less urgently necessary. Kingsley Martin had become oddly excited about horror comics, and wanted me to write an article urging Parliament to legislate about them. I decided to shuffle out of this because I thought I saw what a separate Act on this special issue would do to our campaign. He was rather annoyed with me and then found that the editorial staff as a whole were not much interested in the horror comic menace. Aylmer Vallance reminded him of the Victorian children who, on Sunday afternoons, were given as an improving book to study that classic of homicidal depravity, *Foxe's Book of Martyrs*. Janet Adam Smith, then literary editor, recalls that Kingsley at that time was always showing her revolting illustrations in American comics, in the hope of kindling her anger and involving her in his holy war. He talked about it to everyone, quoting Dr Robert Wertham's book *Seduction of the Innocent* as his Bible. Sir Gerald Barry, a *New Statesman* director told him these grimly un-comic comics were produced for and read by American grown-ups, especially Servicemen. "What do their children read, then?" asked Kingsley. "They can't read," said Gerald wickedly. Max Lerner, the American historian and an old friend of Kingsley, told him he was getting too excited about an age-old phenomenon. For the first and only time, so far as I can remember, he fought an editorial campaign alone, supported by people outside the office but getting absolutely no encouragement inside it. The whole thing released such a flood of odd emotions, odder even than the obscenity ones, that I was glad in the end to see the "horror, cruelty or violence" clause in the Society of Authors' Bill rendered superfluous by the new Act. Kingsley wrote the proposed article about horror comics himself.

Then in March 1957 Lord Lambton drew a good place in the ballot for private members' time, brought in our Bill again, won a second reading for it, and got it referred to a Select Committee. When that Parliamentary session came to an end in August, our Bill of course died with it; but the Select Committee did not. Its report was an encouragingly liberal document,[1] and the accompanying Minutes of Evidence provide a rich quarry of contemporary opinions, prejudices, and serio-comic official practice. They also record myself as rubbing shoulders, so to speak, with other witnesses as oddly assorted as MacDonald Baker, the Scotland Yard solicitor who, I genuinely suppose, had influenced the BBC against me in the libel action, T. S. Eliot, E. M. Forster, the Metropolitan Police Commissioner (Sir John Nott-Bower) and the Director of Public Prosecutions. The result was yet another Bill, which Roy Jenkins this time got through the Commons and Lord Birkett got through the Lords, and it received the Royal Assent in 1959. It gave the Herbert Committee almost everything it had wanted, including the right to call expert evidence

[1] *Report from the Select Committee on Obscene Publications*, HMSO, 958, 123–1.

—not about the alleged obscenity of a book, which remains always a matter for the court, but on the question whether its publication might redound to the "public good".

For our pains, we came in for some heavy criticism. Before the 1959 Act the penalties had been "at large". That is to say they were Common Law penalties, and the Judges could do what they liked. Therefore no one knew in advance what they could be. Now that they were to be statutory, the Law Officers had insisted on possible penalties of three years' imprisonment plus fines of unlimited amount; and of course, once they were thus set down for all to see, they made the publishers gasp. We were upbraided for not having allowed a sleeping dog to lie, and the 1954 occasion when five reputable publishers had found the dog to be merely shamming was forgotten.

Within a year the new Act was being tested at the Old Bailey, the defendant being Penguin Books Ltd for publishing a 3s. 6d. paperback of *Lady Chatterley's Lover*. This time my presence at the trial was occasioned by a commission from Penguin Books Ltd to compile a paperback to be called *The Trial of Lady Chatterley*. The Judge was Mr Justice Byrne, whom I had seen thirty years before as Junior Treasury Counsel at the Old Bailey; the leading defence Counsel was Gerald Gardiner, QC, later chairman of the *New Statesman* board and then Lord Chancellor; the trial was in Court No. 1; and the inspector on duty kindly accommodated me (as I had once accommodated so many others) in the City Lands Committee seats immediately behind the double row of barristers. The story of the trial is fully told in the resulting paperback.[1]

But the background to it is not. In the lunch-time and other adjournments I sought the company of policemen, court ushers and other officials whose lives had been conditioned by years of duty in a building dedicated to the ventilation of sin. They not only knew all the four-letter words which, if the truth be faced, had been the sole cause of this prosecution. They used them as adjectives and epithets in their own descriptions of life, work, beer and each other. And yet they were unanimous

---

[1] *The Trial of Lady Chatterley*, Penguin, London, 1960.

in condemning *Lady Chatterley's Lover* as bloody filth. "You can't get away with that kind of language in a book," one representative constable told me. "Blimey," he added, "you could never see the end of that road. Where *would* it end? You would have some of these buggers printing anything they liked. Lawrence of Arabia? Dirty bastard." One of the uniformed attendants told me he thought it was wrong to let the jury see it. How would they judge its contents, then? "Read out the bits that matter," he said. They could hear the words spoken but not read them.

I had never known the power of print, the magic of catching a word and pinning it to a piece of paper, to be so powerfully illustrated. Here were the cloudy edges of my own two worlds momentarily overlapping and fused. Or if not two worlds, one world with two languages to be kept eternally separate, a spoken one and a written. Since I left the police and the purlieus of the Old Bailey, I had thrown in my lot, irrevocably, with the written; and most of my new colleagues seemed happy enough to use the liberated words because (I supposed) for them such words added power to prose. Not for me. But a little lesson was in store for me when Mr John Mortimer wrote a Foreword to a book of mine[1] in 1969:

> I would like to form a society for the Defence of Bad Literature. Every writer has, it seems to me, the inalienable right to fail, and I think it's highly inequitable that the talented should be permitted access to erotic fields denied to the clumsy, talentless majority. We should not only be asked to defend to the death other people's right to say things with which we disagree; we must also allow them to do it in abominable prose.

When the thirty-five expert witnesses had extolled the merits of *Lady Chatterley's Lover*—literary critics, moral theologians, dons, priests, publishers, authors, politicians—and the jury had said "Not Guilty", there was a burst of applause in the crowded court which the shocked ushers tried in vain to hush. In the Press room afterwards a reporter said to me: "It's OK as far as I'm concerned, but how the hell can a jury say that book's not obscene?" We didn't know, I argued, whether the jury had said that or not. They might have decided

[1] *Books in the Dock*, André Deutsch, London, 1969.

that it *was* obscene, but that it was one of the obscene works which ought to be published in the interests of literature. "Well, they're the only people who will ever know the answer to *that*," he said. I know that three of them did, but I suspect that the others were completely bemused.

The odd thing was that if the jury had convicted (which was plainly what the Judge wanted), there would have been an appeal on the ground that no "publication" had been proved. The whole case had started from the point where Penguin Books had told the police they were *going* to publish the book. By way of avoiding the involvement of an innocent bookseller, it was arranged that someone from Scotland Yard should call at the Penguin offices and collect twelve copies there. An inspector called. But as the law then stood, he was not a person whom any book could "tend to deprave and corrupt": he was a police officer from the vice squad. A couple of years later in another case,[1] an ivory tower Bench of Judges held that nothing can tend to deprave or corrupt a policeman, or at any rate a policeman who is a member of the vice squad. This loophole was virtually abolished in 1964 by an Amendment Act, but in 1960 it would have been enough to get Penguin Books off on appeal.

The Penguin *Trial of Lady Chatterley* established me as a man with a point of view, on a subject which is as evergreen as football or hanging. But not, I hope, as a man opposed to every form of control over the seedy world of pornography. I was never impressed, may I say, with the accusation that the "pornographers" are "merely out for gain". All publishers are out for gain; and why not? But no one in his senses wants to see official control over what people can voluntarily read or privately pore over. I do want to see some form of protection for the public, which really means protection for me and the people I know, against visual assault, against the insulting assumption that we have all abandoned our dignity (dangerous word), aesthetic feeling, and capacity to experience disgust. I want "the private life" defended against invasion, because it seems to me that the private, innermost essence of a man is

[1] R. V. Clayton and Halsey (1962), 3 All E.R. 500.

his spirituality and the one good product in the evolution of our species.

But I do not delude myself about the difficulty of controlling pornographic display. Even when you have defined "display" (which is extraordinarily difficult), you are still left with a baffling alternative: you must define pornography, obscenity, indecency or whatever the term is to be; or you must legislate for the prevention of disgust, in its modern sense of loathing and revulsion.

Chapter 13

OF MAKING MANY BOOKS . . .

I WAS NOW meeting the people who wrote books, the priest-hood of my youth; partly at the *New Statesman* office, partly through the Society of Authors, partly because I was increas-ingly employed by the BBC as an interviewer—and the common denominator of those whom I was directed to interview seemed to be that they should have written a book. I was lucky in not being asked to interview for "news programmes", holding a microphone in the direction of some hurrying diplomat, shop steward or pop star at a crowded airport; or asking a miner's widow at the pit-head how she felt now that she had lost her husband. My interviewing, an hour or more at a time, was done, comfortably and leisurely, in studios or in the victims' homes or hotels. It ranged from Danny Kaye to Dr Margaret Mead, Sir John Gielgud to Georges Simenon, Beryl Grey to Margot Oxford, Sir Julian Huxley to Lord Beveridge. And at that time the tradition was not yet born that a radio interviewer had to be hostile. If you had said, for example, to Dr Margaret Mead: "But don't you think you've gone much too far in your book?", she would be likely to reply, "No, I do *not*. But your question suggests that you do: so let's begin by finding out what you know about it." If you wanted your colloquist's reaction to some current criticism you didn't begin, "But surely . . ." You asked, "And what do you say to the criticism that . . .?" Nor was the unanswerable qualita-tive question yet in use—"How angry were you?" "How serious is this problem?" "How frightening was it?" "How difficult did you find it?" Or (a recent example): "How lethal are these weapons?" You had a conversation. A long one with Pamela Frankau led to the pair of us—I can't think why—doing a weekly man-woman radio discussion of listeners' domestic and emotional problems. We broadcast about these in the mornings at half-past nine, and as we talked I always had three imaginary listeners in my mind's eye. The first was a woman washing-up, the second a bricklayer with a portable radio, and the third a fat man with a white moustache driving a big car. The first two were grinning from ear to ear and the third was scarlet with apoplexy.

I asked Pamela once if she could see why we were supposed to be good at it. "It's because we've both got deep voices," she said, making hers sound deeper than ever. (It was an extraordinary and unforgettable sort of voice.) "Sounds wise and well-informed. Actually I don't think you're any wiser than I am, but you can get an octave lower and sound like it." She used to show me personal letters from listeners saying that they would prefer to listen to her alone, and I would accuse her of writing them herself. I was able to show her one letter from a man who said he had known her father, Sir Gilbert Frankau, and upbraided me for consorting with a woman whose declared hobby was playing roulette. One consequence of these programmes was an invitation to myself to conduct a "readers' problems" page in *Britannia and Eve*, which lasted exactly one week because my replies were considered too cynical.

If all this is name-dropping, then the names are being dropped with nostalgic gratitude, for it is also autobiography. These people, to whom I was a complete nonentity, forgotten, perhaps, the moment I had left them, were important to me. Some of them had a lasting effect on my thinking and, I genuinely believe, on my rather malleable personality. A New York radio station used to ask once a year for six one-hour interviews with famous British writers, which were duly recorded by the BBC and sent over. One year I was the interviewer they asked for. We were still then in the days of recording vans, crews of radio engineers, huge lengths of heavy-duty flex draped from fourth- and fifth-floor windows, and a "talks producer" to sit and twiddle the knobs. It was thus that I went and talked to Sir Norman Angell, one of the pagan gods of my adolescence; and found him, a tiny little man, living alone at the age of eighty-three in a cheap small bungalow near Haslemere. It was a saddening experience. Here was this extraordinary and almost fabulous man, a Nobel Peace Prize winner and author of forty books which included that devastating indictment of war, *The Great Illusion*, ending his days in relative poverty and loneliness. "I've lived too long," he said. "The people who would listen to me are all dead. No one will listen now." He gave me a signed copy of his ingenious *Money Game*,[1] a sort of "Monopoly" outfit by means of which a chairman or banker with a "block of gold" rules the roost and builds up a credit economy on some imaginary island like Tristan da Cunha. The simple ingenuity of it was astonishing. I was even more surprised when Kingsley Martin the next day remarked to me that "Angell really wrote only one book—*The Great Illusion*. That was in 1910. All his other books were re-statements of it." That certainly wasn't true of *The Story of Money* (1930), *Peace With the Dictators?* (1938), or *The Press and the Organisation of Society* (1933). I have a feeling that Norman Angell was one of the most neglected and yet most percipient prophets of our time. The evening before I went to see him he had collapsed in his little weed-grown, shrub-gloomy garden, lost consciousness and lain out there all through a rainy night, to be found in the morning by the postman. He said he was none the worse. That tough little man lived another ten years.

The other authors in this series of interviews were Sir Arthur Bryant, Rosamond Lehmann, Nicolas Monsarrat, Hesketh Pearson and Dame Rebecca West. Hesketh Pearson, who had recently published his biography of Bernard Shaw, reminded me that Shaw had said, "When you read a biography, remember that the truth is never fit for publication." At that time I dreamed occasionally that I myself might write a fresh biography of Shaw, but was continually—and of course luckily—deterred by the need to earn a living. And when I found Hesketh Pearson, who had brought "popular" biography to the status of a home industry, living in obviously straitened circumstances, the deterrence was final and beyond argument.

At about this time I was commissioned by Longmans Green & Co. to write a history of the Rotary movement in Great

---

[1] Published by J. M. Dent & Co., London, 1936.

Britain.[1] The editor of its magazine, *Rotary*, was Roger Levy, an old friend of mine, and he asked if he could put my name before his Publications Committee as one of the possible writers. (Why they didn't get him to write it I can't conceive.) Longmans agreed to publish, I was given access to all the records, papers and meetings of "Rotary International in Great Britain and Ireland", and away I went. I knew nothing about the Rotary movement, not even that it got its name from an early Chicago habit of meeting monthly in its members' private houses "in rotation". I had read somewhere that Sinclair Lewis said of it in America (where it began in 1908) that "a Boy Scout is a Young Rotarian and a Rotarian is a Boy Scout in long trousers". In the police service I had never known a Rotarian—though, as I was to discover, there are many police members. I knew policemen who were Freemasons, and always thought it significant that most of them seemed to join a Lodge at the time when their minds were turning to their prospects of promotion. I never saw any evidence that it made a difference to their chances, but it is possible that some of them, putting their trust in it, were thereby lulled into laziness and failure. The difference between Rotarians and Freemasons (though some men are both) has always seemed to me that the former try to do some good in the community while the latter look after each other and their children—and do it magnificently. I suppose both organisations incidentally serve the universal, and harmless, appetite for mumbo-jumbo and convivial mysticism.

The Publications Committee gave me *carte blanche* to say what I liked about Rotary in my book, and many criticisms certainly suggested themselves as I went along. What I clearly remember about these is that, however smart and original I thought they were, every one of them turned up, sooner or later, in the movement's own highly self-critical literature; and that whenever I wanted to say something pungently observant I had merely to quote the recorded words of some exasperated Rotarian of the past. I was surprised to find how many familiar institutions had been conceived and established

[1] *Towards My Neighbour*, Longmans, London.

either by Rotary Clubs or, where there had been opposition in the Clubs, by small groups of men who knew each other because they were Rotarians: foundation scholarships, funded concerts, white sticks for the blind, theatres (the Birmingham Rep., the Little Theatre at Bristol), wireless for the bedridden, works councils, youth movements. I concluded that it was much better that the Rotary movement should exist than that it should not; and added some good friends to an ever-widening circle. But I never wanted to be a Rotarian.

It was this experience, more than any other, which showed me that to have deserted the police and invaded the literary world was a barely permissible thing. My metamorphosis was accepted with special difficulty by the main body of the Rotary movement, who already had their favourite for the job of writing their history. My champion was the chairman of their Publications Committee, a remarkable man named Herbert Schofield who had been President of the movement and was, incidentally, the founder of the Technical College which became the Loughborough University of Technology. (It started in his back-garden shed, where in 1915 he was making small parts for a war-time munitions factory—as thousands of other enthusiastic amateurs were doing.) "If a man cannot change direction," he once said to me consolingly, "he can never avoid disaster." My appointment as their historian had to be ratified at a colossal annual conference at Blackpool, and such was Herbert Schofield's prestige and popularity that it was done without difficulty. Incidentally, he had had to overcome the further complication that I was known to be on the editorial staff of the *New Statesman*, which was not the favourite reading of many Rotarians.

But it was surprising how many of the delegates, in conversation afterwards, seemed to hope that since I had unavoidably been in the police, I had been there for perhaps a few months or at the most a couple of years? To this day, people who want to know if it is true that I was a policeman will glance round and lower their voices when they ask me, as if I had served a prison sentence, defected from Russia or managed a brothel. The most memorable of such occasions, if perhaps the least important, came when I was acting as "technical adviser" for a Harold French film at Elstree. He had had a succession of leading ladies, none of whom stayed the course, until Dawn Addams was brought over from Hollywood. He didn't then know her, but after the first day he was obviously a much relieved man. Unfortunately she had lost her ration book (clothes rationing was in its last days) and needed some clothes. She had completed a form of application for a new book and it could be attested by the signature of someone in the police service who was "not below the rank of inspector". Harold French introduced her to me and said I would no doubt be pleased to sign. "Not in that capacity," I said reluctantly. "But Harold says you're a police inspector?" asked Miss Addams. Not any more. That kind of authority didn't carry over into "civilian" life. Harold French thought no one would know; and when I still showed signs of reluctance Miss Addams deliberately switched herself on and I, with some sort of shambling and desperate gallantry, had signed within minutes. I never quite got over this.

An author once complained to Oscar Wilde that there was a conspiracy of silence about his books. "Join it," said Wilde. But the man was not writing an autobiography, which is silence laid bare in what Henry James called "the terrible fluidity of self-revelation". I have heard many authors complain about this "conspiracy of silence" business, and yet I have a strong belief that book-sales are not proportionate to any amount of noise, any volume of advertising, any chorus of praise. I have a personal story to support it. At about this time—the mid-fifties—I was much interested in the quasi-philosophical problem of "selfhood", the mystery of being a person, and the application to my own life of *cogito ergo sum*. I gather that it's usually a problem of adolescence and that most people grow out of it smoothy. That it may even start long before adolescence appears in the question put to his father by a nephew of mine at the age of four: "Do dogs *know* they are dogs?" But I think that my exposure to the law and its practitioners, to its historians and thinkers, and even more to the absorbing bewilderment of reading Russian novels, had nourished in me a special state of mind about "the private man" and his growing vulnerability in the modern world. "No man would, I think, exchange his existence with any other man, however fortunate," wrote Hazlitt. "We would rather not BE, at all, than not be ourselves." And I was cornered and frightened by what Dostoyevski had said in *The Idiot*:

> Every man has reminiscences which he would not tell to every-one, but only to his friends. He has other matters in his mind which he would not reveal even to his friends but only to himself— and then only in secret. But there are other things which a man is afraid to tell even to himself. And every decent man has a number of such things stored away in his mind. The more decent he is, the greater the number of such things stored away.

The indecency of autobiography will account, I hope, for any superficial quality in my story. Privacy is, in a strange way, the product of literacy—people didn't worry much about privacy until they could read and got ideas into their heads—and I can now see the muddled state of my own thinking as the effect of a lifetime's undisciplined reading on an ill-prepared mind. But to narrow this down to the relatively crude and simple world in which I had watched men struggling and twisting under the microscope of the law, I was absorbed in the concept of individuality and a "right of anonymity". I decided to write a book about it, the only book I have ever produced from what seemed an original idea and the only one not commissioned in advance. I called it *Personal Identity*. When it was finished I put it away for six months, so that I could reassess it calmly before deciding whether to inflict it upon some publisher. I felt extremely shy about it. When I re-read it I was hotly embarrassed at what seemed to me its unique blend of ingenuousness and fraudulent pomposity. It sadly failed to sustain any intelligent discussion of the philosophy of personality. It "began big" and tailed off into a mere rehash of famous or poignant stories of mistaken and usurped identity. I put it away again.

Then, about a year later, in the course of the Herbert Committee's enquiries, I made the acquaintance of Fredric Warburg the publisher. "Have you got any ideas for a book?"

he asked me one day. With some hesitation I told him about *Personal Identity* and he asked to see it. "You wouldn't like it," I said, "and I don't want it turned down: I'd rather keep it as a work of unpublished genius." But he insisted ("You might allow me to be the best judge of whether I like it?") and sent a boy round to the *New Statesman* office to collect it. It was back within a week, accompanied by a letter from Fred Warburg beginning, "It is with heavy heart . . ." I rang him up and tried to comfort him, without once saying "I told you so."

A week later I had a call from Michael Joseph. "I hear from Freddie Warburg you've written a book?" We went through the same performance and a boy came to collect the manuscript. A month later came a letter saying that Michael Joseph Ltd would be pleased to publish it and offering an advance on royalties of £250. About a week before its publication I ran across Daniel George in Fleet Street. He was one of the judges for the Book Society's monthly recommendation; though I don't understand how he got time to read the books he was commending, because at that time he was reading twenty novels a week, God help him, as literary critic for the *Daily Express*. "Congratulations!" he said. "We're recommending your book this month." I held on to some railings. "Does that mean it will have one of those little paper armlets ound it, saying 'Recommended by the Book Society'?" He roared with laughter at the word armlets. "Once a cop, always a cop," he said woundingly.

The critics' reception of *Personal Identity* was widespread and encouraging. People wrote me kind letters, and I thought I noticed a whiff of the sweet smell of success. In the event, *Personal Identity* never earned the £250 which would have repaid my advance from Michael Joseph, and within a year or two it was "remaindered". As the canny and experienced Warburg had foreseen, commercially it was a flop. But it was not killed by any conspiracy of silence. It may even have died of house-top exposure. I still glance at it sometimes with the special kind of affection accorded to an idiot child.

But Victor Gollancz, who didn't miss very much, had seen it. One day at a meeting of the Executive Committee of the National Campaign for the Abolition of Capital Punishment he reminded me about it. Gerald Gardiner was at that time the chairman, and we were holding our meetings in his chambers at King's Bench Walk. The committee was sitting in a semicircle round his desk, waiting for the proceedings to begin, and Victor Gollancz whispered in my ear: "I want you to write a book for me." I asked what it would be about, and he said *Crime and Punishment*. "It's been done," I said. "Dostoyevski." No man for such trifling, Victor went on to explain that it would be a plain man's guide to penal philosophy, based on the eternal controversy about the "freedom of the self" and the choice between good and evil as a freewill option.

It came out as *Commonsense About Crime and Punishment*,[1] because it was one of a series in which selected authors explored their supposed common sense about race, religion, Christian ethics, young offenders, Russia, Africa, China, the Arabs, and Victor Gollancz alone knew what. The writing of it was a valuable exercise for me, putting me to the necessity of clarifying ideas which had been jostling for recognition in my mind for about twenty years. I had just been exposed to the vigorous and experimental thinking of Californian and New York penologists, in the course of a six-week visit to the USA which came about in the following unexpected manner.

In 1954 I had been asked by the British Social Biology Council[2] to "edit" for publication a long research report about prostitution in London. The publishers were to be Secker and Warburg. It was the work of a social science graduate named Rosalind Wilkinson, who had been engaged by the Council

[1] Gollancz, London, 1961.

[2] This Council, now defunct, existed "to preserve and strengthen the family as the basic social unit", and for that purpose it disseminated biological knowledge as a means of emphasising the social responsibilities of individuals, of eliminating "commercialised vice" and of reducing the venereal diseases. Its president was the Earl of Cranbrook and among its officers were Professor Winifred Cullis, Sir Julian Huxley, Dr Kenneth Walker and Sir Basil Nield, QC. The chairman of the committee on prostitution was Dr Hermann Mannheim of the LSE and among its members was T. E. James, later Professor of Law at King's College, London.

for the job, had lived among the prostitutes in the West End
and some of the inner suburbs, and had come up with a
manuscript which was so vivid and human and at the same
time so factual and carefully documented that I should have
liked to see it published unchanged. But it ran to about 200,000
words, and the Council felt able to publish a book of no more
than 90,000. I suppose I was approached on the strength of
my *New Statesman* articles, and Mrs Wilkinson, I believe,
agreed to my editorship on the same grounds. I met the
"steering committee" of the Council, got my instructions,
and set to work. I was soon regretting the undertaking. It
was butchery. I think that if anyone decimated a book of
mine in that fashion I should raise the roof. Mrs Wilkinson
raised the roof. She vehemently objected to publication in the
"edited" form and there ensued a long dispute about copyright. In the course of this I found myself on the wrong side
in a tussle with the Society of Authors, with which I was
already much identified and which had advised Mrs Wilkinson
that, since she had never signed away the copyright, it was
hers. The lawyers advising the British Social Biology Council
were equally emphatic that it was theirs—if you were engaged
and paid to do an academic research, they said, your report
belonged to your paymasters in the absence of a clear statement
that it was to be yours. The Council decided to go ahead and
publish, leaving out Mrs Wilkinson's name and calling her
"the Research Worker". Even at the time, although I could
see that this was inevitable, I thought it was rather a shame,
since my name appeared on the title page and anyone might
have supposed it was my work.[1] I felt still worse when, as
time went on, I discovered that many people did in fact think
it was my work, though I never lost an opportunity to disabuse
them. But at no time did I feel quite so bad as at the cocktail
party which celebrated the day of publication. Mrs Wilkinson
had received much help and encouragement from that doyenne
of East End social workers, Miss Edith Ramsey—who, moreover, had taught her at the London School of Economics;

---

[1] The book was called *Women of the Streets* (Secker and Warburg,
1954).

and Miss Ramsey, who was very much on her side, came
to the party determined to make a bit of a scene. I had long
admired the work of Miss Ramsey, knew she was coming,
watched the door nervously, and didn't know what she looked
like. When she arrived she looked rather like Margaret Ruther-
ford on the warpath. She declined a proffered drink with
a sweep of her arm, marched straight up to me, and told me
I ought to be ashamed of myself. "I am rather," I said, looking
round to see how many exits there were. "And it's all the
worse because I'm having to dodge bullets going both ways.
But, if I may say so, I'm slightly mollified by the opportunity
to meet you at long last." This made absolutely no impression,
and with one eye on the Press men she made a short speech
denouncing the British Social Biology Council, its steering
committee, and me. Then she left. The next morning the
newspapers made rather a meal of it. Years later, in a BBC
radio programme arranged in her honour as a distinguished
champion of adult education and housing for the poor, I
had the pleasure of interviewing her for the listening multitude.
She was very gracious and kindly, remembered the row, and
told me (off the air) that my reaction to her strictures
had very nearly disarmed her. But not quite. She still
thought the treatment of Mrs Wilkinson's report was an
outrage.

    Now it was as a sequel to this episode that Tom James, then
a law lecturer at King's and a member of the guilty committee,
told me I ought to go to California and do some writing about
American prisons and parole systems. It happened that one
of his former students, a solicitor named Rex Cowan, who
shared his interest in criminology, was planning to go shortly
and renew some contacts he had made during and after the
war. Rex was a child during the war, and had been evacuated
to America with a shipload of children from well-to-do families.
He returned there to read law and criminology, became a
graduate of the California Delinquency Control Institute, and
is now a London magistrate. (He stopped practising as a
solicitor in 1972 when, with a team of professional divers, and
as a sort of holiday task, he found the long-sought wreck of the
Dutch East Indiaman *Hollandia*, which sank off the Isles of

Scilly in 1743 with a huge cargo of silver.) It was arranged that
Rex and I should go to America together and that he would
introduce me to criminologists, police, lawyers, and officials
of the various "Departments of Correction". All I had to do
was get the money: I should need about £500.

Kingsley greeted the idea with controlled enthusiasm, and
said the *New Statesman* would put up £100. At the end of a
circuit with the begging-bowl I had got the rest from the BBC,
John Bull, the *Daily Herald* and one or two smaller sources. I
shall never forget that as I walked up the slope from Los
Angeles airport the first man I met, on this my first contact
with American soil, was Gerald Heard, the philosopher and
mystic whose torrent of books I had been reading for something
like thirty years. He lived at Santa Monica. He looked frail
and, I rather thought, exiled; and wanted more news of his
native England than there was time then and there to give
him.

This is not the place for any account of the penal and police
systems in California, Colorado and New York, of which I
have written elsewhere. But I can't forgo the opportunity to
recall a story of misfortune which may serve as a cautionary
tale for anyone similarly inept. The BBC in London had advised
me not to carry with me one of their tape-recorders, which in
those days would have been a cumbersome equipment in
two metal boxes, each about the size (and weight) of a small
portable sewing machine. The weight would take up all my
air-travel baggage allowance and reduce my permissible
luggage to a pair of socks and a toothbrush. I could borrow
a lighter one in New York, they told me, at the BBC offices
on Fifth Avenue. But the BBC in New York were apologetically
unable to help me; and in the end (in Los Angeles) I was
offered the loan of a "very modern" and relatively small
recorder by a friendly reporter from the Columbia Broadcasting System. With this I made dozens of exciting recordings,
and in New York on the way home I arranged that the BBC's
engineers would make large BBC tapes from them, sending the
borrowed recorder back to Los Angeles and the tapes to me
in London. The tapes, when they arrived, were accompanied
by a note saying that they were all totally unusable. And they

were. The background noise was excruciating (the recorder had had no play-back facilities to warn me). So instead of the feature programmes the BBC was expecting from me there had to be a series of solo talks.[1] I have a suspicion, though, that if someone came back with those tapes today the BBC would use them; and it is based on the wretched quality of the dispatches from "our man in Tel-Aviv" with which the BBC now mutilates its news bulletins, all in the name of immediacy and technical naïvety.

Kingsley had insisted on my coming home by sea. "You will be exhausted," he had said when he studied my proposed itinerary. "This is crazy. I know something about this kind of thing. Book a sea passage and have a rest." So I came home on the *Mauretania*: Rex Cowan, having told me I was crazy if I thought *that* was going to be a rest, said goodbye and went home by air. A rest? The ship was crammed with American children and there wasn't a corner where you could read in peace. There were cinemas, swimming pools, keep-fit classes, bingo, table-tennis, deck quoits, and rain. There were crowds of portly passengers struggling up and down the windy promenade decks in a constant battle to get one big meal shaken down in time for the absorption and temporary storage of another. It was my first "sea journey" and it will be my last. Because there was literally nowhere to sit and read, it seemed to me to promote true boredom to the status of a mystical experience, and it was the first occasion in my life (including all the hours as a bobby on night-duty beats) when boredom had me biting my nails. Even so it hadn't yet dawned upon me that all the scintillating articles I was now going to write had already been paid for, the money having gone on the expenses of the trip.

"Are you going to write a book about America?" asked Kingsley.

"Book? I was only there six weeks."

"Ah, yes. You really need two months for a book about America."

---

[1] Published in *The Listener*, 8, 15 and 22 September and 20 October 1960.

Another member of the anti-capital punishment campaign committee was Arthur Koestler, and we persuaded him that the time was ripe for a revised and paperback version of his hard-hitting book *Reflections on Hanging*.[1] It had been out-dated by the swift pace of events and the passing of the Homicide Act of 1957. He had no time then to do the revision himself, and suggested that I should do whatever rewriting was necessary and that we should sign the result as joint authors. It was published as *Hanged By the Neck*,[2] a "Penguin Special", and I recall the trepidation with which I had sent the revised manuscript to Arthur Koestler for his approval. (It had to be half the length of *Reflections on Hanging* and yet include much new matter; with the result that not more than a third of Arthur's book was retained.) He passed it, so far as I can remember, without a word of dissent. It had a hard-hitting Preface by John Freeman, who was by that time my editor at the *New Statesman*; and under it his name appeared as "J. W. Freeman" for some reason—probably the combined fault of his handwriting and a printer who still didn't know who he was. But I always regretted that we couldn't reproduce, from the Macmillan American edition of the original book— for it was irrelevant—a superb "Preface for Americans" by Professor Edmund Cahn of New York University, one of the best things about the death penalty that anyone has ever written. The Penguin Special drew only one adverse comment, and this was Lord Birkett's in the *Sunday Times*.[3] Abolitionist though he was, he bridled at the "violence" of Arthur Koestler's language, and in particular at an observation concerning the obscurantism of the English judges: "The history of criminal law is a wonderland filled with the braying of learned asses." I remember pausing over that phrase, and funking the task of persuading Arthur that there were lawyers to whom it was less than fair. But Lord Birkett, with whom I had shared radio discussion programmes (and for whom I had devilled when he introduced the Obscene Publications Bill in the House

---

[1] Gollancz, London, 1956.
[2] Penguin Books, London, 1961.
[3] 2 July 1961.

of Lords) wrote me a friendly letter saying that if he hadn't been a judge himself he would have sprung to the defence of the learned asses and shown how they had sometimes brayed progressively. I didn't see why his being a judge prevented this, since he was reviewing in the *Sunday Times* anyway; but one couldn't risk the alienation of so good a man, so courteous an adversary, and so valuable a potential ally in a variety of causes yet to be won.

However, I fell straight into another commitment, yet another book for the groaning shelves. The Electrical Trades Union, and a number of its Communist or pro-Communist leaders, were being sued in the High Court by two other members, John Byrne and Frank Chapple. They wanted a declaration that the elections of ETU officials had for years been fraudulently rigged, in order to ensure Communist domination of the Union. No doubt because of the success of *The Trial of Lady Chatterley*, I was commissioned—this time by André Deutsch Ltd—to write an account of the ETU trial. It was a much bigger job than the Chatterley trial. It dragged on for forty-two days, compared with Chatterley's five. The story was complex, sinister, humourless, and sickening. Life was infused into the proceedings by the fact that the leading counsel "on the side of the angels" was again Gerald Gardiner, QC, and that the Judge was Mr Justice Winn, whose seemingly effortless mastery of that involved story I shall never understand or forget. But the evidence of the Communist ETU officials, as they succeeded each other in the witness-box— beginning always with complacent defiance and exposed always as hopelessly ineffectual lying—was not just another instance of dull men being slowly demolished by a man of acute intelligence. It was the most skilful and courteous process of demolition I had ever seen in a long experience of the courts. In the past, I had hated the spectacle, be the witness never so cocky or detestable. The contest was so uneven, the victim so much like a caged animal being tormented for the public amusement. He might be fairly odious, but so are many caged animals. This time I thoroughly enjoyed it; and looking through the book which I wrote when it was over[1] I can see

[1] *All Those in Favour?*, André Deutsch, London, 1962.

that this bullring kind of enjoyment occasionally shows through. Which it shouldn't.

Many of the defendants in the ETU case could have been indicted in the criminal courts and tried for conspiracy to effect a public mischief, and some of them for fraud. As it was, all they were ever called upon to do was to oppose an application that Mr Justice Winn should declare that their elections had been rigged. By failing in this, they had branded themselves as crooks. But they were not punished. Should they have been punished?

Chapter 14

THE PUNISHERS

DURING ALL THIS time, and rather more perceptibly than these pages may seem to have suggested, Jenifer and I were accumulating a family, answering to the names of Deborah, Jonathan and Julia. They all contrived in some way, and still do, to be at once normal and unusual, strongly individual and community-conscious. I took a great delight in each of these characters in order of their appearance; and since I was older than is normal in a brand new parent this feeling may, I suppose, have combined the pleasure of father and grandfather, a powerful mixture. I have been fond of children, even of other people's, ever since I contrived to forget a few of those I knew at school. It is a fondness which, in recent years, has been brought under severe strain by the unexampled and triumphantly projected soppiness of the ones in the television advertisements. But since my own children have always found these a strain too, their sickly impact has drawn us even closer together than before they were discovered or invented.

We did a great many things together, establishing a firm relationship which sustained only one serious setback throughout the years. When they were respectively about nine, seven and five, I took them one Saturday afternoon to the City of London to inspect the scene of my one-time bailiwick, and in particular to see the City's traditional giants, Gog and Magog, at the Guildhall. Now I will admit that these two wooden figures, with their silly faces and rather tawdry fairground coatings of glossy paint, may be less impressive than a romantically boastful father could wish. But Julia contemplated them with almost tearful disappointment, turning several times from one to the other in deepening scorn. "They're not much bigger than *you*," she complained bitterly. I thought they were, and smarted under the comparison; but the ancient

Sydney Harbour 13 October 1968 with Patsy Zeppel of the British Council, and Inspector Christie of the NSW Police—watching a hovercraft passing at high speed

Rushett Edge, Bramley: my home from 1958

Jenifer in 1973

City of London had suffered a family setback from which it never recovered. The other two didn't like the narrowness of the streets between the high buildings, and Deborah said they gave her claustrophobia, a new word she was using at the time. So I hurried them away to see the statue of Peter Pan in Kensington Gardens and the stamping Guardsmen outside Buckingham Palace; the latter convincing Jonathan, at least, that the British Army was as daft as Gog and Magog.

It happened about then that I was invited to chair a radio discussion on Bringing Up Large Families. The panel included James Fisher, the zoologist and ornithologist, who had six children; an East Anglian farmer who had eight; and the Roman Catholic principal of an adult education college who had, I believe, ten. I think I must have been made chairman by way of consolation for my relatively poor performance in having had only four. We talked about punishment. They each proclaimed, or admitted, that punishment had played an important though sometimes regrettable part in the nurturing of their children, including physical punishment of various traditional kinds. I found myself saying that, although I had been whacked myself as a child, I had not done it to my own children. "What do you do, then?" asked Fisher. I searched my memory for what I did; and had to admit, in the end, that I didn't really punish my children at all. Fisher regarded me with what I took to be zoological interest. How did they behave, then? Or didn't I know—was I so busy that the results of my laxity had to be endured by other people? The other speakers joined in and I began to feel cornered. I was just explaining that it wasn't a planned and enlightened régime, it was probably fecklessness and the inability to do anything resolute. Then suddenly I remembered that I was chairman, called them all sharply to order, steered them to another aspect of the thing under discussion, and breathed more freely.

There was an enormous spate of correspondence about the programme, and the dominant theme of it was that I was mad. The producer, a young woman with a long memory, remembered it ten years later and thought it would be a good idea to reassemble the same panel and find out how its twenty-eight children had responded in practice to the several theories

H

propounded. It was necessary first to find out if we were all still alive. We all were, and we all turned up; Fisher, I remember, sadly crippled by arthritis in the course of the ten years. All our twenty-eight children, we found, seemed to have grown up much the same. There were no thieves, prostitutes, gunmen, rapists, con-men, drug-pushers. No saints or heroes. My older two were happily married, the third was at University. None of mine had ever reproached me for making their lives difficult by neglecting to knock them about while I still had the advantage of height and weight. The panel were disposed to conclude that "corporal punishment" (blessed euphemism), if it did any good at all, did it to the punisher, making him feel that he had acted dynamically in the cause of righteousness instead of shrugging his shoulders, shaking his head with pursed lips, or pretending not to know. Someone mentioned that Samson, apparently under Divine supervision, "smote the Philistines hip and thigh", and that this was an approved punishment for something or other.[1] Walking up Regent Street after the broadcast, Fisher told me he doubted the whole morality of punishment, suggesting to my own embarrassment that there must have been some other force at work in my own household which had had the same effect, and (quite seriously) that perhaps it was love? I demurred on the ground that I occasionally got very fed up with the children, and that my demeanour on such occasions bore no re-

---

[1] Judges 15:8. Looking it up when I got home, I was reminded that Samson had "caught 300 foxes" (how?), tied burning torches to their tails, and driven them into the Philistines' cornfields and vineyards, burning everything up. Why did he do this? It seemed to me that it was because the Philistines, at that time the rulers of Israel, had provided him with a Philistine wife who turned out to be unfaithful to him. So the Philistines, apparently to propitiate the strong man a little further, burned the wife and her father to death. Far from showing any gratitude, he thereupon "smote them hip and thigh with a great slaughter", eclipsing this a little later when he found the jaw-bone of an ass and used it to kill another thousand. The smiting policy seems never to have been truly productive, as Samson's subsequent history shows, though it had the retrospective approval of St Paul in a letter to the Hebrews (11:32-34).

semblance either to the Wrath of God or to any other mani-
festation of love's sterner side. Well, there must be *something*,
he said.

The identity of it has always interested and eluded me. The
problem presented itself during another "panel" broadcasting session, with myself again as chairman but this time
with a team so high-powered as to reduce chairmanship to
rubber-stamp level. They were Bertrand Russell, Lord Hailsham (in his first incarnation under that name, that is to say
before his second interlude as Quintin Hogg), and Sir Robert
Birley, then headmaster of Eton. We were to discuss the censorship of books, plays and films, a subject on which everyone
has unchallengeable and yet opposing views. They all thought
the line should be drawn *somewhere* and showed the usual
concern about "public" decency and children. Inevitably we
came to the question of law-enforcement. Did they want
people punished? Would they be content, I asked them merci-
lessly (since I didn't myself have to provide an answer), that
men should sit in prison because of things they had written, as
Tom Paine had done, and John Bunyan and Daniel Defoe?
Bertrand Russell, who *had* sat in prison for something he had
written, rose to it. He would absolutely prohibit cinema
placards portraying scenes of shocking cruelty and violence,
he said in his incisive and nasally didactic voice. He instanced
a placard then to be seen all over London, advertising a film
of Japanese prison-camp life called *The Knights of Bushido*. It
depicted a kneeling British prisoner-of-war about to be decapitated by a gigantic Japanese guard with uplifted sword. That
kind of thing, said Lord Russell, should be prohibited under
pain of imprisonment. Thinking it over afterwards, I didn't
see how you could altogether do without punishment in this
imperfect world. But you must be absolutely certain of your
motives (a rare achievement), certain that you were punishing
the right man, and as certain as you could be that the public
knew what was going on.

In 1958 there came into being the Albany Trust, founded
"to promote psychological health in men and women through
research, education and social action"; and to press for reforms
in the laws about sexual "deviance". (Deviance, I came to

realise, meant discovering what most other people did and then not doing it.) In 1956 the subject of male homosexuality suddenly swept everything else from the front pages of British newspapers; the crises of Hungary and Suez, petrol rationing, the vast Johannesburg "treason trial", the petrifying dangers of the "Cold War"—all were eclipsed because a group of young men with famous names had been accused of homosexuality. Their much-publicised trial at Winchester was used to create the impression that the police (or perhaps it was the Home Office) were, for some unexplained reason, embarking on a nation-wide campaign. The truth was that a particular chief constable, suddenly confronted with evidence that was literally thrust upon the police, sent it to the Director of Public Prosecutions and touched off the sexual scandal of the century. Everyone loved it. The prosecutions and the prison sentences which followed, coupled with a spate of newspaper correspondence and (in particular) a courageous editorial in the *Sunday Times*, led to an unexpected request from the BBC that I should compile and narrate a "radio documentary" on the subject of homosexuality as a social problem.

In the course of assembling my speakers I realised that I needed, above all, an educationist, since this was primarily a problem for parents. I rang up Sir John Wolfenden, whom I had met a number of times in BBC studios and who was then Vice-Chancellor of Reading University. He had written a powerful article saying it was high time we stopped punishing the private behaviour of a helpless and often valuable minority of our fellow-citizens. "I'm sorry," he said; "I would have been very interested and perfectly willing to take part, but a very recent development has made it impossible, or at least most undesirable. I'll leave you to guess what that is." I guessed at once. The Government had been persuaded to set up a committee on homosexual offences (it had decided, very oddly, to require the same committee to look into the question of female prostitution); and he had been invited to be its chairman. "I think I know what you mean," I said, and asked him if I was right. "You just wait and see," he replied, "but I'm sorry I can't be with you."

When the Wolfenden Report came out the following year[1] it said "in some areas—it may be in most—the police deal only with such matters as obtrude themselves on their notice, not going out of their way to substantiate suspicions of covert irregular behaviour. What we have found is that there may arise particular local campaigns against this kind of offence, either as the result of a deliberate drive by the police or by reason of local public indignation."

The radio programme comprised a series of "linked" interviews with people as various as probation officers, psychiatrists, anxious parents, declared homosexuals, clergy and lawyers—including Lord Hailsham; and its conclusions and recommendations were similar to the subsequent Wolfenden Committee's. It brought me an enormous correspondence, affording evidence of a social problem so vast and tragic that I felt impelled to do what little I could towards changing the criminal law and the climate of public opinion.

The letters were not all commendatory; a small minority gave me a dressing-down because one of my interviewees had been a man who served a prison sentence and thought it had done him good. "Looking back," he said (and I quote from the script),

> I can't help feeling that unless I had been brought before the law and sentenced, I would never have been brought face to face with my problem and wanted to tackle it in the extremely difficult way one has to tackle this problem in later years: and I would say to those who are contemplating a change in the law that this is a fact that might be borne in mind.

I thought he was so a-typical and his testimony potentially so dangerous that I wanted to leave him out. The producer was insistent that he should stay in, to "present a balanced picture". It seemed to me that he unbalanced it significantly; but even so I wasn't prepared for the letters it provoked—one of which said that the introduction of this particular speaker was "as dirty a piece of chicanery, intended to deceive your listening public, as it is possible to conceive. . . . The irreparable damage you have done is this: the more uninformed of your listeners

[1] *Report of the Committee on Homosexual Offences and Prostitution*, HMSO, 1957, p. 48.

will at once say 'There! If HE can become a decent citizen, so can all the others.' You have completely killed any likelihood of reasonable acceptance of the homosexual condition."

He could have been so sadly right, but events show otherwise. I believed at the time, wrongly, that public opinion must be changed first and that the change in the law might then be acceptable. In the event, mainly as a result of the Albany Trust's work, the law was changed first and public opinion (with purple-faced exceptions) fell into line. We called our organisation The Albany Trust because at first it used to meet at the flat in Albany, Piccadilly, occupied by J. B. Priestley and his wife Jacquetta Hawkes. Its first chairman was Dr Kenneth Walker, the eminent surgeon and sexologist, and I was its second. Our patrons included Professor A. J. Ayer, Sir Julian Huxley, Dr Joseph Needham, Lady Stocks, Dame Sybil Thorndike and Angus Wilson. We were specially lucky in the man we eventually appointed as director, Antony Grey, who could run anything from a flag day to a Federal Parliament. The funds came from private sources in individual sums ranging from a few shillings to £1,000 at a time, the bigger amounts coming at the inevitable times of financial crisis and imminent collapse. Most of the recognised grant-giving foundations displayed surprisingly small interest and enthusiasm; giving us, on the whole, every sort of assistance short of actual help. In 1967 Lord Arran, with the Albany Trust organisation at his disposal, got through the House of Lords a Sexual Offences Bill which, said an indignant Earl Montgomery, "your Lordships should hit for six right out of this House". There were similar exhortations in the House of Commons, but no batsmen. The Bill was through by a big majority. The persecution of minority sexual behaviour, and its attendant blackmail, were greatly reduced though by no means over. And the extent of the problem of psychosexual difficulty was now gradually revealed for the first time. As might have been expected, the Albany Trust and its tiny office staff found themselves overwhelmed with entreaties for help from thousands of people who felt that society was now offering them understanding rather than imprisonment. Arrangements were made for the necessary "counselling" to be available elsewhere and, as I write this, there is a companion organisation called Parents' Enquiry which helps families to cope with the newly-acknowledged phenomenon of childhood homosexuality. It seems quite a step forward, leaving the punishers slightly less angry, interested in spite of themselves, but still uneasy.

Unfortunately the uneasiness is nourished by the behaviour of a small minority of the manumitted victims, to whom the new attitude of social tolerance seems to be socially intolerable, and who feel that the centuries of ill-treatment should now be avenged in any way currently available. So organisations like the Gay Liberation Front attach themselves to everyone else's standard-bearing anti-establishmentarianism, hold aloft their own little placards calling upon each other to unite in something or other, and disrupt public meetings for no other perceptible purpose than to flaunt an identity they were formerly constrained to hide. There are still anomalies in the sex laws to be removed, inequalities to be redressed, frightful suffering that could be prevented; but none of it will be done by shouting at meetings, writing on walls with aerosol paint-sprays, or bringing up the rear in processions calling for a Third Airport or more pay for child-minders.

Apart from this absurd behaviour, I have noticed no serious consequences, or even recognisable consequences, of a change in the law which put England and Wales on the same level as most parts of what we go on calling the civilised world. There are still the same old discrepancies in local police activity against men who solicit or misbehave in public places; sometimes reflecting a new and very odd statutory differentiation between "public" and "private", sometimes showing that the Chief Constable disapproves, more than other Chief Constables, of unusual sexuality. But nothing has been proved about punishment. The need to continue the prohibition of public "indecency", and to protect young people, has involved the retention of imprisonment for the minute proportion of homosexuals who flout the ordinary decencies or debauch children. But I suppose no one pretends, even to himself, that this changes the nature of the man.

I have no "theory of punishment". The mere phrase suggests

that there is a kind of scientific axiom by which we can predict and control misbehaviour. But the three conventional purposes of punishment—retribution, deterrence, and reform—are simply moral pronouncements that we must not punish except to redress moral guilt, deter the offender and others, or reform the offender himself. Because there is no theory, neither is there any consistent practice.

It was in this frame of mind that I received an invitation from the Home Office to serve for a session on the Parole Board then being appointed for the first time, under the Criminal Justice Act of 1967. Prison parole was no new thing in this country. The Victorian age had had its "ticket-of-leave" system; prison governors had long had a discretion to give a suitable prisoner parole leave for rare occasions—to be married, to go to a funeral, to see a prospective employer. For many years there had been a "day release to work" scheme for long-sentence men nearing the end of their time. The public had never known much about all this, mainly because nothing went wrong. Beyond it all, and still less known to the public, individual prison governors had allowed parole in some non-specified emergencies that might never have commended themselves to the prison-watching Press (or even, if the truth must be told, to the Home Office). But now parole was being made statutory, open and formal, and a prisoner's eligibility for it was spelled out as "having completed at least one-third of his sentence, or twelve months, whichever is the longer period". This was different, and it was all rather sudden: the public had not been carefully prepared.

There were sixteen of us on the first Parole Board. When our names appeared in an official announcement in *The Times*, a neighbour of mine sat next to me in the train and taxed me with it.

"I see you're on this Parole Board thing," he said sternly. I admitted it.

"If a judge decides that a man shall serve three years," he went on loudly, "who are you to say that he shall be let out after only one year? What are the judges for?"

Unhappily the train was still standing in the station, and there would have been a deathly silence in it, but for my neighbour's discourse and the rustle of many newspapers being lowered and folded as the passengers settled to listen. You don't get this kind of thing every day.

"It's this Roy Jenkins," he said in a kind of indignant bawl. "The innovator. The Great Reformer. The law says a certain type of thug shall go to prison for *x* years. Along comes Mr Lefty Jenkins and says no, I'll let him out after a third of that."

Mr Jenkins, I murmured, was doing something that would have been done sooner or later by any government.

"Is he? I don't remember anything about paroling prisoners in any of the election programmes. Friend of yours, is he? Well, so far as I'm concerned he can clear out just as soon as he likes. And here's something you could tell him from me—"

"Do you know if this train stops at Wimbledon?" I said.

"Course not. It's a fast train. Why do you want Wimbledon?"

I didn't, but I grabbed my brief case, scrambled out, got in again at the rear of the train, and settled down with a sigh of relief. I was soon to discover that the man I had escaped from was expressing a view that was unexpectedly widespread, and had much support from the Press.

Those early days of the Parole Board afforded a perfect example of the British political genius for having premature babies and at once feeding them with beef and two veg. Every prisoner considered for parole (at first about forty a week, but now probably five times as many) is the subject of a special file of papers prepared at the prison. And when we began, everything about this was improvised and amateurish; many of the papers were irrelevant, some were presented in triplicate, the photocopies were greasy and illegible, and there was on average 24 hours' solid reading to be done every week.

I think we all took our duties very seriously, and after a few months there was a *volte face* in the newspaper references to us that must have been truly comic to anyone who knew the facts and didn't have to dodge the missiles now coming from both directions. Our impudence in meddling with judicial sentences still enraged the original critics, but there was now a growing army who thought we weren't meddling enough. To the latter, who were very popular in the prisons, we were heartless con-men, posturing hypocrites who had encouraged the hope of freedom in thousands of prisoners whom we were now too timid to release. There were sneering references to our assorted membership, to the fact that we included not only two psychiatrists (why was a criminal always supposed to be a sick man?) but also two High Court Judges and two Recorders (wasn't parole supposed to be outside the scope of the judges once they had passed sentence?). Above all there were jocose references to the fact that our chairman, Lord Hunt, was the famous John Hunt of the 1953 Mount Everest expedition: he might have been good at climbing mountains, but when it came to the operation of a parole scheme he could only produce molehills. And so on. I suppose it's all part of the British method of founding new institutions, throwing them in at the deep end, and not merely letting them learn to swim but throwing things at them as they flounder. Thus it was in the beginning with fishery rights, the labour exchanges, the health service, the school-leaving age, a host of innovations left to work out their own *modus operandi* or drown if they couldn't.

The Parole Board meetings taught me two valuable lessons. One was that all the members seemed to share my view that "punishment", as such, was futile except as a relief for righteous anger, and that imprisonment served the sole purpose of keeping society's beasts of prey out of circulation. We owed our existence, as a Board, to the official Government view expressed in a White Paper in 1965—*The Adult Offender*:

> Experience shows that there are some who just will not make friends with society ever. Such evil-doers must be kept apart for long periods; in the exceptional case, even for life.

But, said the White Paper, such irreconcilables are the exception not the rule; and

> the rest differ infinitely. Many are disturbed, unstable and immature. Long periods in prison may punish or possibly deter them, but do them no good—certainly do not fit them for re-entry into society. Prisoners who do not of necessity have to be detained

for the protection of the public are in some cases more likely to be made into decent citizens if before completing the whole of their sentence they are released under supervision with a liability to recall if they do not behave.

My second discovery was that men who become High Court Judges do not acquire, with the full-bottomed wig and the scarlet robe, some special pomposity that sets them apart. The High Court Judges I came to know best were Sir Eustace Roskill and Sir Arthur James (both now Lords Justices, but otherwise I should think still the same). Both were utterly serious about the job and the merits of the parole system (which they did much to develop as we went along), both were hilariously good company, and both were men with whom, if I *had* to share a desert island, I should be happy to share a desert island. I wish I could pack the High Court Bench and the Court of Appeal with such men. I remember a difficult case in which, with all its pros and cons, most of us felt that we needed expert guidance. Lord Hunt turned after much discussion to Mr Justice James. "Arthur," he said, "perhaps you could sum it all up for us?" The Judge, without hesitation and using the notes he had been making (as we all did), reeled off a list of all the conceivable reasons why the man should have parole. It seemed a crime to have imprisoned such a man at all. Then he did the same with the reasons why he should *not* have parole, and we saw the impossibility of letting such a man loose on the public. Finally: "I think he ought to have parole," he said, and told us why. And by a majority decision the man was recommended for it.

One curious thing about those early days of the Parole Board should here be recorded and I hope I am doing no one an injustice. It seemed to me likely that, in the course of the first twelve months or so, the Board's collective attitude would grow more lenient and generous with practice; a reversal of the process by which the jury in a criminal court gets tougher and more cynical with every case it tries. And this might well have happened but for the gradual elimination of one serious defect in a system which, as I have said, we were largely making up as we went along. In the early days the documents told us almost nothing about the details of the prisoner's crime. This wasn't surprising, for the dossiers were compiled at the prisons, where the staff knew little more than that a man had been labelled, so to speak, with theft, robbery, rape, fraud, incest, grievous bodily harm, and so on. We kept on asking for more information. When it wasn't forthcoming a man may occasionally have missed his chance of parole, but it's more likely that men were paroled who would have been turned down if we had known the horrifying stories behind some of those labels. "We must know what the chap *did*," I remember Sir Arthur James saying. And as we got to know more, a potential drift towards undue leniency was modified by a more detailed knowledge of what the chap might do again.

I don't know about the other members of the Board, but after about eighteen months of this I found myself often comparing two salient documents on a prisoner's file, usually at opposite ends of it. The first related how a man (to take one example) had stopped at a petrol filling station at night and asked the attendant to put some air in his tyres. As the man stooped to comply, the customer bashed him unconscious with a heavy spanner; then robbed the till in the cabin and drove off. The other document set out his reasons for wanting parole. This usually said he was drunk at the time (I got the impression that the only kind of offender not "drunk at the time" was the man convicted of causing death by dangerous driving); and continued with a plea for his dear wife and three lovely children. . . . After eighteen months I was feeling that the Parole Board needed more judicial balance than I could bring to it; that my ideas about punishment were in some danger of moving over towards those who enjoyed seeing it inflicted; and that the end of my two years' stint would come none too soon.

Then I had a letter from Dr John Robson, Secretary for Justice in New Zealand, saying in effect that he wanted me out there to do some lecturing. Once more, my old police comrades would have said, the devil was looking after his own. He was also exhibiting a remarkable sense of timing.

Chapter 15

ROUND IN SIXTY

I THEN WENT round the world in sixty days. John Robson and I had corresponded for some years about aspects of criminology in our two countries. New Zealand seemed to me a perfect laboratory for sociological experiment, and was in fact experimental to a degree that was sometimes dismissed as crazy by the older countries. England, as one of the older countries, had in the past given New Zealand some fairly poignant encouragement by sending its murderers and crooks out there to "make a fresh start". And here I cannot forbear to quote from a letter I had recently from a New Zealand academic who prefers to remain anonymous:

> There is some despondency about further British migration here. The surprise of the last election was the success of the Values Party, which favours a total prohibition. The Party's support comes from the young intellectuals, the liberal-radical wing, environmentalists and "quality of life" people. We have already a quarter of a million Britons here; and the danger seen is that of importing Powellism, venereal infections (of which we have been relatively free), and the like. A thoughtless immigrant appeared on television recently to say he had come here "to get away from the Blacks", and had to be told that the problem of accommodating him to New Zealand society was rather greater than that presented by the West Indian entering Britain. . . . There is a lesson in the fact that no one objects to *Dutch* immigration. I am sure that Britain could equally keep the door open by not issuing passports to plainly unsuitable aspirants. It causes periodic frothing that released British criminals are encouraged to "make a fresh start" out in New Zealand. I know of a number of English murderers who are here on such advice.

Plus ça change, except that in the old days they were sent out there in chains. But I knew nothing of this when I went in 1968.

I was insulated from it by the cosseting circumstances of my visit. "If you can come," wrote John Robson, "I think I know how to get the money." Everyone said I should go. My wife (who would have loved to come with me if we could have scraped up the additional funds); the *New Statesman*, which would get some antipodean articles without having to pay my fare; and the Parole Board, which would look forward to a detailed memorandum about parole in New Zealand and Australia. John Robson, it turned out, got the money through the British Council, from whose London offices on 28 February 1968, I had a letter which startlingly said:

> Our representative in New Zealand told us some time ago that you were in correspondence with Dr J. L. Robson, Secretary for Justice in New Zealand, and that a six weeks' visit to New Zealand and Australia combined seemed to be a distinct possibility. Our representative in Australia has told us that the visit would be most welcome. . . . If, as I hope, you are prepared to undertake this tour the British Council would be prepared to meet the cost of the return journey first class by air, to pay for local travel on Council business within New Zealand and Australia, and to make you an allowance to cover the cost of accommodation, subsistence and incidental expenses throughout the tour. . . . This is a letter to enquire if you are interested and, if so, to ask when the tour can start and how long you can spare for it.

I set off from Heathrow on 18 September 1968, having arranged to go out by way of New York and have a day or two there with my daughter Brenda. She was still book-editing, now with the Johnson Publishing Co. of Chicago; but she and Engelbert, whom I now met for the first time, were living in Greenwich Village—in fact in Washington Square—to be near the University of New York (where Engelbert's professorship embraced astro-physics, cosmology, and relativity; and if that isn't a frightening combination it will do until something worse can be arranged). Greenwich Village, if you can get used to the dilapidation, the old mattresses and discarded refrigerators (some of these at least twelve months old) put out among the dustbins on the pavement, is an exciting and heart-warming place, though I could see from the newspapers that it sometimes overdoes the excitement. Brenda and Engelbert took me to a hot Italian restaurant one evening. It was filled with the nations of the earth, and it had huge artificial trees hung with fairy lights in a room so high that the ceiling was out of sight. I had been there an hour before I realised that the trees were real, that we were in the open air (it was too dark to see the sky) and that the heat was what was left over from New York's roaring daytime.

New York always defeats me, though I want to love and be loved by it. I have many friends there, they seem reluctant to live anywhere else, they like to be visited, and they know only a small piece of it each, the few streets around where they live. Outside that is an area known only by taxi-drivers. The greatest of New Yorkers (though they don't seem to recognise this) was Elwyn Brooks White, and it was he who said: "Many a New Yorker spends a lifetime within the confines of an area smaller than a country village. Let him walk two blocks away from his corner and he is in a strange land and will feel uneasy till he gets back." Whenever I have been lost in New York, which is to say whenever there has been no one actually holding my hand, the man I have asked for directions has always been one of White's disoriented locals. This includes New York policemen. A New York policeman will be so put out if you ask him for a street more than four blocks away that he will nearly stop chewing.

At Tahiti, where the humidity was such that every face was wet and everyone moved slowly, I learned the following lessons. One: do not suppose that the swarthy Gauguin officials will be pleased to see you. Two: do not suppose that the loss of airport baggage is something that happens only to other people. It was at Tahiti that I had to change aircraft for Auckland. I remember watching, through the sweat that ran into my eyes, as the baggage for Honolulu was being transferred to the plane I didn't want. And as I watched I imagined the plight of some poor chap whose baggage was being transferred by mistake, and felt sorry for him. It wasn't until I got to Auckland, 3,000 miles further away, at 7.30 on a Sunday morning, that I found the poor chap to be myself. My baggage had gone to Honolulu and then back to Los Angeles, looking for me everywhere. I had arrived in New Zealand without even a toothbrush.

In the course of some long flights on this world tour I had many hours for writing, in aircraft which were steadier than any train and never more than half-full. For the first time in my life I kept a diary.

Auckland, Sunday 24 September 1968. The two most hectic days of my life, not excepting two wedding days. Meetings, formal and informal, with a host of kindly people; entertained within an inch of my life, five Press interviews, three radio talks and two television discussion programmes, a University lecture (to the Auckland Law School) and another this evening to a public meeting put on by the Ministry of Justice (i.e. John Robson). *Auckland, Monday, 23 September.* [Which suggests a confusion about dates that was only too real. I had lost a whole day somewhere, the fate of all those who chase the setting sun around the world.] Press and radio interviews in my hotel room. Little did I imagine how this was to snowball: once you have appeared in the papers as someone pontificating on television, every other paper in every other town lines up for your arrival. *Rotorua, Thursday 26 September.* Brent's Hotel. This is a beauty spot surrounded by hot springs, geysers, blue and green lakes, and an all-pervading smell of sulphur that affects the throat. Went to see the famous trout streams at Fairy Springs—thousands of huge trout in water so clear that you can see the beds of the deepest streams; and the trout come to take the food from your hand, sometimes illustrating that they watch your eyes to see if you know they're coming, and then making you jump out of your skin as they seize the food when you are least expecting them. Then to the famous Buried Village of Tarawera, wiped out in a volcanic eruption in 1886. The Falls of Te Wairowa, 300ft., link the Green Lake with Lake Tarawera below—marvellous spectacle.

Every morning in these hotels they bring you, unasked, a pot of tea that makes about six cups for one person, and some biscuits. If you don't want this you have to hang a card on the outside handle of your door proclaiming that you don't want it. Otherwise you will get it.

I thought this was a highly civilised custom, setting the New Zealanders apart from any other tribe the human culture had thus far evolved. It showed that if there is a New Zealander who doesn't want tea in the morning he is a crank, an oddity, proclaiming himself as lepers once did. With the tea was always a copy of the *New Zealand Herald*, a paper with a good foreign news service and syndicated articles by people like Tony Howard and James Cameron.

> *Taupo, Saturday 28 September*. The Lake Hotel. A two-storey wooden Wild West kind of building with unexpectedly splendid interior. During licensing hours the din is indescribable—New Zealand and Australian pubs are noisy beyond belief and it is difficult to understand how their roofs stay on. Some special evenings the noise goes on until very late, and on those evenings, ominously, the room maid comes in with a tray-load of ear-plugs from which a choice can be made to suit all ears.
> *Sunday 29 September*. Ngauruhoe National Park. Chateau Tongariro 5,500 feet up, in the snow-line and, but for the still-active volcanoes, all a bit like the surface of the moon.

I had briefly met John Robson in Auckland; he came up there to visit the new maximum security prison at Paremoremo, and stayed at the Great Northern Hotel with me. Thus we met in the flesh for the first time, after ten years of correspondence. A quiet, small, powerful personality, with a way of saying "I can see just what you mean" instead of (more truthfully) "You are talking absolute hogswash." This means that he listens carefully to criticisms of his plans and then goes right ahead with them. Accordingly, New Zealand in the past ten years has seen the reorganisation of its prison and probation systems, the abolition of the death penalty, and the (much criticised) decision to build the new Auckland prison at Paremoremo—a prison designed to afford maximum freedom and movement *inside* by making escape "impossible".[1]

> *Friday 4 October*. Wellington to Mount Cook. Up early for flight from Wellington Airport to Christchurch (400 miles, one hour),

[1] John Robson told me, though, that he wasn't *absolutely* sure it was right to destroy all chance of escape, even if you could. And he doubted that you could while there were (*a*) helicopters, (*b*) corruptible prison officers, and (*c*) tradesmen's vans going in and out of prison.

there to pick up a Government car and drive to Mount Cook, the N.Z. millionaires' playground, 13,000 feet up in the Southern Alps. Perfect flight. The Hermitage Hotel and its surroundings are beautiful beyond words. A place where many people would (they say) like to end their days. I can see why, but I don't want to end mine anywhere. I don't seem to know anything yet. *Wednesday, 9 October*. Christchurch. I was to go and see Paparua Prison but instead the Superintendent, Myles Carew, kindly came to the hotel to see me (I was terribly short of time). Thus at 4 p.m. I was able to go to the Christchurch Supreme Court and meet Mr Justice McArthur, who was to chair my meeting in the evening and not unnaturally wanted to meet me before he did it. Very friendly and courteous and olde worlde, and he had just read my *Punch* article[1] about Julia's biology homework; he said it exactly reproduced his experience with his own daughter. Bond thus established between us. . . . The lecture at 8 p.m. at the Chamber of Commerce Hall was, I think, a success. It was on "Protest and Police in Britain" and satisfied all sides, even the police coming up afterwards and wringing my hand, which was preferable to their coming up and wringing my neck.

On the day I left New Zealand for Sydney I had to be up at 6.30 a.m. to catch a 7.45 Qantas plane from Wellington airport. To my astonishment Dr Robson and Eric Missen, his Assistant Secretary for Justice,[2] were there sharp at seven o'clock to see me off. It was extraordinarily nice of them, to the point of being embarrassing: it was as though Sir Philip Allen, then Permanent Under-Secretary at the British Home Office, had rolled out at 6 a.m. to see me off somewhere; and much as I admire Sir Philip, that thought *does* raise a grin.

The diary goes on and on, through Sydney, Brisbane, Canberra, Melbourne, Adelaide, Perth, Singapore, Bangkok, New Delhi, and Cairo. And from it all, the recollection which envelops and dims everything else is the beautiful, vast and exciting city of Sydney, where the whole Australasian culture comes, as it were, to the boil.

Because of the friends I made there, I should like to live in

[1] 14 August 1968.

[2] Missen is now Secretary for Justice, John Robson having left the Department and gone to teach criminology at the University of Victoria, Wellington.

Sydney, a town that "has everything". But, once installed, I should feel insecure and unsettled until I had coaxed a lot of family and friends out there to join me, and they would not want to go. From among a bewildering succession of people I retain memories of four who will be part of my mental furniture for as long as I may now live. One of them, alas, died the year after I met him. This was Mr Justice Barry of the Supreme Court of Victoria, with whom I was able to spend many happy hours. He was dying, they said, when I met him, for although he was back at work he had had a massive cancer operation, the success of which seemed ultimately unlikely to everyone but him. Back in England I reviewed a book of his in the *Justice of the Peace*, published just after his death, and perhaps I may indulge myself by quoting from it here by way of enshrining a tribute to him in my own story:

Sir John Vincent Barry had the three-dimensional view of moral philosophy that makes a good "Common Law Judge"—and, strange to say, often distinguishes the lapsed Catholic; accordingly he had a deep suspicion of all Acts of Parliament and statutory instruments, which he handled as if with rubber gloves. But he had also the unsentimental humanity that makes a persuasive penal reformer. Among penologists there is a world-wide free-masonry whose common creed founds itself upon "natural justice"; and Barry, for his contributions to the literature of penology alone, would have been sure of a place in their pantheon. Moreover I would rank him, as a fastidious literary stylist, with Wendell Holmes, Frankfurter, Cardozo or Lords Atkin and Macmillan. Among the books he wrote he was most proud, justifiably and I think a little conceitedly, of his biography of Alexander Maconochie, the penal administrator whom Britain sent out to govern Norfolk Island, whom Australia still venerates as a brilliant reformer, and whom the British Government recalled when he was found to be treating convicts as though they were human. I met John Barry in Melbourne in 1968 and we had kept up a correspondence (privileged on my side, punc-tilious on his) that was to me of such value as to make it difficult not to prolong now this typically obituary language.

But J. V. B. himself seemed to me a (reluctant) believer in enlightened self-interest as a useful social principle—he traced it to Adam Smith's *Wealth of Nations*:

Man has almost constant occasion for the help of his brethren and it is vain for him to expect it from their benevolence only. He will be more likely to prevail if he can interest their self-love in his favour, and show them it is for their own advantage to do for him what he requires of them.

But he tended, himself, to make men forget their self-love and get them doing things because, quite simply, they rather loved him. I watched him interviewing, as chairman of the Victoria State Parole Board, a young prisoner eligible for release. It was an effortless bridging of the youth-and-age gap that I shall never forget; we all got to know the boy as we sat and listened. Mr J. H. Edwards, his "Associate" for twenty-two years (in England we would call him the Judge's clerk, but his duties are more varied and academic) wrote to assure me that "the good Lord lost or destroyed the mould after creating J.V.B.". He wouldn't have said that to his face, though I would guess that, in the years that they worked together, he took many risks. The Judge was grimly gentle with those who took risks unawares. When a clumsy counsel, having secured a decree *nisi* in a weak divorce action, jumped up and asked for costs, J.V.B. said: "You remind me of the man who narrowly escaped from a lion's den and then went back for his hat." That was all very well, but John Barry was always going back for his hat. As a controversialist he courted danger—loved it, I think. He dodged it all because he could rely on making his adversaries laugh and they forgave him. (I'm told he did little laughing himself, but if this gave him strength it was, I would say, as a by-product of shyness.)

I don't know whether there are really great men, but because John Barry increased the self-esteem of so many who knew him, and will do the same for many who never can, I can delegate the real obituary note to G. K. Chesterton: "There is a great man who makes every man feel small; but the really great man is the man who makes every man feel great."

This particular gift, this unconscious knack of streamlining and balancing the personalities of others, was also possessed by Patsy Zeppel, who represented the British Council in Sydney and was, in a sense, my impresario while I was there. The truth about this deceptively shy young woman, though she was (I *think*) unaware of it, is that she was also my Svengali.

If the other cities of Australia have any recollection of my performance on their lecture platforms, they may find it possible to believe—and to forgive—that what I lacked, outside Sydney, was a Patsy Zeppel. For me, she did in Australia what John Robson had been doing in New Zealand; though, as you may guess from the photograph on page 224 the process may well have called for less effort. The way she goes about her business, that is to say the British Council's business, may be said to have justified the whole idea, whatever it was, that we should have a British Council at all.

And my quartet of memorables is completed by John Robson (of course) and Stuart Perry; the latter, when I was in New Zealand, being City Librarian in Wellington. A kind of walking book, perfectly bound and finished and containing, it seemed to me, everything a man needed to know; and, still like a book, forcing nothing upon you but waiting to be opened and consulted when the mood took you. After my first lunch with Stuart Perry, I stopped in the street to write on the margin of a newspaper a saying of (I think) Lichtenberg's which Stuart had passed on to me:

A book is a mirror. If an ass peers into it, you can't expect an apostle to look out.

Let me conclude my account of this tour, which meant so much to me, with a few more diary extracts:

Sydney, Sunday 13 October. 9.30 a.m. Called for by Inspector J. W. Christie of the Sydney Water Front Division, NSW Police, and taken (with Patsy Zeppel) on a police-launch tour of Sydney Harbour. A huge bay with countless inlets, about forty sandy beaches, a naval dockyard, cliff-top villas, and the incredible new Opera House built to look like a gathering of yachts in full sail. Inspector Christie demonstrated to us how the police launch could do 35 knots, which had been useful a week earlier when two escaped prisoners had stolen a speed-boat. This was impressive and exciting until there appeared behind us Sydney's first hovercraft, making its maiden voyage; which overhauled and passed us as though we were riding at anchor. [I hope the picture facing page 224 adequately portrays our joint astonishment.]

Being due at a farewell party for Professor Rupert Cross[1] at 2.30, I bought some sandwiches and ate them in Rushcutters' Bay Park, watching meanwhile some teenage boys playing soft-ball cricket against a tree and comporting themselves as if at a religious exercise. They shaped like professionals, cutting, slicing, driving, and then maintaining classic stances as if for eager photographers. They clapped solemnly when someone was bowled or caught. They were completely absorbed. God help us, I thought. Where will it all end?

5 p.m. Radio recording for the A.M. programme at 8 tomorrow; a daily kind of Robert Robinson pot-pourri, very well done.

6.30 p.m. The "Guest of Honour" nation-wide radio programme so much talked about. Found I was expected to have written a script. No time for that now, so I ad-libbed for fifteen minutes and got away with it. The producer, Marcus Ashton, said he was always short of English books for his book-review programmes. British publishers simply would not keep him supplied, he said. Yet ABC does many more book programmes than the BBC does.

Sydney, Tuesday, 15 October. Morning in magistrate's court. Deafening din outside in the echoing corridors, where the waiting witnesses and their children fret, gossip, quarrel, and play. Why are so many court precincts built with glazed bricks, producing the noise of a crowded indoor swimming bath? The swing doors into the court rooms don't meet in the middle—there's a gap of an inch; and you can hear what people are bellowing *outside* but very little of what's going on *inside.* You have to guess what the charges are—vagrancy or begging because the prisoner looks a Skid Row type; obscene language because the prisoner is shown a piece of paper and indignantly shakes his head. (Apparently he is not asked whether he can read as well as utter such language.) "How do you plead?" he is asked *by a police constable,* who, astoundingly, sits in the place—and does the job—which in England we allot to the Justices' Clerk. Some of the prisoners seemed not to know what this question meant. They must have

[1] I had always hero-worshipped Rupert Cross. He was then, and still is, Vinerian Professor of English Law at Oxford; to my mind the greatest academic lawyer of our time, a distinction achieved despite total blindness from babyhood. And when I arrived in Australia he was just finishing a year as visiting professor at the University of Sydney. I found myself staying at the same Sydney hotel with him, and he paid me the paralysing compliment of coming to one of my lectures.

thought it was an intimation that they would be well advised, if they wanted to propitiate the Court, to go down on their knees while pleading. There was a bevy (is that the word?) of prostitutes, some of whom seemed little more than children, though this may have been partly because of their ultra-mini skirts and pain-stakingly babydoll make-up. New South Wales has a real problem here. The law requires the corroborative evidence of the man solicited, if soliciting is to be the charge. So the police arrest the girls for "offensive behaviour", for which the magistrates seem to require no corroboration at all. The girls get a 10-dollar fine (£5) and take it as a business expense just as in the bad old days at Bow Street. The demand for prostitutes is unusually high because of the hundreds of American servicemen on short leave from Vietnam, and because Australian immigration policy admits European males almost indiscriminately but no women.

The evidence in these courts is typed (rather noisily) by another police constable, who sits facing the first one just below the magis-trate's bench.

I remember being very shocked at all this. In England we had abolished the expression "Police Court" because of its implica-tion that the police ran the whole show. We now had magi-strates' courts. And where the words POLICE COURT were indelibly sculpted over the door of the building, we either looked the other way or pretended that we were antiquarians. More, we were in process of replacing our policemen-jailers and policemen-ushers with non-policemanly figures who would merge more congruously into a background of impartial justice. The Sydney courts seemed to me to be serving up some pretty rough justice; though their magistrates—all career stipendiaries, like the French judiciary—know their job, their law, and (above all) their policemen both thoroughly and cynically.

It was in Sydney, the day before I was to leave for my stay in Canberra, that I had what I suppose was the biggest disappointment of my life. Shortly before I left England I had received from the Centre for Studies in Criminal Justice in the University of Chicago the offer of a twelve-month research Fellowship. It was a tempting offer. Did I want to write a book, was I trying to finish a book, which might fit into the

University's publishing programme and for which I needed rest and quiet and freedom from financial worry? They could pay me 18,000 dollars plus my flight fares, and they would not expect me to do any lecturing unless I wanted to. It was enough money to have taken Jenifer with me, and perhaps Julia (neither of them had ever been to America). But I had been stalling on it because I was also involved with Purnell and Sons and the British Printing Corporation in a projected "part-work" on *Crime and the Social Order*; a vast affair of ninety-six weekly parts, of which I was to be General Editor, and for which I had assembled (mainly by correspondence) an editorial committee of great distinction from all over the world. I had already compiled a long synopsis (for which I had been handsomely paid); but the whole thing was being repeatedly postponed because of "staff changes", sudden new ideas, commercial misgivings and a gradual (and no doubt from the first inevitable) reshaping of the scheme, down from academic criminology and forensic science towards blood and thunder, guts and murder, squalor and vice and the things that *sell*. The preparations, if you could call them that, had been going on for two years, and although I was under contract to BPC to continue with the project I was already minded to extricate myself from it as soon as possible.

At Sydney University I talked about it to Gordon Hawkins, an old friend of mine who was a lecturer in criminology there. He was one of those I had tentatively involved in the projected BPC part-work, and he rather guardedly thought it had possibilities. (It turned out that he was relying on my judgment to an extent that I subsequently found extremely sobering.) But he was also involved in the Chicago Centre for Studies in Criminal Justice, was actively fostering the proposal that I should go there, and on that very morning had had a letter from Professor Hans Mattick of Chicago which, in effect, put me on the spot. I had at last to make up my mind. The Centre had a "legal and funded life", said this letter, only until August 1970:

We are sanguine about the continued existence of the Centre beyond that time, but prefer to treat it as an open question. The proposition for Rolph, therefore, is that we would have to work out something within that limit. My own preference would be a six, nine, or twelve-month stay beginning in March 1969.

And this was already October 1968. I knew it was impossible, and at last I wrote to Chicago and said so. It wasn't the fault of BPC in any sense that involved "keeping me on toast". They were paying me a retainer, I felt beholden to them, and it drifted on for another year before I finally decided to free myself in case there should arise any offer similar to Chicago's. BPC agreed with perfect courtesy, and *Crime and the Social Order* quietly died. It wasn't the chance to live in Chicago that I mourned so much: I knew nothing of Chicago beyond its marvellous lakeside buildings, and of course its much-publicised crime figures. But I knew that the work going on under Professor Norval Morris in the Centre for Studies in Criminal Justice was exciting and imaginative work, and I wanted to be drawn into it for a time. I think the non-story of the Chicago fellowship was the biggest disappointment I have had. As A. C. Benson said: "There still remains the intensely human instinct, which survives all the lectures of the moralists, the desire to eat one's cake and also to have it." The sad thing is, I can't even remember either eating or having it.

Before I leave the Australian scene, I wish to record three zoological experiences which have an out-of-the-way importance. The first is that in the Tiddinbilla Nature Reserve at Canberra I was obliged to spend a long time scratching a kangaroo's chest while he stood with his front paws on my shoulders and his eyes ecstatically closed. He was very large. Each time I decided the moment had arrived to stop scratching, his eyes came half open and revealed an unfriendly glint, the unmistakable message being that the scratching had better continue. Uncertain about what kangaroos can do to you, I continued until my arm ached. My companion and guide was Peter Hewitt, of the British High Commission in Canberra. His wife Joyce and their three children were with us; and they, occupied with other things like emus and parrots, all seem to have supposed I was enjoying myself so much that I couldn't bear to break away. In the end Peter realised my predicament, found some food for my kangaroo, and enticed it away; and we all then left the scene walking warily backwards. It then turned out that Peter Hewitt didn't know what a resentful kangaroo can do to you, either.

Secondly, in the Cleland National Park near Adelaide I was allowed to nurse a fat koala bear, which the curator called *phascolarctus cinereus* and which weighed two stone. These are supposed to look like Teddy bears, but in fact they look more like very fat old dogs with parrots' faces. Nature has gone to great trouble to ensure that they shall not grow conceited. Mine put his arms round my neck, and as he did so I noticed that they terminated in strong hands equipped with two thumbs and three fingers, each with a fingernail like an enormous tin-opener. Cuddly as he was, I would rather have him on my side than against me.

Thirdly, I saw, and therefore at last believed, a duck-billed platypus (*ornithorhynchus paradoxus*), nature's deliberate mistake; and was assured that very few Australians could make the same boast. What I did not see, throughout my tour of Australasia, was the Southern Cross; and each time I asked an Australian to point it out to me, he confidently took my arm, extended his own to the night sky, and then was ruefully unable to do any more. The Southern Cross therefore remains for me, as for all the Australians I met, an article of faith. They clearly believe it to be up there somewhere.

I left from Perth on 14 November. When I had arrived at Perth airport a week earlier, and mumbled my way through the now familiar interviews with television and radio men, the place was occupied by swarms of flies. In one television picture of myself that I saw later in one of the University common rooms, I was constantly pawing at my face with both hands to beat the flies off. When I got back to the airport to leave for Bangkok, there they all were again, seemingly millions of them. And this is the place to say that, for one Englishman at least, flies are Australia's one and only curse, the main reason why I could not, after all, live in that otherwise delectable land. I recall that I was taken on a Saturday afternoon to the Royal Perth Yachting Club, where on Saturdays the élite of Western Australia disports itself at a kind of

weekly sailing and wine-bibbing jamboree. There is an extensive
marina along the Swan River, with lawns and marquees;
and a military band playing, I was sad to notice, for the entertainment of a crowd that took absolutely no notice of it, in a
setting that was so startlingly like the places where my father
had played as a bandsman in my childhood that I had an
almost frightening sense of *déjà vu*. Then I realised that the
dresses of the ladies, all with their picture hats and their long
white gloves and parasols, made the whole scene absolutely
Edwardian. The effect was completed by the fact that they
nearly all wore veils, as the posh ladies unaccountably did in
my childhood, and my mother and aunts would do on very
important occasions. (They even kissed you through them.)
I asked my hostess why the ladies of Perth were wearing veils.
"Oh, the flies," she said. "The flies are awful if you don't have
a veil"; and I can lay hand on heart and reveal, such is my
stupidity, how never till that moment had I realised that the
true function of a woman's veil, at least in the Western world,
is to keep the flies off. I wished I could have had a veil; or, like
some of the men, a big hat with strings hanging from the
brim and little corks to keep the strings dangling.

But in Bangkok the flies were worse. It was they, as much as
any sense of reverence or tourism, that induced me to take my
shoes off and escape into the fabulous Temple of the Emerald
Buddha. And a note in my diary at Bangkok (which most men,
I suppose, would suppress) shows how blind I must have been
to the magic of the East:

> The ornamentation of these sacred buildings, to say nothing of
> their immensity, is finically detailed and painstaking, and—at
> close quarters—slightly tawdry. I blushed to find myself reacting
> as I do to those beaten copper or stamped tin coal-scuttles you
> see in Co-op furniture-shop windows in England. I wouldn't mind
> betting I am the first Englishman ever to have had such a
> philistine thought in the presence of these world-famous and
> timeless marvels. Took some photographs of the Temple and
> other buildings, and huge grinning statues of gods with daft-
> looking animals' heads; and I thought, as I knew I would, of the
> measureless and miserable poverty which had made possible all
> this fabulously expensive arty-craftiness. I'm rather allergic to

the mysterious orient, and its ageless indifference to the sufferings of those who, in such inconvenient hordes, have had the temerity to survive babyhood . . . I think I never saw human beings so perfect as the Thai babies and very young children. They look so angelic that the world ought to belong to them. Almost nothing will ever belong to them.

I seem not to have fallen for the magic of New Delhi, either. A difficult man to please, perhaps; too chock-a-block with Forster and Kipling and Edward Thompson, Rabindranath Tagore and Gandhi and the ideals of inter-racial brotherly love:

New Delhi, to the air traveller, turns out to be a ghastly, filthy pandemonium of a place. It was my very first impression of India, Jewel of the East; and my first practical experience of it was a visit to the men's loo, which reminded me of provincial France at its—well, not quite worst. The immigration official, a little rat of a man with a cigarette hanging from his lower lip, spoke to everyone curtly and reluctantly, as though they were all spies or crooks trying to evade detection and arrest. The Customs man was worse: not to me, for he never looked at me or my baggage, but to almost everyone else. New Delhi airport admittedly looks a mess, it's undergoing reconstruction, it covers you and your baggage with cement dust and plaster. Its din is infernal, the noise of hammers and drills not quite drowning the endless, plinking, infinitely boring music from the distorting loudspeakers (or the incomprehensible gabbling of the women announcers). But that doesn't excuse the cruel insolence of these horrid little frontier guards, who treat their own compatriots the worst of all.

As I sat in taxis and buses, bouncing and bumping along the appalling roads and sampling their countless pot-holes, it seemed to me that the drivers—all drivers—charged through the hordes of cyclists with a total indifference to their safety. Whether a cyclist was killed or injured just didn't matter a damn. How often it happens I don't know, but on one trip from the Oberoi International Hotel to the Old Town in Delhi I saw three smashed bicycles, at intervals, by the roadside. The cyclists, I must say, joined in the game of fatalism: their conduct was suicidal in a way I have never seen elsewhere.

There was a final vignette on the way home which impressed me so vividly and painfully that I can see it now as clearly as if I were still watching it. At Cairo, three turbanned brick-layers were repairing the wall of an airport building, kneeling beside each other and working away conscientiously. Suddenly, as if at some word of command, they leaned forward together and put their hands and foreheads on the ground; and I realised that they weren't bricklayers but Muslim airport employees answering the midday call to prayer. And then there passed between me and them a young Egyptian policeman in a khaki uniform, with a younger man handcuffed to him. I wrote in my diary:

> The prisoner turned to look curiously at the praying Muslims, and the policeman turned with him, struck him violently on the back of the neck (I couldn't see whether with any kind of weapon) and then jerked the handcuffed wrist so that the prisoner perforce stumbled after him. Then I lost sight of them. It was over in seconds, and it remains with me for ever. I can extract no moral or meaning. One thing of course stays in the mind. The treatment of the prisoner, whatever he was supposed to have done and wherever he was going, accorded with all that I had heard about the Egyptian police and penal systems. Having said which, one should acknowledge that the policeman might, like his prisoner, have been from anywhere in the world and merely in transit, as I was, through Cairo to some distant part. There is a sense in which policemanship, seen as a form of power over the helpless, is stateless and universal.

From Cairo I had the first-class section of an Air India 707 all to myself. And my diary ends:

> It wasn't until Heathrow that I discovered who my fellow passengers had been, the people in the "economy" part of the aircraft at the rear. They were all Indian and East Pakistani immigrants, about 150 of them. Their bundles, all rolled and strapped and exactly alike, seemed as if they would never stop pouring out of the big baggage doors on to the moving baggage platform. I never saw their owners. I was as insulated from them as if I'd been Enoch Powell. But if I were Enoch himself, I could never have been accorded better treatment, anywhere and every-where, as I went *Round the World in Sixty Days*. And since these

immigrants were all said to be joining members of their families already over here, I could but hope they would be as glad to see theirs as I was to see mine. Mine arrived, complete, on the very stroke of time—Jenifer, Debbie, Jonathan and Julia. "He looks exactly the same!" said Julia for some reason. And they took me home, shivering because I was still in my Simpsons of Piccadilly tropical twopiece and the London temperature was just below freezing; shivering because of the excitement; and shivering because of a delayed sense of the many things that *might* have gone wrong but didn't.

Chapter 16

CLIMAX

I HAD BARELY got one foot back into my normal whirlpool when I was taken away from the Parole Board for a further interval. I had put in a long report to the Home Office about my impressions of parole systems in Australia and New Zealand, pointing comparisons from which, it seemed to me, our system emerged rather well. Soon afterwards I was told that the Home Secretary, Mr Callaghan, wanted to see me.

With my background and experience, this had an inevitably threatening sound. It was as though I had been told to see the headmaster after prayers, and I tried in vain to convince myself that I wasn't uneasy. I had often had a feeling that successive Home Secretaries would have been glad to sign some sort of *lettre de cachet* that would get me out of the way, and I had been told as much by at least one man in the Home Office Press Division. Still, this one was Jim Callaghan, whom I knew to be on the side of the angels; and I waited on him with only half-bated breath. He wanted me to do a special job for him, he said. His interest in prison reform didn't really begin until he had arrived at the Home Office and had seen something of the work that was going on. "I then realised," he told me later,[1] "from my own visits and talks with officials, that if I had known so little about it all, other members of the public who were not in my fortunate position must know even less." So he had asked the various Home Office departments concerned to let him have memoranda from which a readable account could be compiled. When he found that these memoranda were a foot high on his office desk, he decided to get them painlessly summarised by some professional writer who was already interested in the subject. When I was with him

[1] In reply to a letter I wrote him in 1973, asking whether I could tell this story.

in his office he placed his hand on top of the pile of documents. It was overwhelming, he said. Would I write a pamphlet of, say, 15,000 words condensing it all into some easily digestible form? "Something I can pick up and *understand*," said the Home Secretary, "and something we can publish as a White Paper for everyone else to understand." I should have to make my peace with Lord Hunt, he added, about a further release from the Parole Board. I disappeared for three more months, taking all the Departmental memoranda with me; and I should like to record here that, even if I had shared the general view (which I did not) that the Home Office wallahs were a lot of muscle-bound reactionaries, those memoranda would have quickly disillusioned me. And in due course I came up with the White Paper called *People in Prison*.[1]

The result was, I thought, very curious. If you are writing, anonymously of course, a government White Paper, you do not berate the Government for its complacency, its errors of omission, its lack of drive and innovation. Mine made certain wry admissions about this and that, and I was genuinely surprised that every one of them was allowed to remain in. But perhaps the general tone of the White Paper could be judged from paragraph 24:

> The work of the prison service is inherently complex because a prison must be, in most respects, a micro-copy of the world outside. People live, eat, work, and sleep in prison; there must be hospitals, chapels, classrooms and workshops within the perimeter of the prison, as within the confines of other "total institutions". There is the further responsibility for security. "Rehabilitation" itself is complex. There is no such person as the average offender. How should there be, when all human beings are different? All generalisations about the characteristics of people in custody are therefore suspect. (There are exceptions even to the generalisation that people in custody are there unwillingly.) The prison service has to deal with offenders, some of whom are dangerous and many of whom are afflicted by emotional and personality disturbance and social inadequacies. It is also true that the

[1] Cmnd 4214 of 1969, HMSO.

prison service has to cope with many with whom other social agencies have in some way failed.

Not exactly tabloid newspaper stuff, but (said *The Magistrate* for March 1970) "a most readable and informative account which, if read widely, should lessen the feeling that more repressive measures are called for". *The Times Literary Supplement*, on the other hand, said on 19 November 1970 that

> although the policies discussed in the White Paper *People in Prison* are cogently argued, and in a humanitarian vein, a future generation might see this document as the penological counterpart of that Home Office classic at the time of Munich, *Protecting Your Home From Air Raid Attack.*

And they might indeed. It was Hugh Klare who had called attention, in a letter to *The Times* on 2 December 1969, to the kind of thing that *People in Prison* ("a useful document, containing many good things") would not have been allowed to say anything about:

> Visiting facilities in some prisons are atrocious. A wife and her children may wait for an hour in an unsuitable waiting-room only to find, when admitted to the visiting room, that the husband is not there: he was sent to another prison the day before.

And yet I believe this cautious and non-polemical pamphlet to be one of the most important pieces of writing I have had the chance to do. It called attention to faults and difficulties in the system without pretending that they were inherent. Its purpose was not to say "Look, here's a list of the things we ought to be doing". I did not find that it either induced or reflected any complacency in official circles, where there was and is a healthy impetus for improvement, research, and the adoption of new ideas, kept in check by those twin dragons, the Treasury and the public belief in vengeance. I did find that it showed reformers where they must concentrate their energies. For a few years yet, perhaps, it may be the New English Bible of the "correctional services". Copies went to the Commonwealth countries, and in due course it was commended

I

to me in letters from friends there who knew nothing (and still know nothing) about my connection with it. But it's time that someone was revising it, for exciting developments in the world of British penology have been ushered in by the Criminal Justice Act of 1972.

In 1970 I was invited to address the Annual General Meeting of the Camden Council of Social Service. The meeting was in Camden Town Hall, and afterwards there was a large sherry party at which I discovered, for the first time, that my audience had included dozens of people I had known for years. Suddenly, and with an odd feeling amounting almost to fear, I saw that Kingsley Martin was approaching me, sherry glass in hand. This was disturbing for two reasons. First, my old friend Kingsley had been dead for two years. Second, he had gone much smaller, dressed as a woman, and put on spectacles, which rather improved his appearance. Luckily I came to my senses before the apparition spoke. "You are Mrs Irene Barclay," I said, "and we have met before, and you are Kingsley's sister. You are also exactly like him in appearance, and you gave me a severe shock, but how do you do?" Irene Barclay had made so considerable a mark in the world, quite independently of her brilliant brother, that her impact on my own life at this stage justifies a brief digression.

She was the first woman ever to become a chartered surveyor—as one of the first-fruits of the Sex Disqualification Removal Act of 1919. She was among the founders of the St Pancras Housing Association (which she served as Estates Manager and honorary secretary for forty-eight years); and she was Housing Manager to several others, all as the result of commissioned housing surveys. I hope that some day she will tell the story of the slum property surveys she and her business partner did, during the twenties, in Somers Town, St Pancras, Southwark, Stepney, Birmingham and Edinburgh, and the outcry these aroused among the owners—for they amounted to revelations and should have led to revolutions. Called upon to address West End audiences about rehousing schemes, she enjoyed making their flesh creep with her accounts of sodden and bulging brickwork, of chimneys full of holes, of rotten floors and staircases, and of myriads of bed-bugs.

"Directly these old buildings were touched," she once wrote
to me, "bunches of thousands of these evil-smelling insects
were uncovered. I remember seeing a cross taken down from
a wall; its exact outline remained for a moment in living
bugs." The realities of slum clearance are known only to those
who have seen such things; and in my early days in the police
I had seen my share. Getting the money needed to change it
all, coping with ground landlords, persuading slum-dwellers to
move, these are the realities of slum clearance, and Irene was
one of the realists. "They didn't know it couldn't be done, so
they did it." Irene was also vice-chairman of the Family
Service Units, which engaged her absorbed attention for
twenty-five years.

She asked me whether anyone was at work on a biography
of Kingsley. I knew, at least, that no one had been commissioned by the *New Statesman*, and I had seen no letter in the
literary or daily papers announcing that someone was about
to begin and would like to borrow letters, etc. Irene and I
thought it was time somebody started on Kingsley, mainly
because his contemporaries were all getting old. I remembered
learning from Mr Robert Gittings's splendid biography of
Keats the astonishing fact that no one who had known Keats
personally, among that immense circle of writers and literary
gossips, had ever *written* anything about him. Personal memories
of Keats died with his friends. So, for that matter, did personal
memories of Shakespeare and Homer, with the result that
people argue against their having existed or in favour of their
having been syndicates. But while we were casting about
for the best man to write Kingsley's biography, and I was
sending Irene lists of names, she suddenly asked me why I
didn't think of doing it myself? I saw then, without letting
on, that this was precisely what she had intended from the
start. She had approached it with the skill of a woman accustomed to the unobtrusive but successful arranging of things.
I made evasive noises for a time, but the idea grew upon me;
partly because I had known Kingsley for thirty-five years, as
a man quite different from the one in his autobiography,
and partly because I now knew scores of his eminent contemporaries who would probably talk to me freely. The firm of Victor

Gollancz agreed to publish the book; and this was a happy development, for Victor and Kingsley, who had regarded each other with affectionate disdain for many years, had sunk their differences to run many a three-legged race in sudden urgent causes. On matters like the Second Front, the post-war treatment of Germany, the Suez crisis and CND they always came together (if I may change the metaphor) like two straws in a pond. Each crisis surmounted, they disengaged themselves, drifted to opposite shores, and fell to regretting each other once again. . . . However, the contract was signed, and away I went.

How, if you are not a biographer, do you begin such a job? Engage a secretary, a research assistant? I once had a secretary, for two months. At the end of the first month there arrived from the Commissioners of Inland Revenue a huge parcel of foolscap-sized books about P.A.Y.E. income tax; a year's reading at least. It was a foot high. As I looked at it I knew what it must be like to have a nervous breakdown. At the end of the second month my poor secretary had one, and I never saw her again. Thenceforth I typed all my own letters, made my own appointments, answered every phone call, licked my own stamps, and above all sorted, classified, labelled and stapled the enormous mass of papers that Kingsley had bequeathed to the Library of Sussex University. But one thing I knew you had to do was put a letter in *The Times* announcing the start of the proceedings and asking for letters.

The Times replied coldly that it published requests of this kind "only on extremely rare occasions"; of which, clearly, this was not one. I then watched the correspondence page of *The Times* for the rare occasions that were, and in the course of a few months a series of published letters from more eligible biographers enabled me to assess Kingsley's relative importance (not to say mine) in the estimation of *The Times*. The approved subjects included Clement Attlee, Lord Goddard, Scott Fitzgerald and Peter Fleming. Then I came to know that this kind of letter is often intended as no more than a Keep-Off-The-Grass warning to other would-be biographers, a pre-emptive banging-in of pegs, which might not produce the promised or threatened biography inside ten years, or at all. As I was soon to discover, there was enough material already in

Kingsley's papers to sustain half a dozen volumes, and any further influx would have been frightening. It was a lucky escape. As it was, a similar letter in the *New Statesman* produced letters from all over the world.

The ensuing round of visits among those who had known Kingsley Martin filled a period of fascinating enquiry, beginning in Hereford with those who had known him as a baby. He had lifelong friends and enemies, admirers and critics; he was loved by many, hated by some. Everyone acknowledged him as a born journalist and an erratically brilliant editor; but from that point they diverged in a way that was as entertaining as it was bewildering, and taught me much about human nature. I've heard it said that good biography is not to be written in this way, by tape-recording the recollections of sought-out people and weaving them into the story. But I don't know why. I wish there were tape-recordings of talks with Leonardo, St Augustine, Henry VIII, Lincoln, millions of recordings available to all. I thought that in thirty-five years I had got to know Kingsley Martin, but it was in those months of listening to his contemporaries (some of whom have since died, even in so short a time) that I learned the kind of man he was. Without them I should have written, I suppose, a mild panegyric, for to me he was always a good friend, loyal and solicitous and unaffectedly extrovert; though I always knew that, behind all his cleverness, he was an odd mixture of insecurity, ingenuousness, and borrowed sophistication.

I was well launched on *Kingsley* when I received an invitation to address a Conference at Princeton University. On 8 February 1971 Professor M. H. Wilson of the Politics Department at Princeton had written an article in *The Nation* suggesting that the activities of the Federal Bureau of Investigation, which was threatening what the American citizen still seems to regard as his privacy, should be subjected to an independent investigation. And independent meant something quite different from a Senate hearing on the FBI budget; or an enquiry by a House Appropriations sub-committee using FBI agents to enquire into their own work; or even an enquiry by the Department of Justice (of which the FBI is nominally a part). It meant as thorough a study of the FBI as could possibly be undertaken by a totally independent group of some fifty lawyers, scholars, journalists and former government officials. Such a study group was accordingly convened at Princeton by the Woodrow Wilson School of Public and International Affairs, working with the US Committee for Public Justice; and I was invited to go over and contribute a paper on *The British Analogy*, which really meant the Special Branch as the nearest thing the British have to a Federal Bureau of Investigation.

Now this involved little interruption of my work, and indeed there were a number of people in America whom I wanted to talk to about Kingsley. Moreover, I wanted to see Princeton University, where he had held a visiting Fellowship for a year. This time it was possible for Jenifer to come with me, and her enjoyment of it all was so infectious that I found myself actually prepared to enjoy New York. And so was she. While I was doing my New York interviewing she wandered about the shops of Greenwich Village, basking in the cosmopolitan friendliness, seeing no one killed or mugged, occasionally stepping round a horizontal soak or junkie, watching the open-air chess matches in Washington Square Garden, and generally storing up impressions for use in books to come. (For a few days in New York we were guests of Engelbert and Brenda.)

The Conference itself, on 29 and 30 October, was superbly organised. Its proceedings were published the following year,[1] and one of its more interesting proposals was that the function of "gathering intelligence", whether on domestic subversives or foreign spies, should be separated (as in Britain) from that of criminal law enforcement. The best hope was thought to be that the President of the USA might one day appoint a commission to study the whole "national security" apparatus, domestic as well as foreign; and the contributors, myself included, hoped that any such commission would begin by reading our book. There is no sign of this happening yet, but when they come to it they are likely, I think, to feel the scales actually falling from their eyes.

Kingsley was published on 12 April 1973, the sixtieth birthday

---

[1] *Investigating the F.B.I.*, Doubleday & Company, New York, 1973.

anniversary of the *New Statesman*. So there was a great celebratory party in Stationers' Hall, in the City of London, at which there gathered 500 distinguished guests to whom the entry of the *New Statesman* into its sixty-first year would be a matter for jubilation, despair, amazement, dismay or utter indifference. The newly published biography of the *New Statesman*'s greatest editor was, so to speak, the *leitmotif* of the evening; and its author, as he sidled around the packed hall trying to pick up snatches of conversation about it, found that everyone was talking about something else. At last a very small thin man, with white hair, piercing eyes, and a Central European accent, pulled my sleeve. I had been talking to him earlier about the accepted notion that a biographer should be an idolator, arguing defensively that I was neither. "I am just leaving," he said. "I wanted to remind you of something that Thomas Carlyle wrote about hero-worshipping:

> If a book come from the heart, it will contrive to reach other hearts. All art and writing is of small import otherwise."

I may have got the words wrong, but I think it unlikely because of the way they drummed in my mind when he had gone. I dared not ask his name, because something told me he was well known. And no one afterwards could tell me who he was. He quietly dramatised, and did it for me alone, a sense of the evening's occasion. I knew that for me it was a climax, and I think other people knew it was too.

Still, it was climactic mainly in the sense that I had written the story of my longest-running editor, and that an important job was done. I have said that he was the *New Statesman*'s "greatest editor", but I think that for my part it's an accepted judgment, rather than a pronouncement. It happens that I'm the only member of the editorial staff to have worked under five successive editors: Kingsley Martin, John Freeman, Paul Johnson, Dick Crossman and Tony Howard. Among them all, of course, Kingsley stands like a monolith because he was there for thirty years, building the paper's circulation from 12,000 to 90,000. I have offered elsewhere my own assessment of that astonishing feat; but this is the point at which to say, though all the subsequent editors inherited me as part of the furniture, so to speak, as they came to office, that they not only accepted but re-established me, whatever consequential changes there may have been in other respects. I survived four new brooms. They all made their changes in the paper, of course; none seeming to me of great significance, and all greeted with proper indignation by that loyal body of grumbling readers who avail themselves of every opportunity to complain that the *New Statesman* is not what it was.

None of Kingsley's successors could now have the excitement, as he did, of turning a loss-making "coterie paper" into a profitable commercial enterprise. They faced logistic and survival problems such as he never knew. They faced the inevitable decline in circulation which, from 1960 onwards, depressed those periodicals unwilling to believe that most modern thinking takes place below the waist. None of them, however, gave way to gimmickry, and I found undiminished pleasure in working for them all. I had known them all, of course, before they were appointed; they had all been contributors and three of them, in fact if not in name, had been deputy editor. John Freeman seemed to me the ideal man to usher in any kind of new era because he was deliberate, unflappable (on most days), knew where to commission an article and how to discriminate among those he had not commissioned, and was much aware of the paper's secondary role as a kind of ombudsman (which was where I came in). I knew he had no intention of staying for more than a few years; though in 1965, when Harold Wilson appointed him British High Commissioner in India, I saw that he was reluctant to go. He and I were the last two at the office on the night when he left—it was very late and he had been sorting some books and papers he wanted to keep. The occasion would have surprised the many people who have always regarded him as an unemotional man.

He and Paul Johnson, who was to succeed him, had effectively been running the paper for about five years when Kingsley was induced to retire and John took over. Accordingly Paul's succession seemed likely enough and, to most of us, highly desirable. But not to Kingsley, who in his retirement went around unashamedly lobbying against Paul's appointment on the ground that he was a Roman Catholic. He seemed appalled at the prospect of a Roman Catholic editor, worried to the point of obsession. I had by that time been made a director of the company, in succession to Sir David Low who had died in September 1963; and when Kingsley pressed his misgivings upon me he was, I think, exasperated at the obtuseness with which I dismissed them. I remember saying that it must be the first time Kingsley Martin had ever lined up with the Vatican, whose disapproval Paul had seemed to me to be courting for years; but it was not a good thing to say.

And then Paul, after five good years in the course of which Kingsley saw—and handsomely acknowledged—that his anxieties had been unfounded, decided that he had had enough and wanted to do some writing of his own. Dick Crossman was appointed, and the paper entered upon sixteen months that would have worried Kingsley far more, had he been alive, than anything to do with Catholicism. I always liked Dick Crossman, always forbore to argue with him because I like winning (or dislike losing when I know I'm right), and supposed that so good a journalist with so eclectic an experience, much of it editorial, was bound to turn out all right. But, as it transpired, Dick was not merely unable to suffer fools gladly; he took the Aristotelian view that, since knowing what is right doesn't make a man wise, you don't have to suffer him either. I had some share in Dick's appointment, and none in his dismissal, but found myself in the complicated emotional state of regretting both. I shall pour no further oil on those troubled embers, but welcome the opportunity to say that I am glad to have worked with and for him, and that so far as I can recall he is the only man who has been able to show that extra-sensory perception can be used to argue with someone too slow to get his own thoughts out in time. As I write this, the editor is Tony Howard; and he is setting out, with what seems to me ample equipment, on an editorial stint which (be it long or short) will at least be as difficult and eventful as Kingsley Martin's.

Chapter 17

AS I WAS SAYING

It is from the diminishing band of people who do not publish their memoirs that you can still get a detached, if slightly bilious, assessment of autobiography: an unrivalled vehicle for telling the truth about other people, a vice as common now as adultery and hardly less reprehensible, a book that should always begin with Chapter Two. You know the kind of thing? It seems to me that there are four excuses for having written this one. First, I was asked to. Secondly, I've enjoyed doing it. Thirdly, its double-barrelled aimlessness may seem sufficiently unusual. Fourthly, through what seems to be an exceptional memory I can begin in babyhood; my story opens at a time when, according to Father Ronald Knox, the average person is merely a loud noise at one end and no sense of responsibility at the other.

But being now (I suppose) old, I feel what may be an old man's desire to tidy up, draw a few conclusions, offer some sage suggestions. To be frank, these belong in earlier parts of the book. But there, because they would have held up the story, they would have the more strongly tempted any reader to skip; and they are much more important than the story. To set them out is a self-indulgence, of course, but it is of a kind which is different and, just conceivably, more useful here. That kind of self-indulgence, which will be brief, is what now follows.

"The atom bombs are piling up in the factories, the police are prowling through the cities," wrote Orwell in *Shooting an Elephant*, "the lies are streaming from the loudspeakers— but the earth is still going round the sun . . .". Bombs and police and official lies having supplied the back-drop of my life, I approach the end of it with a fear of all three; and the effect of the fear is to fuse them into one powerful and of course frightening concept. The disturbing thing is that they all seem indispensable, a fact which I have found hardest to accept in relation to lies. In middle life I was attracted by the scientist's concept of truth, as something that stands the test of experience — "Ethical axioms," Einstein says in his own life story, "are found and tested not very differently from the axioms of science." In a television "brains trust" programme I heard Bertrand Russell invited to comment on Keats's words in the *Ode on a Grecian Urn*:

> "Beauty is truth, truth beauty"—that is all
> Ye know on earth, and all ye need to know.

I cringed with approval, so to speak, as I saw what was coming. "Well of course it's utter nonsense," said Lord Russell dismissively, and he would say no more. Neither Keats nor Russell knew what he was talking about, I decided, and neither would have understood the other's language. I had seen truth denied and trampled on a million times, often to the sheer gain of society; and I had played my own part in the preparation of police reports which I knew to be false in the quasi-respectable sense of *suppressio veri*. I had come to accept that lying must sometimes be an instrument of government, when "the truth" in public hands might lead to public disorder and perhaps disaster. Sometimes it was right to tell official lies, sometimes wrong. The report of the Warren Commission on the Kennedy assassination seemed to me, at least for the time being, an occasion when it might well have been right, though the truth about that must some day come out; while it was manifestly wrong in the case of the *Sans Everything* hospital enquiries in 1968[1] concerning the ill-treatment of helpless geriatric patients in hospital. Respected statesmen like Stanley Baldwin had blandly admitted in the House of Commons that with the best of intentions they had knowingly misled "the nation". Stafford Cripps, whom I once admired beyond reason,

---

[1] *Sans Everything* was a book edited by Barbara Robb, and published by Nelson in 1967, a compendium of real-life stories about hospital cruelty so horrifying that the impulse of every decent citizen was to dismiss it as false. It was true. What was false was the subsequent White Paper which virtually exonerated the hospitals and, by inference, branded Mrs Robb and her team as liars.

had lied about the Government's intention to devalue the currency (as any Chancellor must lie if he is pressed by untimely questioning). Eden had lied to us about Suez. I had lived through two world wars in which special departments of State had been set up for the purpose of telling lies. In 1941, when the British Government urged the unbelievably gullible British people to give up their saucepans, frying-pans, and front garden railings so that aeroplanes could be made out of them, the art of official deception had reached its most cynical depths or its most poetic heights, depending on what view you held about the use of mass stupidity as a kind of aperient for the release of patriotic fervour. I cannot remember a single criminal trial, a contested civil action, a suit for maintenance, in which there was no perjury. It was all tacitly accepted. But as the slow explosion of society scattered its members more and more widely, leaving them marooned on lines of instant communication known as "the media", they came to distrust and disbelieve official spokesmen as never before. I cannot believe that the devastating effect of this process on the national life and character has ever yet been fully appreciated.

It is for that reason, and because I think it relevant to what follows, that I have written thus about liars of high estate and (sometimes) lofty motive. The late Editor of the *Yorkshire Post*, Sir Linton Andrews, said to me in a radio interview: "Truth in reporting? Well, you see, the truth is many-sided. It's like an obelisk—no man can see all its sides at once." I've sometimes recalled that for comfort; remembering too that the side a man is looking at may be the side he is allowed to see by those who increasingly control the sources of information. But the abiding impression I retain from a long life is this: that lying identifies with self-preservation as what Samuel Butler called the first law of nature. If, for example, a policeman is in some kind of disciplinary trouble and you give him the prescribed form on which he is to set out his version of the facts, he will lie; always if he is guilty, often if he is innocent. And so would almost anyone.

The police system, no doubt like many other systems of which I know less, is therefore rotten in important parts of its foundations. But what is unusual about this is that the rot has spread downwards from a summit which is obscured from the policemen by clouds. Not even, that is to say, from venial chief officers but from departments of State and their readiness to lie for the common weal. And this is the atmosphere in which corruption comes to seem excusable, if not inevitable.

I used to worry a great deal about police corruption, and try to think up suggestions for getting rid of it. The same idea seems to have presented itself to a young man I taught in the School of Instruction. He had hardly been in the Force twelve months when, moved by an obvious sense of outrage, he made a series of written allegations charging his senior officers with corruption. Within a week he had been "allowed to resign", as a sequel to a disciplinary charge of bringing unfounded allegations against superior officers. Most of us knew that what he had said was absolutely true. None of us said so. Why? Because we had no proof that could possibly avail against the mass lying we should thus provoke, even if we would have wanted to produce any.

The Crown Colony of Hong Kong has a Statute under which a police officer can be called upon to explain why his standard of living is beyond the scope of his police pay. At one time I thought this might be a useful addition to English law. But when I saw my seniors (many of them totally innocent men) being called upon by the Commissioner to produce their bank passbooks, cheque stubs, Post Office Savings Bank books and other evidence of their comfort, I realised that, whatever might be necessary in a Crown Colony, there was available in this country a kind of do-it-yourself common law machinery which, though it had all the finesse of a six-shooter and a sheriff's badge, was quite as effective as any Act of Parliament could be. The suspended police officer in England either did as he was told or—if he was lucky—resigned. He would not have this kind of luck if there was evidence against him that went beyond the mere state of his bank account.

Moreover, I believed for a long time that corruption was not to be cured by higher pay. "More money," I told myself, "is today an appetite that grows with what it feeds on."

Higher pay would merely fertilise lusher tastes. The idea received a setback when I found, on visits to America, that the highly-paid FBI is probably the least corrupt policing organisation in the USA, if not in the world. (Not much is heard about this, for there is little excitement in police virtue.) The speakers at the 1971 Princeton conference to which I have referred[1] would have been unlikely to forgo any opportunity to charge the FBI with corruption. But they made no mention of such a thing. Moreover in New Zealand, where the police are not popular, I heard on all sides that at least they are not corrupt; and their pay affords some startling comparisons with that of other public servants. The youngest constable, on joining, gets 4,891 dollars a year[2] which in New Zealand is 200 dollars more than the pay of a male bank clerk at the age of thirty-five. A New Zealand secondary school teacher (without degree) starts at 3,300 dollars and rises to 5,882, while the starting salary of a university lecturer is 5,862. Compare these with the 6,000 dollars of a constable with twenty-five years' service. A New Zealand Member of Parliament gets 7,604 dollars, which is well below the pay of a senior police officer. All this is not to say that a highly paid police service in this country would be a popular police service; but if, as in the banana republics, police popularity were to be a marketable commodity, the market would be cornered by the wrong people.

I feel, now, that we should be more honest and less hypocritical if we treated corruption as at most quasi-criminal, and set up (by special Act of Parliament) a *permanent* tribunal on corruption in public life. The consequences of a mere denunciation by such a tribunal should be drastic enough for anyone—policeman, local councillor, Member of Parliament, or whoever—without worrying about the conventional clamour for specific punishment. Punishment for corruption, as for many kinds of misconduct, is ineffectual and often barbarous: where it sees corruption as a moral offence against the state, it has lately reached its apogee in Rumania, whose shopkeepers are being publicly executed for what we should call "fiddling".

[1] p. 261.   [2] These are 1973 figures.

In this country the policeman who is forbidden, rightly in my view, to accept the smallest of Christmas gifts from members of the public, watches on his own television screen the delivery at No. 10 Downing Street of Christmas bounty from a national association of turkey farmers. If my suggested tribunal had a motto or an emblem on its coat of arms or stationery, it could be "There but for the grace of God". Its adverse findings would have the same effect on public servants as a rebuke from the Press Council has on a decent newspaper—they would very much rather that it didn't happen; with the little extra, in the case of the public servant, that his promotion prospects would be strikingly reduced.

In much of the foregoing there is, I am venturing to hope, an implied recognition of right and wrong, with a basis more disinterested than mere expediency and a goal rather higher than "just reward". First as a policeman, and then as a man who has written for half a lifetime in the public prints about "social justice", I had always believed, as Thoreau did, that "it is not desirable to cultivate a respect for the law, so much as for the right".[1] I was always oppressed, and the oppression is now so great that I try to avoid thinking of it, that the wisdom of man through 3,000 years, such wisdom as often lifts the mind to the topmost towers of reason, has nevertheless left man so foolish and so spiteful. When my brother Harold and I talked our adolescent way through the jungle of church-going mumbo-jumbo, we decided that we were Huxleyan agnostics. We belonged among the "don't knows" of religion. Man could not, we concluded, in the nature of things *know* anything about a spiritual existence, whether of God or of man or of immortality. To hear my father speak of T. H. Huxley at one time, you would have thought Huxley was the man who invented atheism. On the contrary, he held that there *might* be a transcendental universe and that atheism, which would have none of it, was a negligible kind of dogmatic materialism.

But when it came to the acceptance of a God, my brother and I eventually agreed to differ: we could find no common ground,

[1] Henry David Thoreau, *Civil Disobedience*.

for in his declining years he was uncertain whether he would even call himself an agnostic. I felt, and still feel, that there is a central intelligence which it is convenient to call God. Admittedly I can sometimes perversely feel, as Jules de Goncourt felt, that "if there is a God, atheism must strike him as less of an insult than religion". But religious belief came in the end to seem a more rational thing than atheism; and of course it was warmer, you could put it on like a kind of spiritual overcoat in which to savour your mystery, and poetry, and the inexpressible magic of great music, and the sense that there was power outside the slippery-walled round-house of thought.

As the children of my second marriage grew old enough to begin questioning, I would take them to our small village church so that they should not be denied that dimension to their lives. (I have long reproached myself that I did not take Brenda similarly, though she would probably have out-done me in reproaches if I had.) The time would come when they would reject it, of course, but then at least they could know what they were rejecting. Well, they didn't reject it. And to me a church, whatever its denomination, is still a place where, having parked my smart-aleck sophistication outside, I can achieve some kind of humility and feel (or imagine) myself to be in touch with the infinite, sometimes almost regardless of what is going on in the building. With memorable exceptions, I like the people I meet there, perhaps because they do not know me very well; but I like the stillness, the peace and the emotional agelessness of an empty church even more.

"I am an agnostic," said Clarence Darrow (it seems to me complacently); "I do not pretend to know what many ignorant men are sure of." In that sense, so am I, though I can see the lazy arrogance of it, the tired abdication. But to be an atheist, for a man so to declare himself, can mean but one of two things. Either he is a fool, in whom incredulity has become a faith, or he is a man of superhuman percipience, a science-fiction kind of man with huge intellectual courage.

In the nineteen-thirties, the court probation officer at the Old Bailey was a genial, elderly, soft-spoken Irishman named Michael Walsh. He was serenely happy as a Roman Catholic, though not uncritical of his Church. We became good friends, perhaps because he nourished my ego, soothed my worries, and loved books. He wrote little pieces for the evening papers that might have come straight from Oliver St John Gogarty. And he used to quote Browning at me:

> All we have gained then by our unbelief
> Is a life of doubt diversified by faith
> For one of faith diversified by doubt.
> We called the chessboard white—we call it black.

Which enables me to say that in both the lives I have been writing about, though I could never "call myself Christian" because of what Christianity has tried to do with the simple teachings and the sublime charisma of Jesus, I was always more at ease among Christians than among hard-boiled non-believers. But to some extent I felt emotionally lonely in both worlds. Looking back on both of them, as it is now time to do, I see that they are almost as isolated from each other as I from them. Between them, though, they gave me two lives, each one richer than many a worthier and wealthier man's. I seem now to be setting out on a third; and the excitement is no less because there is so much to learn. Henry Ford said: "Anyone who stops learning is old, whether it happens at twenty or ninety. Anyone who keeps on learning not only remains young but becomes constantly more valuable regardless of physical capacity." Valuable to whom? But one must go on learning.

INDEX